Transcendence

Transcendence

A MEMOIR

Rebecca J. Brock

LUMINARE PRESS
WWW.LUMINAREPRESS.COM

TRANSCENDENCE: A Memoir

Printed in the United States of America

Luminare Press
442 Charnelton St.
Eugene, OR 97401
www.luminarepress.com

LCCN: 2023909408
ISBN: 979-8-88679-294-2

For Sammy

I will never stop loving you.

Contents

Prologue

There comes a moment in everyone's life that is sudden, shocking, and leads to a *total paradigm shift*. In a flash, *everything* has changed, nothing is the same. If you live long enough, you might have several of these momentous disturbances.

In the tarot community we call this a "Tower" moment. In traditional tarot, the Tower card illustration is depicted as a tall tower, built on top of a mountain, with lightening striking it as a couple of people fall from the top. It represents destruction, chaos, and it is *always sudden and shocking*. Sometimes a tower moment can be a good thing, but mine wasn't. My Tower moment was the day my son Sammy died.

Interestingly enough, "tower moments", while always unanticipated and surprising, can also represent a *sudden revelation* or *an awakening*. And that's exactly what happened to me. All of a sudden, *everything* that I thought was important and sacred was reduced to frivolity. *I knew that my life would never be the same.*

We are all going to die, it's literally the *only thing* we can ever be sure of. Absolutely *no one* gets out alive. Yet we fear death as if it is the end of the world, *but it is not. Death is merely a transition to another realm.* We never really cease to exist, we just leave our physical body and return home, to the place of Pure Love and Consciousness.

If you have ever read about people's near death experiences (where they die briefly and come back), it's always deeply spiritual and profoundly revealing, and most say that they never want to leave that place. There's no pain and no hunger; only that feeling of pure love. *Sounds like Heaven.*

After losing Sammy, I had a supernatural experience, more like a mysterious *awakening,* and my life unexpectedly became *surreal.* The Game of Life, I realized, was not about the accumulation of as much money, material possessions, and power that one can grab. The man who dies with the most toys is certainly *no winner.* Beyond the veil we are all the same. I knew that no one could bargain or bribe their way into heaven; it's our actions, choices, and *intentions* we have that will *determine our fate.*

I've never been an overly materialistic person, but I do love the comforts of luxury. Nevertheless, in a matter of seconds, the truth of the material realm was revealed my consciousness. *None of it is real, it didn't hold any significance because we can't take any of it with us when we die.* I also saw very clearly that every evil in this world since the dawn of mankind came from those who placed too high a priority on the material realm. It was the very thing that *caused* people to lie, cheat and steal *in the first place.* The love of money, greed, and the power that they gained from it has caused some humans to commit the most horrific crimes against their fellow men. At that moment and still today, I would give everything I have if I could just have Sammy back alive.

I also became aware that absolutely *nothing* will remain hidden forever. *The truth will always be revealed, one way or another.* It's not only God that knows the intentions of our heart, but the *entire spiritual realm.* Nothing can be concealed forever because we are all *connected* by the Divine Matrix, the

Universal Mind of which we are all *One.* Also, any person in a physical body can *learn* how to tap into that knowledge and every horrific crime will *eventually be exposed,* and not because they will suddenly announce it on the news. People on planet earth are awakening at a rapid pace, and soon *everyone will see what I see.* I'm using this newly obtained knowledge of the interconnectedness of everything and the Divine Matrix to *manifest* the life I've envisioned.

Life isn't as serious as I had first supposed, and God is not angry and won't punish us for our sins like I had been taught to believe my entire life. The whole purpose of life was *to learn,* we incarnate into a physical body in order to spiritually evolve. Apparently Planet Earth is one the best school rooms in the cosmos because of how dense and *evil it is.* One has to evolve *out of it* and *come back to unconditional love,* and any soul who hadn't mastered that yet was going to *keep reincarnating until they got it right.* I knew I was meant to understand this concept in this lifetime instead of repeating karmic cycles.

We are all on our own path, and my reason for being here may not be someone else's. We all get to *decide* for ourselves, our reason for being here, we make soul contracts with others before we get here and we come here to fulfill them.

Ultimately I came to understand my life purpose. Besides bringing my sons into this world and being a mother, it is to *write this book.* When I started writing I realized my life purpose was *much more* than just this book. It took me years to even begin writing, because just thinking about it made me burst into tears and I would have to relive that dreadful night. Also, I felt inadequate to be the one to write something so mystical and was embarrassed to share parts my story because I've made so many mistakes. There were even things that I did *not* want to disclose, but I was shown that it was important. I sobbed and tried to negotiate with my spirit guides, but I had already agreed *to speak my truth* when I began writing.

"The question isn't who is going to let me,
it's who's going to stop me."[1]
—Ayn Rand

I had to muster up the strength and courage to share my story because it is deeply personal and revealing. But I knew I had been in this exact place before in other lifetimes. Yet I either hadn't had the courage to speak up or had been burned at the stake before I was able to fulfill my mission. So here I am, *back again,* and this time I needed to *finish the task.* This lifetime was the *first* one where I had complete freedom of expression and I *grasped* at the chance. Besides love, *truth* is the only thing that can *heal and save the world.*

So there came a point where there was no turning back. This book was already written in my head, although it took the strangest twist once I began writing. I wasn't even sure where these spiritual insights were coming from, but now I know these messages were from my spirit guides. While I procrastinated, I knew I would never find true joy or feel fulfilled until I completed my *Divine calling,* what *my soul* had set out to do in this lifetime.

I'm not afraid of what others think of me, I never have.

1. Ayn Rand, *The Fountainhead* (Bobbs Merrill, 1943).

However, after Sammy died I truly no longer gave a *flying fuck*, and the feeling was *pure and exhilarating freedom.* People were avoiding me anyway, maybe because they didn't know what to say. Others steered clear of me because I would always talk about his death, and it wasn't to try and garner *sympathy.* I'm assuming they avoided me because it made *them* uncomfortable. *Those are not my people.*

Once I stopped listening to what everyone else thought I should do with my life, I was able to get clear about what my purpose was and what *my heart* wanted. I was amazed by what happened when I blocked out *all that useless chatter* of everyone else's opinion…that's when I could *tune into my own intuition. I had to follow my heart,* I was the only one living my life! The way I think is probably the exact *opposite* of the way most others think and I'm fine with that, I'm not embarrassed to *be me.* I find it impossible to be normal, but normal is *boring.*

I'm sure I'll have a boatload of critics, *but so be it.* Cognitive dissonance is a real thing, and I'm sure many will disagree with my theories. People may be downright *angry* about them, but someone's reaction to my message isn't something I have any control over. *As far as I know, we still have freedom of speech.* I was upset and disturbed too, when I first discovered the truth. But the day of reckoning is *here, the world cannot keep going on this way.*

Owning our story and loving ourselves through that process is the bravest thing that we will ever do.[2]
—Brene Brown

---

2. Brene Brown, *Rising Strong: The Reckoning. The Rumble. The Revolution.* (Random House, 2015).

This book is not about Sammy's life or how special he is, although he's clearly an extraordinary soul. This book isn't even all about my life, because it wouldn't be that interesting unless you actually know me. This is *my truth,* and *I have stayed silent for far too long.*

This book isn't about grief either, because that topic is super depressing and no one wants to read a book about it. This is my story of how a series of supernatural events have led me to where I am today. This book is the "abridged" story of my life (I'm not telling you everything), and my life is *stranger than fiction.* It is about the mystical moments that made me realize, *without a shadow of a doubt,* that there are things unseen and the Divine plays a role in *all of it.*

The title of this memoir changed several times in the process of writing it. Somehow, every title I chose didn't quite fit. Writing is my *art,* the paper is my canvas, and the words are the colors. The title had to explain what my life was like up to this point. How could a simple title do *that?*

Then I was given a simple word from my spirit guides: Transcendence. I looked it up in the dictionary, just to be sure. Transcendence is "the state of being transcendent or exceeding the usual limits; extending beyond the limits of ordinary experience; beyond comprehension". *Yes, this is accurate!*

But for some reason this description of the word didn't quite satisfy me. So I had to look up "Transcendence" in the Urban Dictionary, I've always been more street wise than book smart and I needed clarification. It said: Transcendence: "When you get over shit by dancing". *YES!* I have been *dancing* my entire *life,* and it is *how* I overcome adversities. I had such a hard time coming up with an appropriate title, and yet *one word* could describe my life!

There is no greater agony than bearing an untold story inside of you.[3]
—Maya Angelou

We've all experienced profound loss, illnesses, and challenges. There is no way around it, it's literally the *reason* we are here. But what I chose to do with what life has given me, well, *that's entirely up to me.* I could have just given up considering everything that has happened to me, and let it *break me down.* I'm sure no one would've blamed me for taking that route. But my fiery spirit, the spark inside of me, *wasn't going down that way.*

Maybe that was the gift I was given for having gone through such a tragedy as losing a child: I give myself the permission to *say whatever I want.* I wasn't going to wait until I was an 85 year old granny sitting around the Thanksgiving table to *blurt it out.* I am going to *say it now.* If people had told me when I was a kid that someday I'd go all Biblical and be shouting about God from the rooftops, I would've looked at them like they had *two heads. Yet here I am...*

I ended up having *the best time* sticking my finger in everything, stating the obvious, and pointing out idiocy while writing this. Once you read my story, you may never look at the world in the same way again. *Proceed with caution!*

---

3. Maya Angelou, *I Know Why the Caged Bird Sings, an Autobiography* (1st Edition: Random House, 1969).

CHAPTER 1

The Day My Life Changed Forever

January 8, 2019 started off like any other Tuesday. Except on this Tuesday, there was a palpable excitement in the air because my middle son Sammy was turning sixteen the next day. We had a scheduled driving test for him to get his license, and he had a brand new car waiting for him in the driveway.

Sammy had just gotten his braces off a couple of days earlier, and he was loving his new look. He had a beautiful girl that he liked, and she liked him too. He couldn't wait to take her out on a proper date. Sammy was literally *on top of the world,* he just could not contain his excitement!

I rolled out of bed and because it was winter, it was still dark outside. I came out to the living room to find Sammy fully dressed, shoes and even his backpack on, and ready to go to school! He had even already made himself breakfast. This was a normal occurrence actually, Sammy was usually ready before his brothers even woke up. I rummaged around in the pantry looking for coffee while wondering how I could've given birth to a morning person.

Somehow I managed to get my other two boys up and ready and gave them each a hug, and my oldest son drove them all to school. I don't remember exactly what I did that day, but I'm sure it was uneventful. I probably did the usual: some work, ran errands and went to the gym.

AROUND 6PM I HEADED DOWN TO MY SONS' SCHOOL TO watch Sammy's older brother play basketball. His younger brother was with his classmates on a school trip, but I knew Sammy would be there. I got settled in and started to wonder where Sammy was. I sent him a text, "Hey baby, where are you?".

He finally showed up and he looked like he was on *cloud nine*. He just smiled and sighed, he had just spoken with that pretty girl I was telling you about earlier. He told me he had just had a DMC. I asked, "What's a DMC?" Sammy grinned and said: "*A deep, meaningful conversation.*" He seemed smitten by the pretty girl, and I thought it was adorable.

Five minutes before the game ended, Sammy really wanted to go home to my apartment to meet a friend, and he wanted me to drive him. I told him: "No! Just stay for your brother, the game is almost over". But he was itching to go, so he decided to take an Uber. As he left the gymnasium, he turned around and waved good bye to me with a huge grin on his face. *That was the last time I ever saw him alive.*

SAMMY HAD LOST HIS KEYS TO MY APARTMENT LONG before this fateful day, but he never really needed them because he was always driven around by either me or his older brother. We didn't even look for his keys that throughly because he was usually with someone else who provided them.

A mere two minutes after the game was over, I headed out to my car and I got a call from my doorman. There was this *edge, a panic,* in his voice, and he told me I needed to come back home *immediately.* I demanded that he tell me what was happening, but he wouldn't. One of my neighbors took the phone, and relayed the same message, with the same anxiety in her voice. *I have never driven like such a maniac in my entire life.* I don't even think I put my seat belt on. Something was *wrong! I could hear it in his voice.*

I pulled up to my building and saw it: flashing lights. It looked like there were *thousands* of lights. There were cops, fire trucks, and ambulances. I raced inside, my heart beating out of my chest. I don't think I even turned off my car or shut the door. I was *panicking.* "*What happened?*" *I was screaming now, what was going on?* I demanded to know! I was already shaking, and I saw the look on everyone's face. It was horrific, I could already tell. It was my neighbor who told me, Sammy was already gone. *What? Gone, as in…dead? How was this even possible?* I had just seen him moments before. How did he die? *Why wouldn't someone tell me what was going on or let me see my son? How could already be gone? I was in complete state of shock. It just couldn't be true!*

I sat in the lobby for hours, I wasn't allowed in my apartment while the police did an investigation. *I was hysterical, I couldn't stop crying,* yet I still wasn't believing he was gone. *Just like that? I had just seen him smiling at me!* I eventually learned he fell from the balcony to his death. The police weren't ruling out suicide, but I thought, *are you kidding me?* There was no possible way Sammy would ever take his own life. Especially on *that day, he* was so excited for his birthday and *had so much to live for!*

The investigation also considered foul play, but again, I knew it was *impossible.* Sammy was loved by everyone who knew him; family, friends, even teachers and school staff. I ruled that out, *I couldn't fathom it.* Apparently, Sammy had gone to the upstairs neighbors and convinced the woman to let him in so he could go on her balcony. He supposedly wanted to see if he dropped something onto our balcony? *I never got the full story.* Her husband was in the shower, she had a hungry infant and five year old and was in the middle of making dinner, so she let him in. He had a trusting face and he was as tall as an adult, so she must've figured it would be alright. He was planning on climbing down to our balcony because he knew we always left that door unlocked. *He didn't make it.*

I don't blame the neighbor, in fact, I don't blame anyone for Sammy's death. I didn't even blame him, even though *I know he knew better. What was he thinking?* It was just a tragic accident, and there was no way to turn back time. I started to get angry, *why would he think he could get into my apartment that way? He knew the front desk had a key!* But in a flash, the anger had vanished. *How could I be angry at Sammy when he was already gone?*

THE WHOLE WEEK WAS AN ABSOLUTE BLUR. I KEPT hoping I would wake up and realize it was just a nightmare. The next day we headed to the airport and boarded a tiny plane with Sammy's body wrapped in a white sheet. No one said a word on the way to New York, we sat there in silence. *There was nothing to say.* Then we boarded a plane to Israel to bury him on the Mount of Olives in Jerusalem.

I had to see his face before we buried him because I couldn't believe it was true! *How could he be dead? My baby!* If I hadn't seen his face, I would've always thought he might still be alive somewhere, and It would've driven me crazy. But he was dead and gone, and my heart felt like it had been *ripped from my chest.* My chest was collapsing and it was so hard to breathe.

The Rabbis placed Sammy in the cold, hard earth according to Jewish Halacha (Torah Law). The dead are to be buried as soon as possible, and are placed in the earth without clothes, without a casket even. God's Law: return the physical body to the earth. *I had to put my baby in the hard, cold earth, naked!* Now I started to feel my knees buckling beneath me. *This couldn't be real.*

I remember the funeral, some people got up and said some things about him, although I wouldn't know who it was or what they said. I couldn't see actually, *the tears were so thick*, I was blinded. I was sobbing so much, that I couldn't hear anything either. All I remember is my friend Dina standing next to me, her arms wrapped around me, trying to comfort me. How can one even comfort a grieving parent? *This is not the way it's supposed to be!*

Having a child is a bit like your heart suddenly growing feet and walking around outside your body. And my heart had been absolutely *crushed.* Sammy was so much more than my child, he was my *best friend.* That's not to say that I'm not close to my two other sons, but Sammy told me *everything* and we were so much alike, *we just got each other.*

We had the same dorky sense of humor, we found humor in things others couldn't. He was the *man in my life*, no one was closer to me or knew me better than Sammy. His brothers always had girlfriends, but we both seemed to be single most of the time, despite us both *trying not to be.* I felt like he was *my person.*

I didn't know was how much my emotional grief would cause actual *physical pain.* The term heart break is not a misnomer, I could *feel* a huge crack, and it went *straight through my heart.* I was completely *devastated*, and I would never be the same. Most of that time period is a *blur, maybe it is too painful to remember.*

THE ONE THING I DO REMEMBER THE NIGHT SAMMY DIED, was that I was lying on the floor saying "I knew it" over and over again. When Sammy was seven months old, I had fallen asleep while nursing him and had what I thought was a nightmare. We lived in a house in Miami Beach, and Sammy's room was on the second floor. In this dream, I *dropped* him off the balcony! I jerked awake with such a violent lurch and was *mortified.* I couldn't understand what this meant, *I would never hurt my own child.*

I called up my sister and told her what had happened, and she suggested it was postpartum depression and told me I should see my doctor right away. I remember he wrote me a prescription for some anti-depressant like it was no big deal, and sent me home. When I picked up the medicine, I saw a sticker on the side that was a warning: "Do not take if you are breastfeeding". *So I threw the pills away*, I wouldn't risk it getting into Sammy's breastmilk.

I decided this whole thing was probably from lack of sleep or exercise.

When Sammy was about eight months old, we had moved to an apartment while our house was being renovated. His older brother was at school, and I had a thought come into my head that didn't come *from me.* I was told: *He's not going to make it to adulthood.* My reaction was, of course, to question it. *What?* I didn't understand what this meant or where this message was coming from. *Again, I chalked it up to something mundane like "losing my mind" from how hard being a mother was.*

I looked at Sammy's face at that moment, and he looked so sad. He wasn't a loud baby like his brothers, who demanded food and attention. He was quiet and observant, taking it all in. *Where was this coming from?* I figured I really was just *losing my mind.* Being a mother is challenging, to say the least. We are on the clock 24 hours a day, seven days a week. *There are no "holidays or "time off" with this job!*

As Sammy grew I forgot about these experiences. I had pushed them down so far into the back of my mind, and made up simple excuses as to why I had had that dream and heard that message. *I'm crazy. Postpartum depression. Fluctuating hormones. Lack of sleep.* The list went on and on. *Oh, how the mind can believe anything it wants!* I had convinced myself it was something *it was not. But now I know what it is: messages from beyond the veil.*

Looking back on my life, I realized I had been getting messages and guidance from my spirit guides and beyond the veil for my *entire life.* I discovered I had psychic abilities *this whole time.* Yet I dismissed them as nonsense, thinking I was being "logical". Maybe because someone told me such things weren't possible. When I was younger, I was probably trying to fit in and be accepted by people. Whatever it was, *it was just an excuse.* For so many years, *I had denied accepting who I was.*

How could I have missed this? I'm guessing my upbringing and conditioning prevented me from believing these messages or that things like this were even possible. But I would become aware of how important every single message I've received over the years would be later on down the line.

I had been practicing daily gratitude for about a decade when Sammy died. I had gone through a really rough patch in my life, and I had been in "victim" mode for *years.* I remember the day when that shifted. I was doing my jog on the boardwalk and ran into another mom from my boys' school. I was telling her my whole, long, *dramatic* story… *again.* I had been repeating it for years. Just at that moment, a close friend who knew the story well, walked by. Suddenly, I was *embarrassed.* How was I still recounting this stupidity and not taking responsibility for my part of the drama I was going through? So I started a gratitude journal, and every day I would record something I was grateful for. I was grateful for my boys. I've always had a roof over my head. Even on the worst days in this dark time, I could find something to be thankful for.

But when Sammy died, I told God I needed a break from all this gratitude mumbo jumbo. It wasn't bullshit though, and *I knew that.* It had *changed my life.* I had seen it work miracles from the very first day I began my gratitude practice. *But I'm sorry God, how exactly could I ever find something to be grateful for in the midst of all this heartbreaking sorrow?* I told God I would be taking a break from it.

The day we returned from burying Sammy in Israel, I was sitting at the Shiva all numb and withdrawn, only focusing on my pain. When I looked up, I was *shown* something to be grateful for. There was my whole dysfunctional family in the same room together and they were all *getting along.* I had friends that were divorced that hadn't even spoken to each other in *years,* and they talking and being civilized. *Wow! Only Sammy could do that.*

I kept being *presented and shown things* to be grateful for. Which I have to admit, I was a little *pissed* about at first. *God, hadn't I told you I needed a break from gratitude? Just for Shiva week, of course.* But I couldn't help being grateful someone had gone into my apartment and covered all the mirrors, because Lord knew I didn't want to see what I looked like that week. I probably would've scared myself if I had glimpsed into a mirror. Then there was food delivered *daily* to my house for a full *month!* Had it not been for the help of others, I probably wouldn't have eaten at all. *I couldn't help myself, I was so grateful.*

I am eternally grateful to the Jewish community here in Miami Beach. I wouldn't have made it through losing Sammy without them. The outpouring of love and support was *incredible.* The Shiva (the 7 day period of mourning for the 7 closest relatives: mother, father, brother, sister, spouse, daughter and son) was pretty much *hell.* All I really wanted to do was just crawl into my bed and not come out for the next *year.* But I had to be present and *greet* people wearing the same torn sweater from the funeral. I dreaded the thought of anyone seeing me in my grief stricken state, let alone trying to have a conversation with them. *Every single moment I felt like dying inside.*

I had posted the Shiva "hours" on Facebook, because I couldn't imagine sitting there for seven days straight awaiting guests that wanted to comfort me. I needed to have breaks where I could just lay down and cry alone. I didn't want to be bothered by anyone, although I knew everyone meant well and were there to comfort me and my family. *But the whole thing was torturous. Thank God for pill popping friends that are willing to share.*

One day that all changed. During "open" hours, a woman that I didn't know came up to me and said: "I just want to tell you something about your son Sammy. My family and I recently moved here from a foreign country. My son goes to the same school as Sammy, and he was having a lot of problems fitting in. He doesn't understand the English language yet, and the other kids were teasing him. One day he was in the bathroom crying, and your son came in and asked him why he was crying. He told Sammy that he didn't have any friends. Sammy immediately said: "I'll be your friend, don't worry!" and introduced him to everyone else and encouraged them to be friends with him too." She told me that her son hadn't had anymore problems since that day he meet Sammy.

I stared at her in amazement. Of course, *I knew this about Sammy*, he went out of his way to make others feel good about themselves. But to hear someone else tell me this story, I was beyond *grateful!* Tears of *joy* were streaming down my face. After this, I felt compelled to write a blog about Sammy, and I felt so *urgent* that this message get out there. I texted my friend who runs the platform my blog is on, and asked him if he could please publish this article right away? I said, "Even though it's Sunday, I know your office is closed and it should be edited first, but *please*-can you publish it *now?*" He did. I'm forever grateful to him, not just for publishing the blog, but because he was the first person that believed in me. He told me I was a good writer.

Originally, I needed to write this post because I got so tired of answering everyone's questions on how he died so suddenly. *It's so rude of people to ask that question*, but I guess it's human nature. That's always the first question that comes into my mind when I hear about a sudden death, especially of someone so young. Although, *I had never dared to ask.*

I was surprised by what came out in the blog. It was like it wasn't even me writing it. In fact, when I went back and read it a couple of years later, I had tears streaming down my face. I was thinking how beautiful each word was and I wondered: *who wrote this?*

HERE'S THE BLOG POST:

> 3 Things You Can Do That Will Instantly Make You Happy
>
> A Tribute to My Son Sammy
>
> As I write these words, I'm still completely overwhelmed with grief over the loss of my dear son, Sammy. He died one day before his 16th birthday.
>
> This tragedy began when he had gotten locked out of my apartment. As teenagers are wont to do, he had lost his keys. Instead of asking the doorman to let him in, he decided to go to the upstairs neighbors balcony in order to try and climb down onto mine (I always left that door unlocked.) He didn't make it.

Sammy was the happiest, most joyful child I have ever met. I am forever grateful for the privilege of being his mother, even for just a short amount of time. His positive, loving nature has affected so many lives.

My purpose of this blog post is not to solicit sympathy from my readers or to raise awareness about the dangers of teenagers doing risky things like this. Although I have recently found out that teenagers do this *all the time!* I vow that at some point in the future, I will do *something* to raise awareness about this dangerous "trend" in the hopes of saving even just one life.

But let's not talk about his untimely death. Let's talk about Sammy's life and use his shining example to improve our own lives and our relationships with others.

What I want to tell you about is what Sammy did that made him happy... everyday.

1. He was GRATEFUL, even for the little things.

Constant, unending gratitude is truly a magnet for miracles. How can anyone be depressed or unhappy when we feel immense gratitude for what we do have? We can be grateful for so many things, it doesn't have to be something grand. Even just being grateful for a beautiful, refreshing breeze on your face can change your entire day.

I want to share a couple of stories of how Sammy exemplified this gratefulness in his every day life. A few days before he died, he came into my room wearing only his underwear. He had that look on his face that he was about to say something funny.

He always made us laugh. Instead, he told me how grateful he was to me for always making sure he had wet wipes in his bathroom! He went on to say that he knew that there were people in the world that didn't even have toilets, let alone toilet paper. But he was extremely grateful that his "ass felt great" (his words). He then thanked me again and gave me a hug and a kiss. I laughed at how cute this interaction was, but Sammy did things like this everyday.

On one other day near his death, I had been running short on time and was rushing around so we could make his brothers basketball game on time. I needed to feed my boys, so in typical single working mom style, I heated up some frozen chicken nuggets and french fries. Sammy ate every bite and then thanked me profusely for the wonderful and delicious (??) dinner, along with his usual hug and kiss.

These are just two stories that stand out in my mind but Sammy did these types of things *everyday, all day!!*

2. He went out of his way to make others feel GOOD.

It's the traditional Jewish way to sit Shiva (a mourning period) after the burial of one of our seven closest relatives (Mother, Father, Sister, Brother, Son, Daughter or Spouse) for one full week. There are many customs and rules regarding this, but the basics is that everyone comes to visit your home to grieve with you and give their condolences. Plus, they came bearing gifts, anything we might need plus so much food was delivered to the house daily! I'm forever grateful for my family and friends and the amazing Jewish community here in Miami Beach for their much appreciated assistance. Anything we asked for was taken care of immediately! We would never made it through that brutal week without their help, prayers, and outpouring of love.

I had never had to sit shiva before, and honestly the first few days I was downright angry. I just wanted to crawl into bed and not come out for a week. Yet I had to be present to greet these people that only meant well and wished to comfort us. But every time I hugged a complete stranger (or even a close friend) with tears in their eyes, I would start sobbing (again). I was starting to think that I didn't have any tears left, but they keep flowing.

On the third day, my attitude towards the shiva completely changed. A women came up to me (another complete stranger) and told me a story about Sammy. She said her family had recently moved here and her son was attending Sammy's school. She admitted that she and her family didn't speak English very well, and her son was having a very difficult time. On his third day of school, he was in the bathroom crying. Sammy came in and asked him why he was crying. He said "I have no friends."Sammy said "I'll be your friend!" without a moment of hesitation and immediately added him on Snapchat. Not only that, he got his other friends to welcome this new kid as well. THIS WAS THE TYPE OF PERSON HE WAS! He went out of his way to make everyone feel included in the group and good about themselves. I can't even count the amount of times he told me I looked beautiful when I clearly was not feeling my most confident.

There are so many stories just like these ones about Sammy, because this was his way of life. It came naturally to him, he didn't even have to think about it.

I believe it's impossible to be unhappy or depressed when you're making others feel good about themselves. Any simple act of kindness has enormous benefit not only for the person, but for yourself as well! Smile at a stranger. Hold the door open for someone without expecting a thank you. Run after a man that just dropped his wallet and give it back to him! Tell someone you love their outfit or their earrings. Tell your coworker how smart she is and how much you admire her. I could go on but...

One applicable quote from one of my favorite authors Maya Angelou says: "I've learned that people will forget what you said, people will forget what you did, but people will never forget how you made them feel." Sammy will be forever remembered because of the way he made *everyone* feel good.

3. He completely TRUSTED GOD and his divine plan.

We spend so many hours of our life that is *wasted*, either feeling guilt about the past or worrying about the future. But once you put your complete faith in God and his plan for you, I can guarantee you will find happiness, no matter what is going on around you!

Sometimes it's so SO hard to do this. I miss my Sammy so much it hurts me physically. There is a huge hole in my heart that will never be filled. I know my life will never be the same. I'll never be able to hug or kiss him or watch him grow to be a man. My sorrow has overwhelmed me and I'm sure it will stay with me for the rest of my life. But it is helping me to share this article with all of you who may be depressed or unhappy because it doesn't have to be this way! Happiness is a *choice.*

So many people struggle through life, unhappy or depressed because they feel that life is unfair. Maybe they didn't get exactly what they want. We push so hard to get that dream job or to get one specific person to fall in love with us and are bereft when it doesn't happen. But what if God has something BETTER planned for you? What if your trials are exactly what your soul needs to learn to make you stronger? I'm still learning to surrender to God's plan for me. But Sammy was one person that had complete *unwavering* faith in God and his divine plan. My goal is to strive to be just like him everyday.

Sammy wrote this paragraph below as a school assignment, one month before he died. It had such a profound impact on me and it completely touched my heart. This was a perfect description of him-these are his own words:

"My Hebrew name is Yitzchak. It was the name of one of our forefathers, the son of Abraham. Its literal translation means 'he will laugh'"and this is my outlook on life. There is a famous quote that says: 'Man plans, God laughs' and it means you are unable to have full control over your life and that Hashem (God) is behind the scenes, pulling the strings. Both of these connect to demonstrate that life can't be steered by anyone and that Hashem has a plan for you. It should be known that everyone has a destiny that only Hashem knows, but you have to make the right choices to become the best possible version of yourself, which I strive to do every single day."

My blog is about dating, relationships and finding love, but I believe this story can be related to our quest to find true love. If we can make a conscience effort to do these three things that Sammy did, we will find true happiness, with or without a partner. When you are truly happy and love yourself you GLOW and are like a magnet to others with the same vibe. Once you can reach that place, love will find YOU.

Sometimes being rejected by someone we were dating and really liked is not an actual rejection, it's God *redirecting*. God has someone more compatible for you that is searching for you right now! Often times not getting what we want is the most wonderful stroke of luck. Always keep believing in love and that YOU DESERVE IT! Be patient and trust in God's divine plan and timing. I've been divorced for 11 years now and had been getting impatient about finding my life partner. But now, because of this beautiful thing Sammy wrote, I more fully trust God and have surrendered completely to Him. After all, he's pulling the strings! I don't mind waiting to meet the One, God knows what I need right now and I trust in his divine plan for me.

Life is so precious, and in an instance, it could be gone. It's amazing the way Sammy's death brought our families closer together. But we shouldn't wait until someone dies to become closer with our families and friends! Bury those grudges and let go of that anger. Forgive someone who isn't even remorseful. Don't stop loving someone just because they stopped loving you. Stop judging other people and accept everyone for who they are. We are all on our own path and are at different stages of spiritual evolution. Respect other people's opinions and beliefs, not everyone is the same, nor should we be. We don't always need to be right or convince someone that they're wrong! Treat every person with compassion and kindness, you never know what they are going through.

But most importantly, tell your family and friends *everyday* how much you LOVE AND APPRECIATE them, because you may not get another chance. The last thing Sammy said to me was: "I love you mom."

RIP MY LOVE!
Samuel Issac: January 9, 2003-January 8, 2019.

Grief: You can't run from it, you can't hide from it, and you can't pretend that it doesn't exist. You can ingest any sort of substance to try and dull the pain, but *grief doesn't go away.* You can try and distract yourself with whatever so you don't have to think about it, yet the feeling persists. *Once grief comes knocking at your door, it's here to stay.*

I'm no stranger to grief, my mother died when I was only one year old. Growing up whenever I told someone this fact I'd always hear: "Aw, I'm so sorry!" My response was always the same: "It's ok. I was so little I don't remember her anyway." and I would continue to dance around with a smile on my face. When I said those words, I think I actually believed them. As if by not remembering my own birth mother, I would somehow be able to escape grief.

But grief doesn't work that way. One day, one way or another, I'd have to deal with it. *And boy, did I.* When my first son was born and I became a mother, I suddenly felt this loss so *intensely.* My step mother had never had her own children, and my sister's daughter wasn't born yet, so I had no one to turn to for advice. Here I was at 25 years old, a motherless mother trying to navigate parenting, all while realizing I had done *nothing* to process the grief of losing my own mother. I had tried to *pretend* that it didn't exist, that it didn't *matter. But it did.* I had no one to talk to for guidance on how to navigate life as a mother, and this parenting thing was so damn hard!

My mother died of Hodgkins lymphoma at the age of 29. The doctor discovered a lump in her armpit the size of a golf ball when I was four months old. *It was already too late, and less than a year later, she was gone.* In adulthood, I faced my own health crises and I couldn't shake this feeling that my mother *had* to have known something was wrong in her physical body. I mean, *how could she not? I had known something was wrong inside of me, so she had to have known as well.*

Yet she told no one, not my dad or my grandmother. I'm certain they would've made her go straight to the doctor and start having treatments of some sort, and her pregnancy with me probably wouldn't have continued to term. She had wanted *so desperately* to be a mother! She wanted to have my sister and I *more than anything in the world.* So now I was finally processing my grief, *but then it started to spiral out of control.* I discovered I been carrying around this unconscious belief that my mother sacrificed her life for *me!* Whether that was true or not did not matter, this is what my subconscious mind *believed. No wonder I was so fucked up.*

"Sometimes God has to break your heart
in order to save your Soul."
—Unknown

With my heart broken into a million pieces after Sammy's death, I had no choice but to surrender to the situation. Then a strange thing started happening, I was receiving messages from beyond the veil, more than I had before. I knew what this was now, I couldn't dismiss them or excuse them as nonsense. Sammy was still so close, and he was letting me know that. I now call these Divine Downloads, where as before I called them "I'm going crazy". I can now actually decipher where these were coming from too. Some were from Sammy, others from my spirit guides, and some were from my higher self.

I could tell the source of the guidance based on the tone of the message. Sammy's were always hyper, he was excited and just had to tell me something! My guides' messages were more *no nonsense, they aren't fucking around.* Their messages were more slow and steady, and quite *serious.* My higher self's advice was the kind you'd get from your funny and sometimes bitchy best friend that you *knew was always right.*

One day I was so deep in my grief from losing Sammy that I cried out to God: *WHY?? How long was this pain going to continue?* Then I was told: *You're doing it wrong, stop trying to get rid of your grief. Grief never goes away. Grief is like a virus.* This message was from my guides. *What? Like a virus?*

So these messages may be from more enlightened beings, *but I've always got questions.* I thought: *What do you mean grief is like a virus?* The response was: *When a virus enters your body, your immune system makes antibodies to fight the virus and your symptoms go away, but the virus never leaves your body. Stop trying to get over your grief, it doesn't work that way.* So I had to ask: *Well, what was I supposed to do instead? I can't keep feeling like this! My heart is so broken!*

In my mind's eye I looked down and saw I was holding an infant, fresh from the womb. He was all skinny, red and *angry,* having been forced from the warm and safe environment of his mother's womb. *What am I supposed to do with this?* I asked. I felt panicked, and my heart started racing. Did this mean I was supposed to have another baby? Good God, *please explain.* I love being a mother, I felt like I was born to be a mom. It is the most difficult (yet most rewarding) role, but with everything I was going through, an infant was *the last thing I needed.* And I knew I could never replace Sammy.

Yet here I was, staring at this infant. I'm not ready to close that door on never having any more children. I've even considered freezing my eggs. But at this moment, I couldn't handle anything more than what I was dealing with. *God, what does this mean?* I listened to Spirit say: *This is your grief. You have to raise it like you would your own child. Nurture him, feed him when he's hungry, soothe him when he cries.*

Eventually, he will become an adult and he won't be around as much, but he will always be your child. He will never go away completely, he will always be a part of you. That answer made sense to me. Thank you God. I realized I'd never "get over" grief, *so I stopped trying. Grief doesn't work like that.*

I spent the next several months raising my fourth child Grief. Before I knew it, he was grown and he left my home. He came to visit his mother from time to time, as any well raised child would, but he never stayed for long. I knew that Grief would always be mine, and the *sooner I accepted this*, the faster I could get back to my happy and joyous self.

Despite Grief being a mature adult, one day I couldn't stop the tears from pouring down my face and I had to face those fears: Who was I to be getting such profound messages from Spirit? How was I actually going to write this book? It had been made very clear to me that it needed to be written. *I am nobody special!* I told my guides. *I was a vain model who spent half of the 90's high on weed and quaaludes! How was I supposed to be the one to write this down, and who would even listen to me?* It didn't make any sense, but nothing has ever made much sense in my life. None of my life thus far had been rational, *so why would I suddenly expect it to be now?*

I became very aware that something profound was happening: *I was having a Spiritual Awakening.* A Spiritual Awakening is a process, and *it's grueling* and at times almost *unbearable.* It becomes *so lonely too,* because it became so hard to relate to people. But I knew I just had to *keep going.* I wasn't sure how I would even know when it was "completed". But once the process had started, like an avalanche… couldn't be stopped. While it was excruciating, I couldn't help but be excited and curious as to what I'd find at the end of this rainbow. I bet it's worth *more* than a pot of gold or any other material item.

I was going down that rabbit hole, and it was too late to climb out. Maybe I would find the fabled inner earth civilizations and reach Agartha. I've heard it's peaceful and abundant down there and all they do there is *create.* It's unlike up here on the surface of the earth, where it seems like all we do is *destroy.* I'm guessing that until the day that I can somehow figure out how to activate the other 92% of my DNA (or whatever that percentage is) that is dormant and *unlock my full potential*, my Spiritual Awakening would not be complete. I haven't the slightest idea how to do that, but I know I'll figure it out. *I always do, I'm determined and I never give up.* I know that there are things the human brain simply *cannot* comprehend, *yet I knew that my soul did.* My soul already has all the answers, I just needed to figure out how to access this knowledge.

I was told by my guides: *Ascension is the goal.* But I had to ask: *what does that even mean?* I had to do a little research. Ascension is the process of ascending (duh) or rising to higher levels of consciousness. Ascension is the conscious participation in our own evolution. Becoming conscious helped my ability to accurately perceive *truth.* As my consciousness rose, so did my vibrational frequency. I went through what's called an "ego death", *the ego is what keeps us separated. Yet we are not separate, we are All One.*

I BECAME AWARE THAT EVERYTHING IS INTERCONNECTED and I moved into a higher realm of love and light. Ascension would open me up to a whole new life with infinite possibilities, beyond the limitations of the 3D existence. *I decided that this was a worthwhile endeavor,* so I proceeded with that goal in mind. I had had enough of the pain and suffering, so this seemed to be heading somewhere better. *Thank God.*

I realized all of my suffering came *from my own thoughts.* I had to detach from my emotions and understand that *I am not my thoughts.* When I was unawakened, I was like a child who created my own problems due to unawareness. Now when I met someone who has not even begun to awaken, their complete lack of self awareness is *painful* to witness.

Once the layers got peeled back and my awakening kicked into high gear, *there was no going back. I had started awakening, and it was impossible to go back to sleep.* I had discovered the *true nature* of our reality, that we are always connected to *Source,* or *God. It is inside of us.*

So Ascension is my ultimate goal, although it may not happen in this lifetime. I'm not even sure what it would feel like or how I would know that I had gotten there. I only knew that life, *my life* in particular, was filled with so much *physical and emotional pain,* that reincarnating again just *wasn't an option for me.* I was determined to learn everything I was supposed to learn *in this lifetime,* so I wouldn't need to come back.

You must be willing to say no to the ordinary, and step into the extraordinary.[4]
—Aurora Ray

4. Aurora Ray, quote from the weekly email www.thegalacticfederation.com.

Having the goal of ascending and becoming enlightened didn't mean I was going to try and become a saint. *I'm no angel.* I couldn't imagine being celibate for the rest of my life. I wasn't about to give away all my material possessions and walk around wearing a potato sack either. However, it did mean I would have to *kill my ego* that kept me separate from others. I had to see past the *illusion* of the material realm; it wasn't real anyway or even all that important. I had to do self reflection with complete *honesty and transparency,* and go within to heal my wounds. I needed to actively work on raising my frequency by embracing joy, love and unity instead of letting myself stay stuck in emotions of grief, anger, greed or jealousy. *I had to forgive quickly and easily. I had to figure out a way to turn my fear into unconditional love.*

Turn your wounds into wisdom.[5]
—Oprah

I was so sick of crawling around like a slimy caterpillar, I needed to spin myself into a cocoon and *transform myself into a butterfly because I needed to fly.* I don't really identify with the archetype of a Phoenix rising from the ashes, I'm not that much of a badass. But I do identify with a butterfly, and seeing a butterfly had always reminded me of my mother. So I was on a *mission* to make such a metamorphosis. I wasn't getting anywhere by just inching along. But I should've been more careful what I was wishing for, because first God needed to wring me out like a sopping

5. Oprah Winfrey's commencement speech at Wellesley College, 1997.

wet towel. Which, as you can imagine, was *quite painful.* But I'm getting ahead of myself.

First, I need to rewind and go back, to explain how I got here. I had stepped into the *unknown* with this Spiritual Awakening, and *t*he farther I went into the mysteries of how the Universe works, the more curious I became. I had opened Pandora's box so of course, *I had to see what was inside.* So many things were being revealed to me, and it was a lot to process. At a certain point I asked for it to *slow down* a bit. The true nature of how the Universe is designed is almost beyond comprehension of the human mind. Understanding of it was going to require I use more than just my five senses. I accepted the possibility that I may not be able to comprehend everything, and I was going to have to be alright with that.

The soul is always on its way to somewhere, *ever evolving.* The only thing constant in life is change, and spiritual evolution is all a part of it. The whole reason we are here is to evolve beyond the physical to a higher consciousness and exit the wheel of karma. Then we are free to fulfill our *Dharma* or life purpose. *I was determined to get off this karmic merry-go-round because it wasn't very much fun. I needed fun, laughter, joy and...Love!*

CHAPTER 2

Small Town, Small Minds

Shortly after my mother died, my father remarried. My maternal grandmother was *livid,* and she fired him. It didn't help that he purchased an engagement ring for his new bride with the company credit card. *What was he thinking?* My dad was the CEO of the company my mother's father had built, a chain of Hallmark stores throughout Maryland, Pennsylvania and Delaware, where I was born. Actually, my grandmother had my alcoholic uncle fire my dad for her. As you might have guessed, there's nothing left of that company or the trust fund my sister and I supposedly had.

My sister and I were uprooted every few years to a different state where my father had found work. We weren't by any means well off, and it seemed like life was always such a struggle. I only knew this because I would overhear my parents talking about money problems and having to move *yet again,* and it worried me. They tried to hide it from us, but as kids my sister and I were both very perceptive. *Plus, we were always moving.* My sister and I were raised right, we are definitely not from the wrong side of the tracks. We always had everything we needed, and we were raised in a very strict Christian Mormon home. We were taught values and morals, had music and dance lessons and lived in decent neighborhood. We had normal friends and did all the same things any kid would do, *up to a point.* My sister and I both played soccer, and my dad was the coach. My sister played the violin, I was into gymnastics, ballet, and cheerleading. We both got good grades and got admitted to good colleges.

My maternal grandmother had been adopted by Mormons, she never knew her birth parents. But Grandma Betty never really liked the Mormon church and didn't identify with it. My mother wasn't raised all that religious, but she had already decided that she wanted to raise her children in the Mormon church. *She just needed to find the right guy that was on board with her plan.*

As the story goes, my mother and father were just friends at first, they weren't dating. One day, my dad and his three best friends were driving back from the Maryland shore and got in a horrible drunk driving car accident. My father, who was passed out in the back seat, *was the only survivor.* The paramedics first on the scene didn't think anyone was alive until they heard my dad moaning.

My dad was in a body cast and in the hospital for *nine months.* So my mother came to visit him every day, and decided it was the perfect time to tell him all about the Mormon church. My dad's parents identified as Methodist, but they weren't by any means religious. My dad was receptive and listened to my mother, and he was hooked. Was he hooked on her or the religion? I'll never be sure. But if getting in a dreadful car crash and losing your three best friends isn't a "Come to Jesus" moment, *I don't know what is.*

I've survived my life solely because I threw myself into *me.* I started with gymnastics, I wanted to be like Mary Lou Retton. She had just won a Olympic Gold medal. When I was doing gymnastics, I was in a focused place where I didn't have to face how horrible my life was. *It was my escape.* I loved it so much that I didn't care that rounding the bars ripped the skin off my hands. *I kept going.* I loved it, I could do a standing backflip and a split...well, at least one side. But then, I starting growing...and growing. I was *way taller* than I ever expected to be.

So I switched to ballet, *I wanted to be a ballerina.* This time it was the skin on my feet that was ripping off, *but I didn't care.* One day I realized it wasn't so much the ballet part that dazzled me, what I loved was *being on stage.* As it turned out, I wasn't the correct "body type" for this profession either...ballerinas have *really long legs, but tiny bodies.* I have long legs, sure, but I also have *an abnormally long torso.* Now, I know this to *be a fact,* because I have been turned down by major designers like Ralph Lauren to be a fit model. Just so you know, a fit model wasn't getting paid to be in a photo shoot, she was getting paid regularly just to go in and *try on clothes.* But a fit model always had to fit a certain size. *This was way before I realized that I don't fit into any mold. I'm not regular.*

For some reason, when the curtains were lifted and the spotlight *was on me, that was where I thrived.* Maybe it was the adrenaline, or maybe it was because I could *pretend to be someone else?* Whatever that feeling was I had on stage, the sensation I got once I was "on pointe" (in toe shoes) and became a "snowflake" in the Nutcracker; was *exhilarating.* I concluded that I had never really felt alive up until that point. *I was proud and happy to be a "snowflake"? For real?*

*Anyway...*I hadn't even discovered acting yet...*oh boy, this story gets so much better.*

The day I had proof there was a Higher Power, and that things unseen were *real,* was when I was 16 years old and got in a pretty gruesome car accident myself. Somehow I had convinced my step mother to let me borrow her car for cheerleading practice after school. All those gymnastics and ballet lessons had *paid off,* and I loved being a cheerleader. I remember feeling like I was going to be a little late to pick up my best friend Celeste, but I don't remember speeding.

It was the dead of winter in Pennsylvania, and there was snow and ice on every road. I decided to take a shorter route, the road less traveled as it were. This street was dense with trees, and there weren't that many houses. Suddenly, the car spun out of control! I was going in *circles. I completely panicked,* I didn't know what to do or how to get the car under control. *The car seemed to be possessed, it had taken on a life of its own.* As an inexperienced driver in an unsafe car, I ended up hitting a tree *head on.*

Good thing I was wearing my seat belt, or I wouldn't be here to tell this story. So instead of plummeting through the front windshield, the force of the impact caused me to knock the side window out *with my face.*

Thankfully the car had stopped at least, and there was a huge dent in the front. *I had wrapped a car around a tree, it was basically totaled.* I saw some steam coming up from the engine, and I wondered what I should do next. Then I glanced in the rearview mirror and caught a glimpse of myself. There was *blood, and massive amounts* of it, gushing from my face. I started to be *really* alarmed, *I knew this wasn't good.* I looked down to try and take my seatbelt off, but found it difficult as I was blinded by blood. Somehow

I was able to gather myself enough to get out of the car. I headed to the nearest house across the street. When I got to the door, the outer glass door showed me my refection and it was *literally straight from a God damn horror movie. Except this wasn't fake blood, it was real blood. It was my blood! Oh. My. God!!* The blood was gushing all down the front of me, and it was *ghastly. My panic turned to sheer terror. Was I going to die?* I didn't have time to think about that.

I banged on the door, and I knew I wasn't being polite about it. I screamed "*Help! Help me Please!*" I was being a *freak,* because well, *how could I not be?* I demanded that the lady let me in to use the phone to call my parents. She wouldn't. I thought I must have scared the hell out of her or that she didn't want her carpet to get all bloody. *But why couldn't she just call an ambulance for me?* This was before everyone had cell phones, obviously. *Couldn't she see the horror I had just seen reflected back at me?* Turns out she was blind, so she really couldn't see. But there was no way she was letting me into her house. *What was I supposed to do now?*

I was losing a lot of blood, and *fast.* I started to feel dizzy and lightheaded and was in a complete state of *panic. By now I was filled with absolute dread, maybe I was going to die.* Besides not being able to see from all the blood, I wasn't thinking straight. My heart was pounding right out of my chest, making the blood *pour out faster. Adrenaline kicked in, and everything seemed to go haywire.*

I went back to the car and wiped some blood from my eyes so that I could see. I sized up the situation. Sure, I was bleeding, but I didn't think a major artery had been severed. *Maybe I was being dramatic. But seriously? Look at the car I had wrapped around a tree...*I decided I needed to go to the other nearest house, but it was set so *far* back from the road. The big tree that I had hit that was practically *in the road* was on their property. Although, there wasn't any driveway or sidewalk path that I could see, everything was covered in three feet of snow. *So how was I supposed to get there?* I stood there in shock, *mouth agape*, for who knows how long. I wasn't wearing the right shoes to trek through that snow. Maybe someone would drive by and could go get some help? I'm not sure how long I was standing there, *but it felt like forever.* I had no choice, I needed help. So I took that first step towards the house.

ONE MOMENT LATER, A MAN DROVE UP ON THIS ICY ROAD. He just happened to be driving down this back road, somewhere in rural Pennsylvania at 7:30am. He got out of his car and picked me up from the middle of the road. I don't think he even said anything. He didn't ask me where I wanted to go, *he just knew.* He carried me through the snow to the house far back from the road.

I don't remember that much about him, but I do remember he had a kind face, brown hair and a mustache. He was so *calm* and *serene. Did he somehow miss the fact that my stepmother's car was wrapped around a tree and blood was gushing from my face? How did he know I was planning on heading to the other house far back from the road?*

What I do recall clearly was that he had on a white button down shirt under his overcoat. I only remember this because I kept apologizing for bleeding all over him. He was unfazed, and told me not to worry about that. *I wondered who he was and how he could be so calm.* Obviously, he would need to change his shirt, and possibly his whole outfit, before he went to work. I felt really guilty about that. It would probably make him late for work and his boss might be angry with him. But he wasn't annoyed about the shirt. He didn't even seemed shocked or panicked from looking at all my blood! He stayed with me until my stepmother arrived.

This woman in the house set far back let us in, *thank God*. She took one look at me, and *freaked out. It must have been really bad.* She called an ambulance and my step mom and got all wound up. Her hands were shaking and she kept saying "Oh my *God*". It was like I was her own child or something. *I must have been a gruesome sight.* Although her reaction was more normal than the guy's calm demeanor. When my step mom walked through the door, she took one look at me and burst into tears. *It quickly turned into full blown hysteria.* I wanted to say: "Mom, that's really not helping", but I don't think I said anything. *That bad, huh?*

A couple of weeks later, my mom was in the grocery store and saw the nice man. He asked her how I was doing. She said I was doing well, everything was fine. She told him I had had to have a bunch of stitches as she was loading her groceries onto the conveyor belt. She wanted to thank him for his help, but when she turned around, *he had vanished. We never learned his name or saw him ever again.*

I remember he was so calm and peaceful, *almost saintly.* I mean, he ruined his outfit and probably his whole day trying to help me. It was almost as if he *knew* I was going to be at that exact spot at that exact moment, and that I would need his help. *I was certain I had met my Guardian Angel. He saved my life.*

I WAS TAKEN TO THE HOSPITAL, AND A PLASTIC SURGEON was called in. He was another cheerleader's dad, and I remember him humming Grateful Dead tunes while he worked. I couldn't feel much, I'm not sure if they numbed me or if I was in shock. He had to pull out huge shards of glass from my face near my left ear, and I needed stitches. The broken glass had come *dangerously* close to my left eye. *Thank God* it hadn't blinded me! I had been saved from a horrible tragedy, and I *knew* that it was *God* and my Guardian Angel that had saved me. I'm sure the seatbelt helped a little too. But to me this didn't feel like an ordinary car accident. I believed I had been saved for some *special purpose, although at the time I had no idea what that was.*

The first time I looked in the mirror after the car accident, *I shrieked! I had seventy black stitches in my face, and I know because I counted them. I was Frank-en-face!* My parents made me go to school the day after I was stitched up. *They couldn't even let me take one day off? Or a week? Why such urgency to show the world what a freak I was?* I wasn't very happy that I was being sent back to school, especially since I had amazing grades and was in the top 10% of my class.

When everyone at school saw me, all I could see was the *shock and horror on their faces. Why, oh why, couldn't my parents let me hide away, at least until the stitches were removed?* I was absolutely *mortified.* I straight up looked like some creature from a horror movie, and I secretly wished that I could just *disappear.* It was the 90's, and horror movies were all the rage, but I didn't want to *be one.* I had only watched one horror flick and it gave me such nightmares that I had to sleep on my back for years afterwards. I had this fear of someone stabbing me, *thank you Friday the 13th.* Yet here I was, a real life horror show, *no special effects required. Welcome to the free freak show, enjoy the entertainment!*

High school didn't get much better after that. People somehow think that if you're a cheerleader or in the "popular" crowd, that your life will be all rosy and special. *But it doesn't work that way.* Being a teenager is just downright shitty, I'm convinced it's probably like that for everyone. I'm decided on this, *so don't try and change my mind.* Kids are *cruel,* and just plain *stupid.* I'd find out really soon just how dim witted they could be, especially the boys. Maybe that's why I always taught my boys to be kind to others *no matter what. No son of mine would grow up to be a bully. I've spent hours and hours making sure of it.*

The first time I drank alcohol, I was hanging out with a few people in my friend Rachel's basement. Her parents were divorcing, so they were clueless as to what we were doing, even though I think they were upstairs. I was pretty oblivious myself, I didn't know there would be alcohol there.

I hadn't intended to drink any alcohol, even when I saw it. And it wasn't peer pressure that made me drink it, *I couldn't give a fuck about that.* For me it was pure *curiosity,* and I had to know what it felt like. The guy who brought the alcohol didn't even want to share it, *I had to ask him if I could try it. Brilliant idea Rebecca!*

It had been hammered into my brain for so many God damn years: "Mormons don't drink alcohol". For Christ's sake, Mormons don't smoke cigarettes or even drink coffee. Premarital sex wasn't allowed, *ever.* Even kissing was frowned upon. *Really?* No one curses either. *Liar, cheater and thief* isn't even in a Mormon's vocabulary. Actually, anything that was fun that made life *exciting* seemed to be off limits. But for some reason, alcohol seemed to be the *worst of sins.*

Well, curiously killed the cat as the saying goes, although I never understood what that meant. I didn't die that night, obviously. Again, I was spared and allowed to live. *Except I was about to feel like I wanted to die. Of embarrassment*, that is. Maybe Mormons abstaining from alcohol would start to make sense after what happened to me that night. *Only it didn't, and I can't explain why.*

I'm a very stubborn person, I can't even hide it. If anybody tells me I *can't* do something, then that's *exactly what I'm going to do.* The more off limits or taboo it was, *the more I just had to try it. For fuck's sake already. How stupid was I? I couldn't help myself.* My strict Mormon parents absolutely forbade *everything.* Hell, I wasn't even allowed to go to a PG-13 movie! The more disciplined my parents became, *the more rebellious I got.* My step mom had even scared away a boy I *really* liked. She would make him come to the door to pick me up so she could *grill him.* I had to make the poor dude lie, because there was *no way* he could say he was taking me to a party. And of course, our stories needed to match. *My step mom was my first cock blocker! I was so pissed yet there was absolutely nothing I could do about it.* My parents strategy of keeping me "pure" and virtuous was not only *not working, it was backfiring.* I'm not even a liar by nature, but I wanted to have a *life.*

I had planned on calling my stepmom that night to tell her I'd be doing a sleep-over. I knew if I had asked her up front if I could spend the night at Rachel's house, she would have definitely said no. She wouldn't even have to give a reason, which was beyond *frustrating.* I hadn't even given her any *reason* not to trust me! *Not yet at least. I think she was projecting her own mistakes unto me. Well, that was quite possibly the worst idea ever.*

I took my first sip of alcohol and felt it burn all the way down my throat and on into my stomach. *Ugh!* It tasted like...*baby aspirin?* It was not very pleasant and I wondered if all alcohol tasted this disgusting. But what *was fun* was the feeling it gave me, almost immediately. I felt light as a feather, like I was floating up...*without a care in the world.* I loved the feeling so much that I ended up drinking *more.* Of course everyone knows that once you get that feeling, you need to *stop* drinking alcohol and start drinking water. *But no one had told me that.* By the time I realized my horrible mistake, *it was too late.* I was so naive and inexperienced, I didn't know jack shit. Soon enough I would *know* things I hadn't known before, and my blissful naively ended *that night. It was the end of my innocence, all within a matter of hours.*

The next thing I knew, my stepmom was there to *pick me up* from Rachel's house because *I had never called her.* I vaguely remember the possibility of puking in her laundry room sink before I completely blacked out. *I had no other memories.* The only thing I knew for sure at that moment was that *I would never drink Southern Comfort ever again. Good Lord.*

The next day we had an away football game. I boarded the bus and headed to the back where the cheerleaders sat. We always had to sit in the back of the bus like second class citizens. God forbid the football players would have to carry their gear a few extra steps. I was the only sophomore to make the varsity squad, everyone else on the bus was a junior or a senior. *I was way in over my head, completely out of my league.*

My Mormon naivety only made it worse. Usually I just tried to keep from drawing attention to myself. I tried to hide the fact that truly, *I had no idea what was going on.*

But that day was different. As I passed a football player, I heard him call me a name under his breath. And then, another player, called me the *same name.* I couldn't even decipher what the word was, and I tried to pretend like it wasn't directed *at me. I wondered what the hell was going on and my head was pounding, obviously. Were these stupid football players calling me a name? What was the name? And how did they come up with this little nickname?* My head was spinning and my mouth was all dry. I was nauseous and could still taste Southern Comfort. *Why would anyone drink that shit?*

I sat down and asked my friend Amy what the football players were saying, *and was it directed at me?* She said, "You don't remember anything from last night?" Oh and by the way, Amy wasn't even at Rachel's house that night. It wasn't a big party, *it was a small gathering.* Besides, the juniors and seniors rarely hung out with sophomores. They were too cool for that. I told her I remembered drinking something called Southern Comfort and the embarrassment of my stepmom showing up to pick me up. But the rest was a blur, because I had blacked out.

Then she told me what had happened. At first, *I couldn't believe it.* It didn't seem possible or even *probable.* I also immediately wondered how *she* could have known what happened that night. She wasn't even there! *No one on the bus was there that night...and yet everyone knew what happened to me except me? Was I living in the twilight zone? Was this some kind of joke?* I kept waiting to wake up and realize I was having a nightmare. *Oh, it was a nightmare, but I was wide awake.*

Apparently, some guy ended up at the party, who wasn't there before I passed out. So when I was completely *blacked out drunk,* he claimed that I "gave him a blow job" and that I had *bit his dick. WHAT? I told Amy that this couldn't be true. That guy wasn't even there!*

Hold on just a second here, I couldn't understand *how* that guy even *got* to our gathering in the first place! I didn't even know he was friends with my friends. *When had that happened?* He was pretty much the most unattractive dude in our grade. I never had glanced at him twice, he was nonexistent. I'm not saying I was a snob, *but the guy basically blended into the fucking background, he had zero personality.* I remember almost everyone from high school, it wasn't that big of a school. But he wasn't funny, outgoing or even *stood for something.* Then I would've paid attention to him. Oh. My. GOD!!!! My face burned red from embarrassment and *anger. How could this story even be true?* Why did seemingly *everyone* know about it? *There was no possible way, I was in denial.*

I was downright *furious* and clearly still refusing to accept this fabrication. If I had had a dick in my mouth, wouldn't I have remembered that? What kind of a fucking God damn *idiot* do you have to be to stick your dick in a girl's mouth who is completely *passed out?* He was an even *bigger bonehead* to go and *brag* about it because *he had just outed himself as a sexual molester. Who would even do such a thing?* He had to know that by telling people what it would make *him look like. Didn't he? He could go to jail, what he supposedly did was a crime.* Apparently, common sense is not so common. *Fucking hell.*

I couldn't even be sure that it even happened, but my reputation was *ruined. I was a virgin! This was the first time I had even tried alcohol!* To make matters worse, no one seemed to care that I had possibly been violated. Yet the molester was suddenly "cool"? *How on earth was this happening?* I felt like I was living in some sort of alternate reality. The psychopath becomes the "hero", and the victim of a *horrible crime* is mocked. *Why is everything so twisted up and backwards?*

If this story is even true, I hope I *did bite his stupid dick, and hard.* He deserved that at the very least. Although, I hoped far worse things would happen to him. To this day I regret not going to the police. He should've been locked up and taught a lesson. But what could I have said to the police? I don't remember anything and there were no witnesses. Plus, I was drinking underage. This is the exact reason *why* so many women get sexually abused and stay *silent. They* will get mocked, and it is their character that is *destroyed* in an attempt to save the dude from a harsher punishment. *But it is the men that commit the crime! It is so unfair!*

So that stupid nickname stayed with me *for the rest of high school.* Why hadn't he gotten a degrading nickname too, like "molester"? *Or "rape boy"? That's an appropriate moniker. How could he not have any repercussions for something that was an actual crime?* Could sticking his dick in a passed out girls mouth be the only action he ever got? Most likely. *What a loser.*

It's not that I was that traumatized by the supposed sexual abuse. It's the *aftermath* of it all that made me *angry.* How was I the one being degraded and called names while he was getting pats on the back? Why couldn't just one boy say to him and all the others, "Wow, that's fucked up, man. Maybe you shouldn't have done that. It's not right."

My friends had pretty much abandoned me as well. I wish at least one of them, upon hearing someone call me that horrible name, would've turned around and said: "Hey douchebag! Why don't you go tell your friend Molester that if he doesn't want his dick bit, maybe he shouldn't stick it in a passed out girls mouth?" But I don't blame them, they were all in hot water too. My stepmom showing up at the party meant we *all* got busted. My only saving grace was that my best friend Celeste wasn't there that night. Otherwise, my step mother would have never let me hang out with her again. Her friendship literally *saved* me and made my high school years bearable.

This is what the whole "Me Too" movement is all about. So many women that have been sexually abused are ashamed and *embarrassed* to say something when *they have done nothing wrong*. NO means NO. And I shouldn't have to explain that a woman that is unable to speak at that moment- *that also means no. Hey, if she could talk bro, she would say no. Let's just assume that, ok? Just in case. What kind of loony bin world do we live in that I'd actually have to explain this?*

This is what the main problem in society today. Women are literally *portals that bring in souls from another dimension, yet we are not treated as such.* Women are given the gift of *creation*, and are blessed with skills and abilities that men will *never posses*. Mankind would *cease to exist if it wasn't for us*. Men and women are *not equal*, we are different. One is not superior to the other. *Yet women are treated like shit. We feel like second class citizens, not as important as men*. We are raped, abused, torn down, belittled, not seen or heard, not given credit for our accomplishments and abandoned. Often we raise the next generation *all alone, without help from anyone else. No wonder there are so many angry feminists, I get it!*

To be honest, *I don't hate men. I love the good men.* Just to be fair, I have to tell you that the bad women *are way more evil* than the bad men. She will claim to be your "best friend", and fuck your boyfriend or husband and never bat an eyelash. She'll marry a man for money, then leave him with every penny she can. She'll trap a man *using a child,* and never feel bad about it. She doesn't care if he's embarrassed of her and hides her away. She doesn't even care if he's in love with someone else, or if he's *fucking other women.* All that matters to her is she got what she wanted. The evil women will stab you in the back, then turn around and smile in your face and pretend like she didn't just call you a *cunt. Evil women are way more sneaky and deceptive* than the bad men. *It's frightening.* It's a whole other ball of wax that I shouldn't get into.

Every man should treat a woman as if she is his mother, sister, or daughter. *The good women should be held in high regard at all times.* Most women are not asking that men treat us as if we are more important than they are. Clearly, both men and women are equal in value, *but we are not equal. We are uniquely different, and for a good reason.* Those angry women that want to "topple the patriarchy" have got it messed up. We can't *take down the patriarchal system. The rise of the Divine Feminine does not have to be the downfall of the Divine Masculine!* What women need to do is re*claim their own power, rise up and work together with men, not try and take them down!* Although, at that moment I knew of at least one male *that should've gone down.*

The Masculine and Feminine are complementary, we are meant to *work together and support each other.* One's strength is the others weakness, and vice versa. The woman creates, loves and nurtures the offspring. The man, because he is blessed with more strength, is *supposed to protect.* Yet today's men are passive and *weak,* they are not held responsible for their actions and they are not living up to their divine mission which is *to protect!* This is why God chose to make men stronger, *because of their divine mission to protect!* But they're abusing their power, and i*t has gone on long enough.*

I am holding all men responsible to step up to their divine mission to protect. I'm starting with my sons. I've already accomplished part of this, because my older son is currently serving in the Israeli army. He didn't *have to serve, he wanted to.* In Israel, all the boys and girls are required to serve in the army. But you can get out of serving in the army if you lost a sibling. My son is not even an Israeli citizen, yet he wanted to serve! He even had to submit his younger brother's birth certificate to prove he has another sibling. This worried me, of course, but he was determined. *You're a good boy, my love. I'm so proud of you honey!*

But angry feminists seem to forget that we couldn't survive without men. *Wouldn't we* all *have been eaten by a saber tooth tiger by now if not for men? We need men.* Personally, I *love the good men.* This unbalance of the masculine not being held accountable has forced women to do everything; we give birth, raise, support, *and protect* the future generations! *Modern women have to do the man's job too. Where are all the real men right now? What are they so busy doing?* Because *women have let men get away with this,* some masculines have become passive *pussies who abuse their power.* Instead, men are taking advantage of their superior strength and power. *They do whatever they want to women without any repercussions. The very people they are supposed to protect, instead they are harming! Something is really off here.* No wonder so many women are *outraged!* Women are exhausted and angry, *and* we cannot keep up this charade any longer.

I hoped Molester would rot in hell. By now I'm sure his karma has come back around to him. But he was now friends with football players, and he didn't even play sports. There was absolutely nothing special about him, *yet suddenly everyone knew who he was.* He wasn't even one of the "nerdy" kids who got into an Ivy League school. He didn't have enough musical talent to be a "band geek". He didn't even have a *personality! This is one of the things I didn't want to share, yet my rant continues. Clearly, I am still pissed about this.* I had actually buried the trauma so deep that I had forgotten about it. *But I've been nice for way too long...*

Speaking of "band geeks", those people were my *friends.* They were talented, and it wasn't fair that they were labeled as "geeks". They were the ones out there practicing every God damn morning, even in the *dead of winter.* They marched around the football field at the crack of dawn before school *to practice. Practice makes perfect, and our band was amazing.* Our school was *known* for our marching band, while the football team *sucked balls.* The football team lost *every single game, without fail.* It wasn't even ever a "close call", they were constantly *slaughtered.* And yet, *those dudes were somehow cool? They were the ones that could slap a label on a girl that had been sexually molested?* And the people in the band, who had *actual talent* and were dedicated, *were the geeks? Am I the only one who thinks this is really fucked up? The whole world is twisted and doesn't make any sense.*

Our football team was such a mockery that it became a joke. On game day we would say to each other: "Hey, are you going to the band game later?" *Everyone went to see the band perform.* They certainly didn't enjoy watching the football losers fumble the ball over and over again. I had to cheer for them, and it was humiliating and embarrassing. I used to feel bad for them, but not after they invented my sub-human nickname. *Fuck them. They probably all still live in that shitty Pennsylvania town. Serves them right.* Why can't people be respected, treated equally and fairly and not be *abused*? Maybe my moral principles were too high, this was high school after all.

I made a commitment right *then and there:* I would *always* stand up for the underdog. I would applaud and *recognize talent,* not who everyone else thought was "special". Being "cool" meant fitting in, and I already knew there was absolutely *nothing special about that!* Anyone could try and *fit in!* What was unique and *special* was someone who wasn't afraid to *stand out!* Someone who stood by their *convictions,* even if it meant *standing alone. Here I was, and still am, standing alone.*

If you don't stand for something,
you'll fall for anything.
—Attributed to Alexander Hamilton

I had to get out of that town. *I hated it!* I had been humiliated, and no one stood up for me or told me that what happened *wasn't right,* except my friend Celeste. No one even asked me if I was alright, or offered a shoulder to cry on, *not even my own parents!* As a parent myself, I couldn't imagine letting something like that slide. I was *mortified* that I was *stuck there* for two more *years.* I wanted somebody to shoot me, or at the very least, hit me with a tranquilizer gun. It was *sheer torture.* I felt especially betrayed by my own father, shouldn't he at least *say something? Anything?* Although, he did nothing to process the grief of losing my mother. Maybe I was expecting too much from him.

My parents seemed to blamed me for this incident. *Or they just ignored it because that was more convenient.* I guess they could rationalize it because I shouldn't have been drinking in the first place. Mormons do not drink *and* I was underage. I felt this smug "you got what you deserved" attitude from them. *What kind of fucked up world is this? So your daughter is supposedly sexually abused, and you blame it all on her, because she shouldn't have been drinking? Really?*

I vowed to get the hell out of that town and never come back. I didn't belong there in that shitty town, I didn't even belong in that *family.* Hell, I don't even think I belong on earth, *yet here I am.* So much for that grander life purpose, this shit *sucked!* I *hated* everyone, my parents the *most!* I couldn't be myself. I couldn't stand up for myself. I had no voice. I felt invisible while at the same time completely *exposed,* with no protection *at all. I wondered if all of life was going to be this way?* Was this just the "fate" of women as the "weaker" and "sub superior" human being? *It wasn't fair. I would try and change it even if it was the last thing I did on this earth.*

I made peace with my parents many years ago, or at least that's what I'm telling myself. I do love them, I just hate their parenting skills. *Seriously. I would never let any child of mine go without therapy when something abusive happened to them, even if they knew better not to do it!* I told my parents not to read this book, *I hope they take my advice, but that's not my problem. I will spare no one in speaking my truth.* I think my parents did the best they could. They were only trying to protect me from *going to hell. The only issue was…I was already in hell.* They were so strict which only made me more rebellious. I felt I couldn't even come to them with any minor problems, they wouldn't understand it. The rift between us grew wider and wider…*until there was nothing left holding us together.*

When my sister left for college, that's when *all hell broke loose,* and I was the one that unleashed it. My sister had been my ally, *we were in the same shitty boat together.* She had taught me how to sneak the car out of the garage when my parents were asleep. She had way more balls than I ever had!! I was at least still trying to "be good", while she just didn't give a fuck. *I admire that about her.* Although, I'm still trying to understand my parents reasoning for completely ignoring the situation. I'm a parent now too, but my boys know they can tell me *anything.* They know they'll get in a lot more trouble if they lie, and they know I'd find it hard to trust them again. I think once my step mom realized she would never have her own children, she just checked out of the parenting thing. I get it, it's not easy. *But in that moment, escaping the hell that was my life was literally the only thing I could think about.*

I prayed day and night for liberation from that hell hole. I couldn't stand where I was, and I felt *trapped.* By this time I was already 18, but I did have to stay and graduate high school. In the meantime, *I felt like wild, caged animal that I had been backed up against a wall. I felt threatened and needed to defend myself. I had to fight for my right to exist… on my own terms! I had to battle just to be me? Something had to change, and fast, or it would not be pretty.*

The only thing I could do was further rebel, because *what did it matter?* And so my life as the "party girl" began. *Maybe it was my destiny.* Or maybe, I was just a teenage girl trying to have some sort of control over her *own life.* My parents were *so proud* of me when they announced the senior superlatives in the year book and all my classmates had voted for me as the "class partier". I'm being sarcastic, of course. *Well shit, at least I made the best of it and had some fun.* Having fun at whatever I was doing became my motto and life long goal that I still follow today.

My mum used to say to me "you can't have fun all the time"and I used to say "Why not? Why the fuck can't I have fun all the time?"
—Kate Moss

I can't say becoming a party girl fucked me up, I was probably already beyond repair. I felt abandoned by my emotionally unavailable father. He did everything he could to make my step mother happy, which usually meant taking her side. My sister and I were only afterthought, and then later, *an annoyance. Were we that bad?* As you can see, my childhood was really special.

The *one man, my father,* who was always supposed to protect me, had *abandoned me.* Although, he certainly cared if I wasn't following his rules. *So maybe that's why I broke some many of them.* That was my *cry* for attention! I broke all the rules, as many of them I was could, *as often as I could. I felt powerless, voiceless and invisible.* I was a broken little girl who sucked my finger until I was eight years old. I had to learn how to soothe myself, and I still struggle with an oral fixation. *I guess I'd always be ignored and pushed aside...and left unprotected. But why the fuck should I just shut up and take that? There was absolutely no way I would...*

I was already pretty fucked up, so I figured: *why not go all the way?* All I had to do was keep getting good grades to finish high school, which was easy enough. I felt grateful because I know academics doesn't come easily to everyone. But for me, it took zero effort. I couldn't understand how anyone struggled with it. I had a near perfect memory, which is insane to think about. All I had to do was *plan my escape*. I had already nearly perfected the art of not being caught for doing illegal activities like drinking beer and smoking weed. *Honey, it's an art, and I'm an artist.*

I just had to keep *dancing*, because *it kept me sane.* When I was dancing, *those* were the only real moments from that time period that I enjoyed. When the band started to play and the cheerleaders did their little dance, *that* was the only time I actually felt *good.* Excluding when I felt good because I was high and/or drunk. *Dancing literally saved me.*

By senior year, I was the captain of the cheerleading squad and choreographing our routines was my responsibility. I excelled at it. It gave me something creative to do that wasn't self destructive. *Thank God.* I threw myself into the task. I don't think anyone else knew how to choreograph or even knew what the word meant. Our cheerleading coach was a joke, I don't think she was ever a cheerleader in her life. She was just a bitch that was overseeing us because we were minors. That's how it works in the life of a teenager who had no control over her life, we needed "supervision". Even when that person was more fucked up than we were. We always wondered what kind of mood she would be in that day. *Was she having her period? Or was her husband not fucking her enough? It was always something.* I guess some people just want to be miserable, and we are all just going to have to let them. Whatever.

Most folks are about as happy as
they make up their minds to be.
—Abraham Lincoln

I also kind of took over the job of the coach, because she wasn't doing much for us except annoy us. I discovered I had incredible leadership skills as well. *My my, the party girl is actually a leader? Who knew? How interesting.* The girls looked up to me, and they came to me for advice. I had already been through high school *hell,* so it turned out I gave some really stellar advice. Even with my "bad" reputation and the fact that I may have been somewhat out of control (and still might be), I found out what I was truly made of. I didn't even know where this wisdom came from, but I had answers. *Sigh...if I could only take my own advice.*

I had just about made it through high school. One day, very soon, I would be *free!* I couldn't wait, the day could not come soon enough. I had gotten into Penn State main campus as a freshman, which was a pretty big deal. You had to have amazing grades and a great resume for admission. I was the only one in my high school that would get to go live on the main campus as a freshman, everyone else had to go to the smaller satellite campuses until junior year. Although, it wasn't *that big* of an accomplishment, a lot of my friends went to Ivy League schools. But I knew Ivy League wasn't in my budget, a state school was really my only option. My parents were already saving to travel the world, which is what they're doing now. They weren't about to help my sister and I with tuition, *but they sure as shit kept hammering into our heads how important a college degree was. I could've used a little help, but I guess they were busy.* Yet I was happy about my situation, and skipped the entire last month of school my senior year. I guess once I went full on rebel, *there was no stopping me.*

I wondered if I would be happy at Penn State. I just couldn't imagine myself in a sorority and trying to fit in with other girls. *I realized I don't fit in anywhere, and I had stopped trying.* Penn State is one of those schools where if you aren't into greek life, you pretty much didn't have a social life. A sorority initiation is probably not as intense as what they did to the frat boys pledging a fraternity, *but still.* I couldn't imagine myself sucking up to some junior or senior "big sister" and trying to make everyone like me. *I had stopped doing that by the fourth grade. It was pointless. You can like me or don't, it doesn't matter.*

So I pondered what life at Penn State might be like. It could be just like the hellish small Pennsylvania town I was already in, *but on steroids. Yikes.* At least I had learned how to drink and have a good time and not black out or make stupid decisions. But I started to have serious doubts about college. At least I'd be on my own and my parents wouldn't be able to control me or scare boys away and I'd be far away from this fucking *hell.* But I told God that I didn't think that was the place I was supposed to be. *Would it be too much trouble, God, if you could show me where I should be? Because I have no fucking idea.*

If everyone is thinking alike,
then somebody isn't thinking.
—George S. Patton

Then one day, a miracle happened. Just one of the many that would occur in my life, for which I am forever grateful. A friend of mine was going to a convention, a "model search" and asked me if I wanted to go with her. I had a free ride and a place to stay, *so of course I said yes!* My parents weren't pleased about this, and did everything they could to place some doubt in my mind that I could ever make it as a model. Being half naked in a photo shoot doesn't align with Mormon values, but I didn't give a shit. *This was my ticket out of this life where I clearly did not belong. God had answered my prayers, He always did!* Penn State would still be there if I changed my mind.

As fate would have it, an agency in Miami Beach and Chicago wanted to represent me, despite my facial scars. *I was over the moon! Finally,* being heads taller than everyone else was a *good thing! I had no idea that it was a privilege to be tall.* I had always wanted to be petite, it seemed more feminine. But of course, the tiny cheerleaders were the ones we were throwing into the air. The tall ones were the ones that *tossed them up and then caught them.* Since I'm afraid of heights (and of being thrown into the air, to be quite honest), it all worked out in my favor. And I can honestly say that I never dropped anyone.

I felt like I had to take this chance. Modeling was my ticket out of this hum drum life that was slowly killing me, *strangling me to death with every mediocre second. I was dying, but had suddenly been resuscitated.* It was a *miracle,* and I said repeated prayers of gratitude to God. I wasn't scared at all, *I was excited.* This was going to be an adventure! It's funny because people often ask my sister and I: "How did two small town Pennsylvania girls end up in Manhattan and Miami Beach?" We are always not quite sure how to respond to this, so we say nothing. But what we are thinking is: *how did you end up still in this small town?* I've never been afraid to be different and take chances. I feel sorry for people who can never imagine leaving their comfort zone. *I'm guess I'm lucky, I've never had comfort zone. It's all been sheer torture so far.*

From that moment on, *I was me. I'd never have to pretend to be someone I was not. I'd be me until the day I died, that I knew for sure.* I *knew* that there were things I could not *see,* but that did *not* mean that they didn't exist. *God does hear and answer my prayers.* Later, I would find out that God only answers my prayers if I asked for the *correct* thing. I would eventually learn how to reframe my request in order to get exactly what I wanted. I knew the human eye can only see a fraction of the light waves, *but there is a whole Universe that exists beyond our measly five senses.* My soul could see and understand it, and I reasoned that absolutely *anything was possible.* I knew that I was being guided and protected for some reason, although I wasn't sure what that reason was or where I'd be going. *What's it gonna be Rebecca?*

There are unseen forces at work in the Universe. These things aren't *supposed to make sense,* but they're all a part of the plan. Supernatural things are *normal, I felt like I was the only one that knew this.* Sometimes, the most illogical thing is the best choice, and *we have to go with.* Following my intuition gave me great results. I was living life on my own terms and that's my secret to happiness, *following your heart.*

Truth is stranger than fiction but it
is because fiction is obliged to stick
to possibilities; truth isn't.[6]
—Mark Twain

The real triumph came when I just *stopped giving a fuck.* I was going to follow my own inner guidance, *no matter what.* I couldn't see beyond the veil but I could definitely *feel* it, *my mother was guiding me.* I was being Divinely led somewhere, for some greater purpose. *I wasn't entirely sure of the plan, but I'd certainly figure it out along the way.* All I had to do was trust my intuition.

Graduation day finally came, and *I was relieved.* That day mirrored my whole high school experience. We all sat there on the football field wearing ridiculous caps and gowns with our clothes underneath. The fabric was cheap, it was scratchy and felt *so uncomfortable, like all go high school.* It was about 100 degrees in July. The school had been shut down the whole month of January due to a massive blizzard that left us trapped in our homes. So we had to get in the required amount of school days in, which meant going to school the whole month of June. *Can you see why I skipped the last month?*

Yet I sat there, like everyone else. Have I mentioned how much I hate doing what everyone else is doing? It was so hot that day, I could barely breathe. *Maybe smoking Marlboro*

6. Mark Twain, *Following the Equator: A Journey Around the World* (American Publishing Company, 1897).

reds wasn't the best idea I've ever had. I sat through the whole *excruciatingly long* tradition of having everyone come up to the stage and get their diploma. I would've been happier if they had just dropped my diploma in the mail.

Then...it started to rain. This was not a little sprinkle, it was as if *the heavens had opened and let out a torrential downpour.* This sudden wall of water didn't seem to faze the Salutatorian *at all.* She was giving her speech, and *insisted on finishing it. Her voice was so monotonous it would've put me to sleep had it not been for the downpour. Yawn.* Someone was holding an umbrella over her head and she kept talking while we all got *drenched. I wonder what she even said. Nobody heard one word of it.* My poor grandmother's hair dye was streaming down her face. It ruined the dress she had bought just for that special occasion, and she was *mortified.* I, on the other hand, only felt a *tremendous sense of relief.* The rain had cooled me off a bit, and getting soaked felt like a baptism of some sort that was initiating me into my next phase of life. *It was over. I was finally free.*

CHAPTER 3

My New Life

In the fall of 1994, I packed up two suitcases and headed to Miami Beach and *never looked back.* I had started a new life, and one that would be on *my terms.* I thought I was so smart and was convinced my naivety had died in that shit Pennsylvania town. I was a fresh faced,18 year old fashion model. I was a "party girl", with an abnormally high sex drive and daddy issues. *What could go wrong?*

Back then agencies wouldn't even consider you for modeling unless you were 5'9". I came in at 5'8.75", which was *good enough.* My dad balked, he didn't understand how I was going to make it. "Where you going to live?" he inquired. "Dad, the agency puts you up in a model apartment with roommates. They take the money out of your paycheck, don't worry!" *As if he had a say.* I had been working for years at part time jobs and I had enough money saved. *I knew I could do it.*

My parents have this ingrained belief that everyone should "go to college and get a *good* job", *working for someone else.* They would say: "Save your money, live frugally and someday you'll be able to retire." They believe this *so much so* that they continue to prod that advice into my head to this day. *But not everyone thinks the same way,* obviously. There's no excitement or adventure in that life. It's like that play *Death of a Salesman,* which, by the way, is *a tragedy.* I knew I needed to have *adventures* or I would suffocate and die a slow and painful death. I *had* to give my life meaning, and discover the secrets of the Universe. *As luck would have it, the fashion industry is full of dark secrets!* I had one way ticket into the school of "how the world really works", *and I grabbed it.* I had a head on my shoulders and by this time I had street smarts.

I arrived in Miami Beach and it was a world unlike anything I had ever seen in my life. The buildings were bright and colorful, in all shades of pastels like pink, peach, and yellow. The atmosphere was laid back and cool. The beach was divine, and the color of the ocean reflected beautiful shades of teal green. The sun was shining, the sky was an incredible blue. *It was warm year round, even in the winter.* People were riding around on bikes or roller blading and they didn't seem to have a care in the world. And everybody was so *good looking. I was hooked.*

I walked into Elite Miami that was located in a swanky art deco building in South Beach. The first thing I was instructed to do by my agent was to "go get a tan". She added in: "Make sure you don't have any tan lines." My jaw dropped, *this was not what I was expecting.* I call this "white girl problems", I was all pasty white and probably *stood out.* So my first day on the job, there I was laying on the beach *topless.* I didn't even know anyone *could* or was *allowed to* lay out topless! *I guess it's a perfectly normal thing people did in Europe, but I didn't know that.*

When I met some of the other models, I finally felt like I met other people that *got me.* These women were tall, gorgeous and confident. Like me, *they didn't give a fuck what anyone thought about them.* During the days when we weren't getting a tan that was a requirement for the job, we would sit around at castings. We would wait for *hours and hours* for our name to be called so we could present our portfolio of our photos and meet the clients. Any single casting could go on *forever,* so we just sat around, smoked cigarettes (by this time I had gotten smarter and had switched to lights), drank diet coke, and rapped about life.

At night, *the fun would began.* We went out almost *every* night, if we didn't have an early call time the next day. We all got into every single club, even my roommate Zoe, who was only 16 at the time. *We never paid for one drink.* We didn't just *get in to the club,* we were moved to the front of the line. *We were treated like royalty* and were partying with celebrities.

One of the first people I met was a really nice French guy who owned the hottest restaurant in town. He would set up a table full of models and give us all free food and drinks. Of course, it made his restaurant immensely popular to have beautiful women around. I was just grateful for the free dinners, otherwise I might have had bowl of Cheerios. I'm still friends with him to this day, *I never forget people who do nice things for me.*

I had the perfect look for this job. I was the blonde "girl next door" and was put into the category of "catalog queen" right away. The exotic girls did more editorial work for magazines, *but the catalogs jobs were where we made the most money.* European catalogs all came to shoot here in Miami Beach, and the Germans especially loved the blondes. I was making *in one single day, the same amount of money that a whole semester cost at Penn State. I couldn't believe it!*

I had finally found where I was supposed to be and what I was meant to be doing. And I've never stopped, *I still model. If you love what you're doing, it doesn't feel like work.*

Most girls would drop out of the modeling industry after a couple of years. Either they didn't like the business, or couldn't handle being objectified and rejected. I never took the rejection of not booking any particular job personally. If the client was looking for a waif brunette, then *they wouldn't book me, an athletic blonde.* I let that roll right off me, *why would I care? I mean, how was I supposed to change who I was?* I was fearless. The clients started to take notice of my unabashed, "I don't give a fuck" attitude, which came off as *confidence.*

Within a few months, I had booked the lead role in the Spin Doctors music video "She Used to be Mine". The small town molesters and loser bullies probably thought I was famous. *Clearly, they didn't know any* better. While the job didn't pay as much as the German catalogs, *it was fun. I enjoyed it so much that I discovered another thing I was passionate about: Acting.*

One day someone gave me the book "The Magic of Believing" by Claude M. Bristol. I devoured every word, I couldn't put it down. It was my very first self-help/law of attraction book, *and I've been hooked ever since.* The book was about how we *become* what we contemplate. How belief *makes* things happen. Coupled with inspired *actions and* following my intuition, I knew I could make all my dreams come true. I already believed it, and *here was my confirmation!*

Reading this book was my first exposure to the power of the mind and the Law of Attraction. *It was a huge turning point in my life.* This thing we call our life, is really all made up in our heads. If we think negative thoughts, that's what we end up manifesting. "We become what we think" or "What you think you become" is valid and true. *I thought I was so smart, but oh, I still had so much to learn.*

So, if I could really *believe* that anything was possible, then I knew could manifest whatever I wanted. Instead of focusing on what I didn't have, I allowed myself to imagine what I *wanted* to have. I have the most active imagination due to childhood trauma, *so I guess there's a silver lining to every tragedy.* I also got into the emotional state of already *having* what it is I desired, and the effect was nothing short of *spectacular!* I was just beginning to discover *manifesting,* and it sent me down a path that very few chose to follow. *But they are the ones that are missing the magic.*

But there was one *super important* missing puzzle piece that I didn't know about at that time. No matter how much I visualized my goals and believed in my mind that it was possible, *it was really my subconscious mind that was running the show.* In the future, I would manifest the life I *thought* I wanted to live, only to latter realize it was the life I had been *programmed to want.*

Until you make the unconscious conscious, it will direct your life and you will call it fate.
—Carl Jung

I was using my positive mindset to manifest, even with that missing piece. I had already accepted that there were things I couldn't see or understand, but that I was embracing nonetheless. My brain couldn't quite grasp these concepts, but my Higher Self *knew damn well what she was doing.* She's an absolute badass. Even at that age, I knew about her. I listened to what she was telling me to do, *I followed my intuition.* I knew that sometimes I'd have to dismiss my logical mind and *go with what my gut was telling me.*

Once my mind was wide open, things in my life took a wild turn. Whatever my mind could conceive, I could achieve. I went to go live the life I had dreamed up in my head. *I made all my dreams come true.* But have you ever heard the saying: *Be careful what you wish for?* It was what my subconscious mind that had "wished" for, what I had been "programmed" to want by my parents, the Mormon church, *and society. It turned out that that life did not make me happy.*

Our thoughts create our reality, sure, but I should've given more thought to all the circumstances in my life. But I've corrected my mistakes, mostly. It's a work in progress. First, I feel the need to clear up some major misunderstandings that have been going on for centuries. I stumbled upon this knowledge quite by accident. *But there are no coincidences in life.*

It is my theory that there is something that has been *hidden* from us. What's been concealed is just how powerful *we are.* "They" are keeping the fact that our minds and souls are so *powerful,* that we can create our own reality, a*nd just about anything we want.* We are all connected by the Divine Matrix, the Universal Mind, because are all creations of the Almighty God. We have within us *all* the answers and the creative abilities that He possesses. *God is within us. This secret has been hidden away. Why do you think that is?*

I had made enough money for tuition and then some, so after the season in Miami Beach was over, I headed to Penn State. I chose Business as my major, and Psychology as my minor. Being a business major was an obvious choice for me, *being an entrepreneur was in my blood.*

My grandfather had built up a massively successful business from nothing. He wasn't anything like my parents that raised me to think getting a college degree and finding a "good job" working for someone else was the only way to go. Even though my grandfather was long gone and I had never even met him, *he had certainly somehow passed down the entrepreneur gene to me.*

I had started my own business at the age of twelve. I was really into this series of books called "The Babysitter's Club"; I had read all of them. So I recruited my sister and the neighbor girl to be in my business. I made fliers and put them in all the neighbors mailboxes that said: "Call one number and you're guaranteed a babysitter!" *It was a great success.* I took all the jobs if I could. I mean, *the idea was mine.* My "employees" were the backup so that if I wasn't available, my business could live up to it's promise. Even at a young age, I instinctively knew I'd never be happy working like a slave for someone else.

Choosing psychology as a minor was also a good choice. Most psych majors were pretty fucked up, *like I was.* We all had childhood trauma, and I'm sure my childhood seemed like a cake walk compared to what some of these other people had been through. I met one girl who had been raped by her uncle as a child! *Jesus Christ!* All of a sudden I was glad to have been raised by Mormons. *Out of nowhere,* the possibility of having a dick shoved in my mouth while passed out drunk *didn't seem like such a big deal.* It really put things into perspective. I guess studying psychology was our way of trying to understand all the bullshit, *because there had to be a reason for all the madness, right?* It's something to think about before you go seek out a therapist.

I figured out right away that I didn't fit in at college either, but *I think I knew that going in.* I had convinced my sister to leave the Mormon college my parents had pressured her into attending and come join me. She was absolutely miserable there anyway, so it was a no-brainer. I made the best of my time there and was determined to *have fun.* On Halloween, I convinced my friends to dress up in costumes, drop acid, and walk around town. *We didn't see one other person wearing a costume. Dressing up for Halloween is uncool? I guess the "anything goes" only applies to South Beach.*

I thought that I was doing the right thing by going to college, but I had unanticipated the *culture shock.* First of all, Penn State is literally the *only* thing in that town. The city is actually named State College, PA. It was freezing there too, and I had gotten used to living in paradise in Miami Beach. To make matters worse, you couldn't even get into any bars with a fake ID, not that I had one. It's not that I cared that much about drinking beer or getting into some shitty college bar, I was more into weed anyway. Only, I went from being let into every fabulous club, drinking with celebrities and not paying for anything, *to being left out in the cold. Literally. And man, it was cold.*

The whole experience felt so *ordinary, and I didn't want to be ordinary.* I had already had a life most people wouldn't be able to dream of having, or wouldn't even think of trying. Honestly, I can't say I learned much that semester that I didn't already know. Except for maybe in my biology class. I learned every stupid name of every single part of the body.

Besides the major organs like the heart, brain and stomach, the other names of these body parts are all at least 12 to 25 letters. *Who is the person that made up all these stupid names? Why so many letters? Jesus.* I memorized them all, got a B in the course, *then promptly forgot everything. College was so well worth the money!* I learned more about life and business in the modeling industry than I ever learned in college. Besides, I know some college graduates that are complete *morons, so there's that.*

I'll admit it, I'm different, some call me weird. Not that I cared what anyone labeled it. *Have I mentioned how much I loathe labels?* For me, it's better than being called average. I'm sure everyone has abnormal experiences, but they're just dismissing them *in order to fit in*. But there are *no coincidences*. I started noticing these things when they happened, *I was paying attention now*. I assigned *meaning* to all the craziness, and once I gave every maverick thing some sort of meaning, *that's when things started to get interesting. I had the will to be different, and I don't even have a ball sack.*

I never set out to be weird. It was always other people who called me weird.[7]
—Frank Zappa

The semester ended and I needed to get back to work to keep up my expensive college habit. It was about to be summer, and I knew there was no work in Miami Beach. Most of my clients only came into town to shoot seasonally,

7. Frank Zappa, co-written by Peter Occhiogrosso, *The Real Frank Zappa Book* (Poseidon Press, 1989 and Simon & Shutter, 1990).

and it *was too hot there in the summer.* So I set my sights on Elite Chicago, the other agency I had met that wanted to represent me.

I got to the model's apartment in Chicago and took a look around. It was pretty basic, like a crash pad. While I was the only one there, there were at least six bunkbeds. *Wow, I guess they could really pack them in.* I had already had dinner, but it wasn't bedtime. I wondered what I was going to do with myself until the agency opened the next morning.

Only moments later, a beautiful brunette walked through the door and introduced herself as Michelle. We eyed each other suspiciously for a few moments. *I wondered, should show her around the apartment? I had only just arrived myself, and the apartment was owned* by *the agency. I thought* that *might be awkward.* So I made some small talk and asked her where she was from. She said she was Iowa, I told her I was from Pennsylvania. I asked her how long she had been modeling and I probably mentioned something about the weather. Typical small talk. Then...*another long, awkward silence.* So I said, "Well, I need a cigarette!". Her eyes lit up and she said, "Oh-me too! Let's go smoke a cigarette!". We headed to the stairwell and lit up, *and that was it.* The rest of the summer we were attached at the hip. We were roommates, sometimes we worked together, and we *always* went out together.

It took me a few weeks to learn how to properly pronounce her last name, but she didn't mind. In fact, she was *just like me!* She was laid back and down to earth. She didn't take herself too seriously and she *always* had fun whatever she was doing. I have to say, I've never had more fun with anyone in my entire life. We both had the same cheerful, optimistic attitude, and being around her only amped that up in me.

After the summer ended, I went and did another semester at Penn State. *I really had every intention of finishing college as I had been programmed that it was something I had to do.* The biggest problem was, models have an expiration date. By the time you were 30, you were "over the hill" and "irrelevant" if you weren't *already famous. Cue the eye roll. It's twisted, I know.* And models don't get famous for being a catalog queen, *not that I cared.* I'm not saying I agree with this concept that women "lose value" as they age. In fact, *I hate it. It is diametrically opposed to my basic belief system.* I would never go back to my 20's, I'm way more confident now. I might have looked really great, but I didn't know my head from my ass. *Also, I was insecure and masked it with a big ego. Quite frankly that's the truth, as embarrassing it is to say.* Some wisdom can only be gleaned from actual life experience. *Society has this all backwards, as usual.* In the institution *of now*, women *decrease in value* as they age, *whereas men do not.* Men become more successful and "distinguished" as they get older. *What a load of crap. This is some fucked up bullshit that I will never buy into.*

I've built my self worth from *nothing,* but I will admit that it's not easy getting older as a woman. Thank God I'm a Capricorn rising, my astrologer says that we seem to stay young forever and seem to age backwards. *I'll claim that!* Every time I feel a slight twinge of insecurity about my age, I have to gently remind myself that getting older is a privilege denied to *so many, like my mother and Sammy. Age is just a number.* Then, I insist on telling myself: *Self: you are the exact same age as Angelina Jolie and you need to calm the fuck down. Works like a charm.*

I really enjoy being in the fashion industry, it is exciting! I've traveled the world and met so many interesting people.

I got into acting through modeling. My agency had something called "the beauty department", which was a nice way of saying they needed a model (or someone who *looked* like one) for a commercial. I discovered I loved acting as well, and in 1999 I joined the actors union SAG-AFTRA. My childhood trauma and spending hours upon hours *alone and all up in my head,* turned out to be quite useful. *I have the most active and creative imagination as a result! Hello silver lining; thanks crappy childhood!*

Acting was a tremendously helpful emotional outlet. I could act silly and goofy, *like I was always doing anyway.* I could be *whoever I wanted to be.* Within reason, of course, I was playing a role. But I felt like I had playing a role my entire life anyway, *so why not make a career out of it?*

What makes an actor excel at his craft is *not being afraid of his emotions.* He can get in touch with them, and bring them *up and out. Also, he doesn't give a fuck what anyone thinks of him. Period.* I can't imagine Leonardo DiCaprio having such an amazing career if he cared what people thought of him. He won a Golden Globe *and* was nominated by the Academy Awards for Best Supporting Actor for his role in *What's Eating Gilbert Grape* in 1993, *one of his first roles.* He played a *mentally handicapped* kid, *and he wasn't shy about it.* While all the other boys his age were probably being bullies and calling people "retards", *Leo was pretending to be one, and getting accolades for it!* He established himself as an A-list actor right off the bat, b*y pretending to be retarded. I realize this word is not politically correct, take a deep breath.* Leo wasn't afraid to *take a chance. I freaking love this story!*

The one who follows the crowd will usually get no further than the crowd. The one who walks alone is likely to find themselves in places no one has ever been before.
—Attributed to Albert Einstein

I knew my life would never been exciting or fulfilling if I didn't take chances. *The magic always happens when I step into the unknown.* I didn't fear rejection or failure, as everything is a learning experience. My determination was to *never give up!* I believed I could make all my dreams come true, and I've never lost hope. *I hold the vision, even if my vision changes.* Even if I didn't 100% believe it, I used the Law of Assumption, *I'd assume it would happen.* I think it's a fancy way of saying: *I had faith.*

What separates great humans from miserable ones is that they push aside their *fear.* They're not afraid of failure, at least they know what *doesn't work.* They hold tightly to their dreams and ambitions, and don't let any amount of rejections or disappointments hold them back. *They stop listening to what everyone else has to say about it.* In fact, they stop telling people their plans altogether. They believe their vision is possible, and t*hey keep putting one foot in front of the other. I would do that too.*

Our thoughts really do create our reality, and I knew I could be or do anything I wanted. While I've never cared what people thought of me, I will admit, *I'm a former people pleaser.* I'm a nice person and I want to make people happy. The problem is, *I couldn't please everyone. So at a certain point, I decided to just make myself happy.* I was the only one that had to live with the consequences of my choices anyway. It was up to me to make myself happy, and I would never *be happy* doing whatever everyone else was doing or *what people expected me to do doing. I was not put on this earth to please other people, and it took me way too long to realize it.* But I've learned to forgive myself. I knew that I could only make myself happy; *happiness is an inside job. I knew nothing external would ever bring me true joy.*

I can't understand why I was even trying to make people happy or listening to their advice in the first place. Maybe they meant well, but in all honesty, they were probably just projecting their subconscious "programs" onto me. Maybe they were trying to deter me because they were jealous they hadn't thought of the idea first? *As if shining my Light might somehow dim theirs?* Or worse, their "advice" was them projecting their own insecurities onto me. Just because they didn't want to take a risk and didn't believe in my vision and thought it was "impossible", *didn't mean I had to. Maybe they're unhappy? There's this saying: misery loves company.* I've never seen a people pleaser get very far in life, *and I was not going to be that way!* I cannot imagine a worse fate than wasting my life doing what others wanted or expected of me.

The greatest prison people live in is
the fear of what other people think.
—David Icke

CHAPTER 4

What Lies Beneath

The day I got married felt like it was straight out of a fairy tale movie, complete with a big, white puffy dress and all the bells and whistles. *I had planned on only doing it once.* Hundreds of people gathered at the Pierre hotel on Fifth Avenue in New York City, and everything was perfect. *Alright, that's a partial truth, no one told me it was the same day as the Puerto Rican Day parade. Also, it was 105 degrees Fahrenheit. Everything else* seemed exquisite: the cake, the flowers, and the bridesmaid dresses. I had always dreamed of getting married like this, and on that day I *felt like an actual princess.* I believed that I had manifested the life I truly desired. *I thought I knew everything. Damn, that ego!* This was everything I had ever dreamed of, *or so I thought.* I had *all this stuff,* it was everything I thought I had always wanted.

What I didn't know at that time was that my knowledge about how the Universe was structured and how everything worked was so *very limited,* it was just the *tip of the iceberg.* What lies beneath the iceberg, what I couldn't see or even fathom at the time, was much more vast and almost *incomprehensible. My life was about to take yet another wild turn.*

I had married young, and had children right away. It was something I had been programed to do, being raised Mormon. Also, maybe I was trying to recreate that mother/child bond that I had missed out on growing up. I have a very maternal and nurturing instinct, and I always wanted to have a family. Plus, being raised Mormon meant *I couldn't be a slut. Yet I had an abnormally high sex high.* This led to co-dependency and holding on to *something I should've let go of.*

MY FIRST SON WAS BORN IN 2001, SAMMY CAME ALONG in 2003, and the baby of the family popped out in 2004. *I had three boys in three years!* To say I was fertile is an understatement. I was a "boy breeder", something I found out later was *an extremely valuable commodity. An heir and two spares.* If I was royalty, *I'd be exalted. Life was beautiful.*

It was wonderful being a mother, so rewarding, yet *so difficult.* My life became all about my children, and giving them what I never had. I sacrificed my career in order to raise my boys myself, I didn't want them cared for by a nanny. *I was the absolute worst helicopter parent until my divorce when I was forced to relax a bit.* Although, somewhere along the way, *I forgot about myself. I always put myself last, and it was a huge mistake.* I had lost a part of myself in the process of raising my boys, although *I have no regrets.* I have to say, I did a damn good job. *They are amazing men, at least I've done one thing right.* But I had temporarily forgotten about my own goals and dreams, and it wasn't a good head space to be in.

One day the most mysterious, mystical thing happened that I couldn't explain. Now I can demystify it: *Everything happens for a reason, there are no coincidences. So cliche, yet it is the absolute truth.*

THE DAY MY YOUNGEST SON WAS BORN, SOME SHIT THAT was absolutely *crazy* went down. First, there was a major hurricane barreling down on us in Miami Beach. I had given birth to him at Mount Sinai hospital, and despite a category four hurricane that had most of the power shut down, everything seemed fine with the birth. He came a few weeks early, which is still considered full term. *He was tiny, the smallest of all my boys, but so adorable and perfect.* Mount Sinai hospital was running on generators, and it was *Yom Kippur,* the Holiest day in Judaism.

About an hour later, the *pain* in my head started. *It was so excruciating, I felt my head was going to explode.* My brain felt like it was in a *vice,* and its grip was *tightening. The pain was intensifying too…Oh, no!* I started to moan, and then *scream. I couldn't understand what was happening!* The nurses were frantic and didn't know what to do. The next two days I was blacked out, I don't remember a thing. *And no, I hadn't had any Southern Comfort.* But I was told what happened to me by OB/GYN doctor.

Apparently, I had sat up in bed, *as if possessed,* and my right eye was rolling around in my head and *I was speaking a foreign language, one that couldn't be deciphered. A language I had never learned. I had only studied a little German in grade school, and French in high school. Too bad cell phones didn't have video recording…that might have been pretty entertaining.* My doctor said: "I didn't know you spoke Hebrew." *Only…it wasn't Hebrew.* Someone said it sounded like ancient Aramaic. *Ancient Aramaic? What kind of crackpot shit was this?* My doctor also believed that I had possibly been "possessed" by some demon. *Since I had no memory of this event, I couldn't even protest.*

When I came to, I was in the ICU. When I opened my eyes, *I was seeing double. Oh no, something was terribly wrong.* It made me dizzy to even open my eyes. I couldn't even walk, I wasn't able to see where I was going! I asked to see myself in a mirror, and I was shocked and *almost fainted.* My right eye was turned inwards, and the pupil immensely dilated. *I was cross eyed! Oh. My. God. Have you ever seen a cross eyed model? That's a rhetorical question, don't answer that.*

When I was in the ICU, a big Rabbi from Israel had sent me a recording of him chanting something in Hebrew. *I had left the Mormon church and became Jewish, more on that later.* I think he was trying to *chant* the "demon" out of me. *Seriously right now? I promise you, I was not, am not, possessed. You guys aren't making any sense.* I don't even remember what happened, but there had to be some sort of explanation. Y*ou can have your chanting tape back now, I won't be needing it.*

I NOW HAD ANOTHER *PROBLEM, THIS TIME WITH MY right eye.* The left eye had almost been taken out by the car accident, but now my right eye was fucked up. *Oh man, I must have definitely had an "evil eye'. What was I going to do about that?* I was certain a jealous person or people were sending me negative energy. *It's been probably been happening my entire life. How could anyone think my life is somehow perfect?* Luckily, we have the very best eye hospital, the Bascon Palmer Eye Institute, right here in Miami. I went to see a slew of doctors, and they put me through a battery of tests. I had bloodwork, an MRI, probably several CAT scans, and psychological examinations. *Who ordered those?*

All the doctors concluded that it was a rare condition called "4th nerve palsy"; it was caused by the fluid build up in my cranium that had put pressure on one of the nerves in my eye. The doctors concluded it was most likely from the epidural, as the cranial fluid in a healthy person is supposed to flow freely up and down the spinal cord to the brain. *Mine had somehow gotten trapped.*

While having an epidural is amazing because you literally can't feel the pain of childbirth, it's dangerous and scary. They insert a catheter into a very specific place at the base of your spine. *It's risky, and the medical professional that inserts it isn't even your doctor.* The technician that had access to my spine was a person I didn't know and had never met. *Oh, the lengths a person will go to avoid pain.* I had hired a doula for my first birth, and had wanted to have an all natural birth. I had walked to the hospital because it's supposed to speed up labor. *I lived on the Upper East Side in Manhattan, it was only a few blocks, but still!* I was thinking I'd be 10 centimeters dilated by the time I got there. *But I was only 3 centimeters dilated, I'll take the epidural please! Hello....pain!*

The biggest problem was that the doctors at Bascon Palmer *had no idea how to fix my situation. How did they claim to be the best?* They could diagnose it, *but I was told there was no cure. No cure? So I'm supposed to be cross eyed for the rest of my life?* The thought of that filled me with sheer *terror.* I'm vain, I like to look pretty. *Or at the very least, not look like a total freak.* I was walking around with an eye patch, *like a pirate. Ahoy! Blimey! It was horrible.* Besides, black didn't always go with what I was wearing. The doctors told me to lie down as much as possible. They told me the caffeine in coffee would help my headaches. *But I had a newborn infant and two toddlers! And you think I should just go lie down after drinking all that coffee? That's your only solution?*

In the end it was an Acupuncturist of Chinese medicine and healer named Dr. Gerald Strauss that saved my life. He was so famous, people would come from all over the world to see him. Some even came directly from the airplane, *suitcases in tow*. Every time I was there, I waited for hours and hours.

Dr. Strauss had actually studied acupuncture in China, with the Chinese. He stuck needles into my neck, and as he did, *I could feel the fluid drain from my head. Thank God there was at least one doctor that had a solution.* Allowing the fluid to move out of my cranium took the pressure off of the nerve in my eye. He also told me to get rid of the eye patch I was wearing. *This was great news for me.* I wore it not only because I looked like a cross eyed freak, but because I was seeing double and *couldn't walk straight.* He had me wear light colored sunglasses, with a certain type of tape on the right side so that I would still just use my left eye to see. He said that if I kept wearing the eye patch, my right eye would become too sensitive to light and then I probably would never be able to use that eye again. *Yikes! Good thing I met you Dr. Strauss! Thank you to whomever recommended that genius.* I went every week for months, and I did everything he said. One day, *I was healed.* Although my pupil in my right eye is still slightly bigger than the left, *I am not cross eyed.*

After my eye had healed, *I went in search of answers.* Many more people besides myself thought I had an "Evil Eye", I'm sure there was more than one person giving me bad juju. *Whatever, I went and bought an evil eye bracelet and got on with my life.* I guess that's entirely possible, but I didn't have time to think about that. I'm the type of person you either l*ove* or *hate, there is no in between. But what people think of me is none of my business.* Besides, I was too busy looking for answers.

Having been "cursed" with an "evil eye" or being "possessed" were not answers that satisfied me, it didn't explain why I was speaking a foreign language I had never learned. I needed to know, and *understand* what had happened. How did I know this language and what was I saying? *Was it a message to myself or to humanity? A warning of some kind? Good Lord.*

Whenever I ask God for an answer, *I always get one.* It can come in any form, a line from a movie or song or from a person, *it could come from anywhere. I just had to pay attention.* This time my answer came from *finding* a book, on my bookshelf, that I had *never* seen before. As many times as I'd packed up the books in boxes when I moved, or dusted that bookshelf, *I had never heard of or seen this book in my entire life. Mysteriously and miraculously, it just appeared. Isn't that something?*

It was entitled "Many Lives, Many Masters-The True Story of a Prominent Psychiatrist, His Young Patient, and the Past Life Therapy That Changed Both Their Lives" by Dr. Brain Weiss. The book was old and tattered and it had a "Used" sticker on the binding. I stood there holding this book and just stared at it. Then, *I got goosebumps all over my body and the hair on the back of my neck stood on edge. What was this book doing here? Where did it come from?* I didn't think it was related to what just happened to me, but I would soon.

How many coincidences have to happen
before it's no longer a coincidence?

I asked everyone I knew; "Is this your book? Did you leave it at my house?" I asked my friends, my business associates, my housekeeper, the nanny, and *everyone else who might have been in my house.* Time and time again everyone said: "No, that's not my book. I've never seen it before". I looked at the book again, and the used sticker glared up at me. *I had never purchased a used book in my life, and yet here it was in my hands.* The book called to me: *You asked the question, so here is your answer.*

I assumed the since the book landed in my lap, I may as well *read it.* I sat down and opened the tattered cover. It's written Dr. Brain Weiss, a Yale educated and clinically trained psychiatrist. He was very traditional psychiatrist at the time, his methods were by the book. It is the story about Dr. Weiss using the technique of hypnosis on a patient named Catherine. He was trying to uncover her deeply suppressed traumas and phobias from childhood in order to help her heal from her intense anxiety and panic attacks. She had refused to take the traditional medication for her ailments.

Dr. Weiss was *shocked and surprised* to discover he had regressed her back to her past, *but not from this lifetime.*

She was remembering her past lives. This was something *so unexpected,* and his logical brain couldn't comprehend it at the time. Nevertheless, *it was happening.* I guess the curriculum for psychiatry at Yale hadn't mentioned anything about reincarnation. Dr. Weiss himself had dismissed any literature on the study of parapsychology, he didn't think it was logical and was skeptical.

Growing up, I had never even heard about reincarnation, Mormons don't believe in it. They think you only get *one chance,* so you'd better be righteous and live with integrity. I'm assuming that this concept kept people in the church following the commandments. Also, Mormons get married in the temple if they're righteous enough or have "repented for their sins"; they believe they are "sealed" to their spouse "for all time and eternity". My dad has admitted that he's not sure how that's going to work in the afterlife, because he's sealed to two women. *So of course they cannot believe in reincarnation.* Whatever goes on in the temple is kept entirely secret. I don't even know what goes on there, and I grew up in the religion. They call it "sacred" instead of secret, *because I guess it sounds less nefarious. But it sounds like a secret society to me.*

I found out from Dr. Weiss' book that at one time in history, there were references to reincarnation in both the Old and New Testaments in the Bible. However, in 325 AD, the emperor Constantine had deleted these references. By 553 AD, the Second Council of Constantinople declared the concept of reincarnation as heresy. *The punishment for heresy was, of course, death. All they had to do was not believe in reincarnation and they could live? That's a great deal.*

Later when I converted to Judaism, I found out Jews believe in reincarnation. Although, it's not one of the basic tenets of the faith and there didn't seem to be a whole heck of Jewish literature on that subject. Whenever I mentioned reincarnation, *everyone seemed to be so afraid of the word.* The concept of reincarnation, that we come back into physical bodies again and again, seemed more logical to me. *I couldn't see how it was possible we only got one chance at life.*

The book was *fascinating,* and I couldn't put it down. Every word resonated as universal *truth.* When I turned to page 40, I unexpectedly became aware of *why* this book had appeared on my bookshelf *and into my hands.* Dr. Weiss writes: "With a new insatiable hunger for any scientific papers that had been published on reincarnation, I hunted through the medical libraries. I studied the works of Ian Stevenson, M.D., a well respected Professor of Psychiatry at the University of Virginia, who has published extensively in the psychiatric literature. Dr. Stevenson has collected over two thousand examples of children with reincarnation-type memories and experiences. Many exhibited xenoglossy, the ability to speak a foreign language to which they were never exposed."

Holy Smokes! I *just just stumbled upon the term for what had happened to me in that hospital.* I wasn't crazy, nor was I possessed. *This was super great news.* I sat there for what seemed like hours contemplating what I had just discovered. I wondered how many other times I had gotten these types of messages or was directed to go a certain way, and had *completely ignored them. Well, now I was paying attention.* I often wonder what my life would be like had I decided to not even read the book that was "given" to me. *I certainly would not be where I am today.*

From that moment on, *I vowed I would never dismiss any messages I received ever again.* Nothing happens by coincidence, it all serves some grander purpose. If it was something someone said to me, it had to be a message. If I came across an article about something I was perplexed about, I knew it was meant for me to read it. *Every person that crosses our path and everything that happens has a purpose.*

The book went on and the turning point for Dr. Weiss was when Catherine began channeling messages from the "Masters". She had no recollection of these messages after she was brought out of hypnosis, her voice even changed while speaking. The Masters told Dr. Weiss personal information about his family and his life, *things he had never told Catherine. He later discovered that the messages from the Masters were for him, not Catherine.* The most arcane and deeply insightful knowledge came from Catherine *after* she had left her body of each lifetime. She recounted there there were *many different* dimensions a soul could go to after death. Each plane she went to after another lifetime was a higher level of consciousness.

Dr. Weiss wanted to know more about this so she prodded her with questions while under hypnosis. He asked her what lessons she had to learn in order to progress to the next level. She said: "...we must share our knowledge with other people. We all have abilities far beyond what we use. Some of us find this out sooner than others. You should check your vices before you get to this point. If you do not, you carry them over with you to another life. Only we can rid ourselves of the bad habits that we accumulate in the physical state...when you are strong enough to master the external problems, then you will no longer have them in your next life."

Catherine goes on to say as an Ascended Master: "We are given intuitive powers we should follow and not try and resist. Those who resist will meet with danger. We are not sent back from each plane with equal powers…some have powers greater than others. Thus, people are not all created equal. But eventually we will reach a point where we will all be equal." *So far I've been following my intuition, so no danger for me!*

More wisdom from the Masters: "We choose when we will come into our physical state and when we will leave. We know when we have accomplished what we were sent down here to accomplish. We know when the time is up, and you will accept your death….Everybody's path here is basically the same. We all must learn certain attitudes while we're in the physical state….charity, hope, faith, love…we must all know these things and know them well." *Of course, there is so much more, I highly recommend this book to everyone I meet.* Reading this book is the single thing that shifted my life and set me on a different path, the one I was *supposed* to be on.

Dr. Weiss was also amazed to discover Catherine's fears and phobias had vanished. Not only that, *she started possessing psychic abilities which she didn't have before.* She had even proved it to her father by choosing the horses that would win at the racetrack. As she left, she handed the winnings to the first homeless person she saw; *she was spiritually evolving as well.*

I felt compelled to re-read this book before I wrote this section because it had been so many years since I last read it. What I found out was how *synchronous* all of this was. First off, Dr. Brain Weiss was at some point the chairman of the department of Psychiatry at Mount Sinai Medical Center in Miami Beach, FL,. *This was the exact same place where both Sammy and his little brother were born and where I had my episode of speaking in tongues.*

It had taken Dr. Weiss four years to work up the courage to write his book, about the same amount of time it took me *to start writing this book*. Not only that, there were similarities between Catherine and I as well. Dr. Weiss described her as "…an extraordinarily attractive woman, with medium-length blonde hair and hazel eyes. She earned extra money modeling swimwear." *It gets weirder:* she had a benign tumor removed from her voice box; I had a cancerous tumor removed from my thyroid, which is the same general area, more about that later.

It was a huge relief to find out I hadn't been possessed, but I still had questions, as *usual*. My next order of business was to run out and buy *all* of his books and try to make an appointment to see Dr. Weiss. *He lived near me, how awesome is that?* I needed to try his technique of past life regression using hypnosis to discover *something* my soul so desperately wanted me to know. But by this time it was 2004, his book was written in 1988. He was so popular by that time that he no longer did sessions with individuals. *Damn! I missed the boat!* A few days later I found out he would be making a speech at my local Jewish Community Center right here in Miami Beach! I went to see him speak, and his voice was so calm and reassuring. *He was definitely enlightened, and I wanted to know more.*

One of Dr. Brain Weiss' books I bought was entitled "Meditation. Achieving Inner Peace and Tranquillity in Your Life" was what completely shifted my *inner* reality. The book came with a guided meditation CD, and I started meditating *daily*. I had never meditated before or had even heard of it, this was all new to me. But it helped my headaches and did wonders for my stress levels. The feeling I got when I was deep in a meditative state *was better than any drug I had ever taken. Believe me, I've probably tried all of them except for crack, heroin, and crystal meth. Because, you know, addiction and death.*

The weirdest thing that startled me from doing a daily meditation practice was that I was becoming *psychic* myself. *Why was this so surprising when I had read about it happening to Catherine in the book? Seriously, sometimes I need to be banged over the head for something to sink in.* I could sense who was calling me on the phone, and I knew what people were going to say *before they would say it. Wild! Needless to say, I was instantly addicted.* Expanding my psychic awareness would help guide me in all areas of my life. I've been meditating almost daily for 18 years. It is the one thing that has *completely changed my life for the better.*

According to Google, about 90% of an iceberg is underneath the water. What I couldn't see, *what lies beneath,* is what I began to explore. *There is so much information under there!* My curious mind *had to know,* and it was a hell of a lot better than my curiosity of what drinking alcohol or doing drugs felt like. *It was way less destructive, a win-win situation.*

I came to understand that we are all connected by a celestial web of energy consciousness. If I could just tap into that place, *the God Source within myself,* I would have all the answers I needed. This knowledge I already had tapped into, *while still only the tip of the iceberg,* posed a *huge* question for me: If people *knew* that not only God, but the *entire spiritual realm,* knew the intentions of theirs hearts, *would they make different choices? I bet they will!* What will people do when they discover that any *human* can tap into this consciousness and see *everything,* the truth; *would there be some people quaking in their boots? The answer came to me: Yes!*

Three things cannot be long hidden:
the sun, the moon, and the truth.
—Buddha

I wanted to do a past life regression so badly, so I asked a bunch of different Rabbis if it was allowed according to Halacha (Jewish Law). Not one of them could give me an answer. They all seemed mystified and a little frightened by the idea. *But no one told me I couldn't do it. As if I ever needed permission to do something?* My ultra curious, truth seeking nature took over, I knew I *had to know about my past lives.*

I know myself pretty well, and I'm the type pf person that was determined to do anything I wanted, no matter what anyone else said or thought about it. In fact, if anyone tells me I *can't* do something, *I take that as a challenge, and go ahead and make sure I do that very thing. Stubborn is my middle name.*

I am headstrong, but I'm a Sagittarius after all. We are the truth seekers of the zodiac, the philosophers, always searching for answers, and trying to understand the deeper meaning of life. Sagittarius people are the optimistic, fun loving, laid back, jet-setting, always adventure seeking, quick witted (and blunt)- *no holding back fire sign that can't (and won't) stop! There's never a dull moment in my world.* So I went about finding a therapist that specialized in past life regression. It wasn't too hard to find the right therapist, and I couldn't wait to see what came up.

In *Many Lives, Many Masters,* one thing that intrigued me was how Dr. Weiss could cure people of mysterious pains and phobias, all by remembering a past life that involved trauma. For example, one of his patients had a mysterious breathing problem, and doctors couldn't identify where it came from or how to fix it. Dr. Weiss regressed him back to a *lifetime where he drowned, and once he remembered that lifetime, the breathing issue magically disappeared.* I was certain remembering my past lives would help me in my current life. *Maybe I wasn't fucked up beyond repair.*

THE FIRST PAST LIFE MEMORY I HAD, *I FELT LIKE I WAS making it all up*. The therapist asked me to look down at my feet while under hypnosis, to see what kind of shoes I was wearing. First, I have to tell you that when you're hypnotized, you don't lose control or don't remember or anything like that. You're always in control, hypnosis doesn't give your brain away to the person hypnotizing you. *That's just nonsense.* You're completely conscious, and in the state of relaxation you become aware of everything that's going on. I told her I was wearing sandals, and I was walking through the sand. She asked where I was, and I said that I was in ancient Egypt, maybe? Then my logical brain took over, and I told myself that this was complete *bullshit, I had to be making it up.*

Then she asked me to go home, to see my family. *That's when it hit me, the emotions. The real tears...oh my God, I couldn't be making this up!* I was a beautiful dark haired woman, and my whole family had been *slaughtered.* I was captured and taken as a slave. I *saw* them all being slashed to death from the cupboard I was hiding in. I felt such intense sorrow and emotional pain. *The intense grief, I couldn't have been inventing that.*

I remembered that lifetime didn't turn out all that bad. My captor ended up being very kind to me. I had everything I could ever want and need, but I spent a lot of time alone. My whole family was gone. It's not like I could try and escape, I'd most likely die alone wandering in the desert. I didn't even know where I was, and I had no family to protect me. Back then (whenever that was, I never could come up a time period) people lived in tribes and took care of and protected each other. *My tribe was gone. Wandering alone in the desert meant certain death, so I stayed.*

In another regression, I was asked again to look down at my feet and I saw myself wearing black boots with a bunch of tiny buttons on them. I was walking down a cobblestone street. The therapist asked me where I was. I said maybe I was in England, maybe in the 1800s? When she asked me to go home to my family, *that's when I began to cry. I was so sad!* Tears were streaming down my face, and I was almost too embarrassed to tell her what I saw and felt. I looked in the mirror, and in that lifetime I saw that I was *super unattractive*. I was too tall, gangly, and super skinny. My nose looked like a beak, and my eyes were too close together. But my ugliness wasn't what the *real* problem. *It was the awareness that I was burden to my parents, because no man wanted to marry me! They were annoyed by my mere presence. No wonder I was so lonely and sad.*

In those days, a woman lived with her parents until she got married and moved in with her husband. No woman lived alone, and marriage was more like a societal contract than a love romance. *I ended up killing myself in that life...*

I walked into a cold river and let myself drift away. No one wanted me anyway. The moment I died, I knew I had made the *most disastrous mistake. We are never supposed to take our own life! It's actually the worst thing one could ever do.* I had come into a body in a physical form to learn, grow and evolve as a soul. I had cut my time short because it I couldn't handle the painful emotions. *We are meant to go through our challenges in order to spiritually evolve. Of course, I would have to come back again and learn what it was that I was supposed to learn in that lifetime.*

After that particular session, I kept seeing disfigured, ugly, and hard to look at humans. *My heart just cried out to them with so much compassion. We all just want to be loved!* No matter what our outer physical appearance looks like, we all have that basic need. *We all want to feel loved, to feel like we belong, like our existence matters to someone.* After that, I never judged a person by their outward appearance, not that I did before. I look for someone's inner beauty, and I usually find it. These souls must have chosen to physically look this way in order for their soul to learn something.

I even remembered a past life with Sammy! I don't think I ever told him about it when he was alive, but I wish I had. I was his grandmother, and he had two other siblings. His father was a traveling salesman who had died on the road; one day he left and we never saw him again. His mother had died during childbirth, I think, and it was just the four of us left.

We lived in a small cottage with a dirt floor. Life was difficult, it was a struggle just trying to keep everyone fed. However, I remember how much *love* we all had for each other. *There was no shortage of love, we were all very happy.*

I remember that we all *helped* and *took care of each other.* This memory couldn't have come at a better time, because I was really feeling the burden of caring for three children as a single mom. After this past life memory, I started teaching my boys to help out more around the house. I gave them chores and reminded them daily that we all needed to take care of each other. When my boys complained that they couldn't have something, I'd remind them how *blessed we were because we had so much love in our home. We had no shortage of hugs and kisses, and those were the important things that really mattered!*

Somehow, every past life memory I had helped me figure out some puzzle or solve some kind of problem in *this life.* I was able to uncover why I had a hard time letting someone go, even if they treated me like shit. I understood why I had certain phobias and fears. At the end of every lifetime there was a profound lesson. *My soul already knew this, but now this knowledge was in my conscious mind as well.* It only enhanced my already loving nature. After these experiences, I wasn't as uptight about everything. *I was able to forgive much more easily.* I didn't hold on to anger or resentment, and I knew that *love* was the answer to *everything. The purpose of coming into a physical body is to learn unconditional love.* Remembering past lives freed me from the one thing I needed to be free of: *I no longer feared death.*

The Jewish community that I had converted into didn't pay much attention to what I talking about constantly, my past lives and the profound experiences I was having. Judaism does believe in reincarnation, *but everyone thought*

I was a weirdo. But my Mormon parents were *horrified when I mentioned it.* I had called up my sister and told her all about the book *Many Lives, Many Masters* when I first read it. The next thing I knew, she was heading up to the Omega Institute in upstate New York to get certified in hypnosis for past life regression, by none of then Dr. Brian Weiss himself! *At least one person was listening to what I was saying.*

I decided I needed to take the road less travelled. I didn't give one consideration to what anyone thought about it, *that was their own personal issue. What people think about me is none of my God damn business.* I didn't exactly know where this path would lead me, I just knew I had to find out. I left behind, for the most part, organized religion, and took my first step on the *spiritual path. I've never looked back.*

CHAPTER 5

My Problem with Religion

It is my opinion that one of the problems with religion is that it *divides* people. While one person thinks their belief system is the only "true" religion, that would make all the others invalid. Let's not forget that more murders have been committed in the name of "religion" than any other reason. I have no idea what the statistics are, *but to find out would be bone chilling.* Think about it: the "holy" Crusades, the Holocaust, and the Armenian genocide... just to name a few. I wondered: *how in heaven's name could religion be a good thing?*

I can only speak about what I know, and that is Christianity and Judaism. I spent the first 18 years of my life at *church,* studying what the Mormon beliefs were, and *therefore what I was supposed to believe in.* I read the Book of Mormon cover to cover. I spent hours and hours at church, learning the Bible and the things I was expected to blindly accept.

My issue with Christianity was that it didn't make any sense. I remember being eight years old in Sunday school, and the teacher telling us that Mary was a *virgin, yet gave birth to Jesus. Say what? Can you repeat that?* I remember thinking: *that's impossible. How would I even know this?* I called bullshit on immaculate conception, even though I was far too young to even understand what sex was. When I looked around the Sunday school classroom, no one else seemed to question anything. They were like zombies, just doing and believing as they're told, waiting for church to end so they could go outside and play. *Clearly,* I *did not belong here.*

Has anyone questioned who Joseph was? No, let's just accept the narrative that Mary was a virgin, yet gave birth to Jesus. Because our mother believed it, and her mother too, and so on and so forth. Just because something has been a long held belief *doesn't make it true.* Was Joseph her brother? Uncle? Husband to be? I kept asking the Sunday school teachers this question, and they never had an answer. *Yet there he is, in every nativity scene and painting on the planet..and his identity has never been revealed. That's not fishy at all.*

What I knew at the time was that God created the whole Universe and everything in it. So why would He *purposely distort His own Sacred Laws of Creation? He would never create something and then go and change it just for one dude, would He?* In my mind, a son being born to a virgin is an impossibility. But…*was it?* I mean, what if Jesus was a creation of some cosmic ultra advanced race of enlightened beings that implanted some alien sperm into Mary? *Today we call that in-vitro fertilization.*

I thought about the possibility that we've all been getting it wrong, or have been *purposely misled.* I'm *convinced* that Jesus' teachings were twisted around to serve the purpose of those in charge, the Clergy. I knew that in past centuries the Pope had more *power* than Kings, but how did he *get that power?* Maybe by twisting Jesus' message to humanity to suit their own evil purposes of *money, power, and control.*

I think Jesus was meant to bring the Light to humanity. At that time humanity seemed to be like animals, giving over to the reptilian brain. People were raping and killing members of their *own family!* Maybe we all needed an enlightened being to put us on a better path. However, evil people used that message of love and light and *God is within you and* distorted it. *They twisted it around and turned it backwards. They've brainwashed us all to think we needed "saving", and made us feel dependent on the church. They've tried to keep us trapped in fear.* They made us feel the need to have to have a priest to confess to, or we wouldn't be forgiven. *We needed them to save us all from eternal damnation? What a mockery of the truth.* Not that Mormons have priests, they call them bishops. *But same shit, different label.* God forbid anyone think they could talk directly to God, only the Pope or Mormon President could do that!

Besides calling bullshit on immaculate conception, my predicament with Christianity was that we were *required* to believe certain things. The whole "accept Christ as your personal savior" and you'll be "saved", didn't add up in my mind. *I hate to break it to you, but I don't think anyone is coming to save you or me. It's up to us to save ourselves.* I had discovered the Divine Spark within *myself,* and I believe that is the key to being "saved".

I now understand what the Christian religion was talking about is what modern enlightened people call the "Christ Consciousness"; it's the Divinity that is *within every single one of us.* Yet, somehow the Catholic Church had twisted it all around to fit their agenda of domination and control. *God forbid* that the common folk know how powerful they really are, they would be too hard to control! How would the church get everybody to give them their money? Has anyone wondered how the Vatican has possibly obtained all the ancient religious relics? Ever wonder where they might have gotten all this stolen art from the Holocaust? The Vatican isn't in Italy, *it's not even in Rome.* It is its own city, state, and *country.* Which means they make their own laws and enforce them. *Isn't that convenient?* I wonder what else they're hiding down there in the vaults? I think the Vatican might be the first, the oldest, *the original,* mafioso crime organization. *Prove me wrong.*

One day I asked my dad what he believed about something, I don't remember what. I'm a rather deep thinker, I always have been. My dad walked over to our bookshelf and pulled out a "Mormon approved" book. I said, "No, dad, I meant, what do *you personally* believe?" *He couldn't answer me. Weren't Mormons allowed to have personal beliefs? Apparently not.*

I'm not trying to invalidate anyone's belief system or trash the Mormon church. I'm grateful I was raised this way; it gave me my moral values and integrity that I still have today. I only heard my dad curse *one time* in my entire life, and he wasn't even angry. I remember it like it was yesterday. We were walking through Arlington Cemetery on one of our many roadtrips to see America. My dad saw this woman and said; "That woman doesn't know where the hell she's going." I was *shocked.* He looked embarrassed because he had slipped. My stepmom would say "damn" every once in a while, but only when she was mad. *The Mormon thing is a little extreme for my taste, my teenage years taught me that. Besides, how did mormons have fun? I still don't know the answer to that.*

When I was 23 years old, I converted to "Orthodox" Judaism after studying it for two years. What attracted me to this religion in the first place was there was absolutely *zero* requirements to believe any certain way. Judaism has 13 Principles of our Faith, written down by Mainmonides, a great Rabbi known as the Rambam. But no one is going to hell if you don't believe in them. But they all make sense, and are the "fundamental truths of our religion and its very foundations." *Every Jew believes differently, according to their own life experiences, and it is acceptable to have personal beliefs! Isn't that great?*

The 13 Principles of Faith are: belief in the existence of the Creator, belief in God's absolute Unity, belief in God's Eternity, belief that we are not to worship anyone *other* than God, belief that God communicates to man, belief that he communicated to Moses, belief in the Divine origin of the Torah, belief in the immutability of the Torah, belief in God's omniscience, belief in Divine reward and retribution, belief in the arrival of the Messiah, and belief of the resurrection of the dead.

The reason Judaism doesn't believe that Jesus Christ was the Messiah is because he didn't fulfill the prophecy. The Messiah, according to Judaism, will rebuild the Third Temple in Jerusalem and gather all the Ten Lost Tribes that have been exiled to Israel. His arrival will bring in 1000 years of peace. *He is a man, a righteous leader, not some mythical creature.* He will become the King of Israel, and re-establish the Rabbinical court, returning Israel to way the way it is supposed to be run. Jews and Gentiles will live together in *peace*. Jesus definitely enlightened humanity, but he did not fulfill these prophecies.

Instead of requiring the belief of anything other than these 13 Principles of Faith, Judaism requires a Jew to keep the Mitzvot. There's a whole list of things you *should* do, and another list of things you should *not* do. Mitzvot are synonymous to what Christians call "commandments". There are 613 Mitzvot to be exact, 248 "dos" and 365 "don'ts". But many of these mitzvahs pertain to the Holy Temple, which was destroyed and has yet to be rebuilt. So today, Jews are required to keep 369 mitzvoth.

WHAT I LOVE ABOUT JUDAISM IS THAT EVERYONE believes the way they want to. Of course, our personal beliefs are rooted in our life experiences, and everyone has had different ones. The rules, in my opinion, are logical. *I mean, why do Christians send flowers to the family of someone who has passed away? The flowers end up dying too, and then you have to throw them away. How depressing.* Jews however, send *food* to the family of a deceased loved one. We are still *living*, and we have to keep going and we need nourishment to keep living.

Judaism has it all figured out, *even if I don't*. The Torah has wisdom we cannot even fathom. *Sammy knew this and he lived it.* If God tells me not to eat a certain animal because it could defile my soul, *who am I to question that?* Any animal that kills its prey, *is not kosher.* Consuming an animal that died a cruel death was also forbidden. This anguish the animal suffered could affect our souls. *I'm not taking that kind of chance, I'll stick with Kosher thank you very much.* Also, kosher laws forbid consuming the blood of an animal, because the blood is the *soul.* This is why red meat is salted, to draw out the blood. Animals that are "unclean" such as pork and shellfish are forbidden. The Torah doesn't explain what unclean means, but today we know these animals *literally eat shit. They're bottom feeders. Are you getting hungry now and thinking about shrimp?* I don't have to eat shellfish to know that shit is disgusting, the smell of it has always made me nauseous. I tried eating lobster only once, and *I almost threw up. I wasn't even Jewish at the time.* Now modern science has discovered that eating shellfish and pork can give humans parasites, which can greatly affect one's heath. *Maybe God does knows something we don't.*

The Bible says that the Children of Israel are God's "Chosen people". It's funny because the Mormons call themselves "the Children of Israel" as well. *This way they can claim to be chosen.* It might sound snobby and high brow, *but the real meaning behind being Chosen is not what you think.* Jews aren't "elite" or somehow more "special" than everyone else. *We were Chosen for a very specific purpose: To be a Light to the other nations. That means,* we are tasked with making the mundane *holy,* and to bring others to *God.* Elevate the world and bring everyone closer to *Him.* We are tasked with making a *heaven here on earth. This is no small task, have you seen what's happening in the world? Personally, I'm up for the challenge.*

This is no ordinary thing, *making Heaven here on earth.* No wonder Antisemitism is rampant, it's probably because they think Jews are snobby. We've definitely gotten a bad rap for loving money too much. Discloser: Jews are not allow by Torah Law to charge interest when loaning money to a Jew, only when loaning money to a Gentile. *So maybe Jews have gotten the reputation for being greedy because if they loan you money, they're coming after it.* But "elitist", we are not. *Well, I'm not. I guess I can only speak for myself.* I think most Jews they feel inferior, most likely due to generations of hatred. The majority of Jews have humbly accepted this "priestly" calling, but not without feeling burdened. In fact, the Rabbis turned me away more than once before I was allowed to convert, which is what they are supposed to do. *I had to understand the gravity of the mission I was taking upon myself.*

People often wonder why I would take upon an extra 362 commandments, as everyone else only needs to obey seven commandments. These are called the Seven Laws of Noah, and are the Universal Moral Laws. Everyone is not allowed to worship idols, curse God, murder, steal, commit incest, or eat the limb of a still living animal. They are also supposed to establish courts of justice. *It's pretty basic.* I find it hard to imagine anyone *wanting* to eat a limb of an animal while it's still living! *Horrific.*

Well I had decided a long time ago that my life would serve some higher purpose. My mother couldn't have sacrificed herself for some small mundane thing, that was obvious to me. I was disillusioned with organized religion, but *I had already chosen a life of service to God* instead of service to self. *I despise egotistical greed and self-centeredness anyway.* I follow my intuition and *go where God is taking me*, now matter where that is. *If I'm on God's side, how could I go wrong?*

Unlike the Mormons, Jews don't believe everyone *needs or should be* Jewish. *What is it with the Christian belief that everyone else needs to be Christian too? For real?* Or that everyone needs to accept Christ as their personal savior, or *be damned to hell? That's crazy talk.*

What we should do is find the "Christ consciousness" *within us*, but I don't like that label, I like to call it the *Divine Spark within.* We already have the power, it's been inside of us all along! Jews aren't trying to get everyone to accept their way of life. They're not proselytizing or acting like Judaism is the only right way to live. *As if! I'm* not trying to get anyone to believe the way I do. *So can everyone please just mind their own business and let me fulfill my Divine mission? Many thanks, that would be great.*

The Mormons proselytize and send missionaries *everywhere,* because if you don't accept this religion, they believe you're doomed. *What a crock of shit,* excuse my language. They'll even do baptisms for the dead, because if a person didn't get a chance to meet some Mormon missionaries and accept the church while they were alive, they feel the need to "save" them. *Are they really serious right now?* The church came under fire for baptizing Anne Frank, *and rightly so!* Maybe that's what they consider fun, trying to save souls that weren't even asking for it. *I'll pass.*

You also need to understand, once the Mormons "got" you, you'll be handing over 10% of your money to their ultra wealthy organization. Don't even try to figure out how much money they have, *it's quite a lot.* While Judaism also has the mitzvah of Tzedakah, which technically means "righteousness", but it often refers to giving charity. *Yet Jews are allowed to give and help whomever we want to instead of giving it to an already wealthy organization that's going to end up telling you what you believe. That sounds more logical, now we are getting somewhere.*

While the finances of the Church of Jesus Christ of Letter Day Saints (LDS or Mormon is the abbreviation) is unknown, just take a look at all the temples they've built *all around the world. They look like castles*, these buildings are seriously ornate. That's where they do all their secret stuff and baptize souls that aren't asking for redemption. I still can't understand how so many people are still buying into it! *Their* brainwashing *techniques must be quite effective. And mind you, these people are all sober.* Yet there are so many Mormons *waking up, and walking away.* Apparently, there's a whole ex-Mormon community that's supportive and thriving. I wouldn't know though, I had already defected to the Jewish side. *Welcome to the Tribe.*

But there are issues within the Jewish community itself that I have a problem with. *It's so splintered, it's not united like I thought it would be.* Judaism has all these different "sects". There are the Reform Jews, whose synagogues look like churches, and they don't keep kosher. Then there's the Conservative Jews, who are more traditional. They're "somewhere in the middle". They eat "kosher style", which means it's not actually kosher, it just looks like it. *Pastrami sandwich and latkes, anyone?* Then there's the other extreme, the "ultra" orthodox, who take the Torah literally and don't cut the sideburns of their hair. I was somewhere in the middle in this place called Modern Orthodoxy. *Oh man, I really don't like labels.* But within the Jewish community itself there is hatred and fear of the other sides! This is absolutely ridiculous. *I had to pause and ponder why I chose this path.*

There are possible other perplexities that are quite alarming. The New York Times recently uncovered that some Yeshivas (Jewish schools) in New York are not teaching the basics of math and science; the children *fail* every test! These institutions are taking *billions* in tax payer dollars and are not teaching children what they are supposed to know. There are parts of the ultra orthodox Jewish community that are *plagued* with *poverty,* dependent on others to sustain themselves and their families because they can't do basic math! They depend on others to support them and their families because they prefer to study Torah and the Talmud all day, instead of making an honest living. *Yet it specifically states in the Torah that a man needs to make a living and study Torah in his free time. How exactly were they getting away with this?*

One day I had just had *enough of all the hypocrisy.* Imagine, I come from a background where people don't even *curse.* Absolutely no Mormon would ever dream of cheating on their spouse or stealing *anything.* But I know Jews, personally, who were ripping off others, even their own fellow Jews. *Robbing them blind. Some were laundering money. Others were liars and cheaters, justifying it in any way they could.* Others straight up didn't pay taxes. The more I got into this religion, *the worse I felt about it. Some of them act very un-God like.* It made me question why I joined the religion in the first place. I was especially distrusting of the guy that *claimed or tried to look the most religious, he was probably the least virtuous person. Why such hypocrisy?*

This is not to say that I haven't found some of the most amazing, giving, and spiritual people within this community that have become life long friends. My standards of who I chose to keep in my life and be in my inner circle are always those that embody a soul that has *integrity,* regardless of their religion or beliefs.

So I made the decision to take what I found useful and resonated with from Judaism, and go by my intuition on the rest. For example, I still have a strictly kosher home where milk and meat are kept *separate*. But the Torah law "Thou shall not boil a kid in it's mothers' milk" is because it's obviously inhumane. *Not that the cow would even know, but I can see the reasoning.* But the law really only applies to red meat, it doesn't apply to poultry. But somewhere along the line, a bunch of Rabbis decided poultry shouldn't mix with milk as well. I guess it's because someone might "think" that they're not obeying Kashrut Laws. I stopped caring what people thought of me and what I was doing, but apparently some others *have not*. But my home is kosher because I believe *God knows what's best for me,* and because it's part of being in a community. I don't want my guests, whether Jewish or not, to feel uncomfortable eating at my table or feel like they can't break bread with me.

I also had a problem with keeping the Sabbath exactly the way everyone else in the modern Orthodox community does. The Torah says; "Remember the Sabbath day, to keep it holy. Six days you shall labor and do all your work, but the seventh day is the Sabbath of the Lord your God, in it you shall not do any work'. By "work" the Torah meant the 39 Melachot, the general categories of labor forbidden on Shabbat. These 39 methods of work was the laborious tasks used to build the Mishkan (Temple) and are things like writing, sowing, plowing, reaping, gathering and binding, grinding, sifting, kneading, baking, cleaning, sewing, tearing, cutting, wiring, erasing, carrying something around, and kindling a fire and extinguishing a fire. I haven't named them all, obviously. *It's a long list.*

My problem was that the same group of people (I'm assuming Torah scholars) that had added that poultry should not be mixed with dairy, had made certain things "forbidden" on Shabbat to keep up with modern times. They included in forbidden Melachot things like driving a car and using electricity…as maybe igniting an engine or using electricity might cause a "spark"? *I can assure you, my iPhone is not on fire.* Listen, I respect everyone and their beliefs and how they chose to observe the commandments, but I was *miserable* on Shabbat when I lived that way. I couldn't talk to my sister on the phone. I couldn't spend time with friends if it was too far to walk. I felt isolated and I was very, very unhappy, especially if Shabbat went right into a Jewish holiday where all those same things were not allowed.

This is my simple religion. There are no need
for temples; no need for complicated philosophy.
Our brain, our heart is our temple;
the philosophy is kindness.
—Dalai Lama

I didn't think that God had intended his commandments to make anyone miserable. Now my Shabbat includes lighting the candles at the appropriate time, and sometimes I have a Shabbat dinner, usually when my boys are with me. *I'm definitely having some wine.* I won't do any work, and often I use it as an excuse to *be lazy and stay in my pajamas all day. It's the best. Shabbat Shalom!*

A day of rest is good for the mind, body and soul, and I don't believe God will "punish" me for doing it in a way that makes me happy. I don't feel the need to do *anything* in order to be accepted by a group.

We are all God's creation, in heaven, there is *no religion. I think it's impossible.* Once we return to Source, we are all souls of pure Love consciousness. Religion makes some people *hate* others, even resorting to violence, and that doesn't seem very God-like. *But let's not forget about the fact that religion is purposely misleading us! This is a terrible situation.*

I believe religion won't be necessary where some of us are heading…towards *enlightenment.* Hatred, division and deception is the *exact opposite* of enlightenment. Of course, I have to tell you that I think the Jews will still need to keep the mitzvots. Judaism is more of a nationality and a way of life than a religion. *Remember the mission, to bring God into the physical plane, to make the mundane holy and to make "a heaven on earth".* And right about now, earth is the exact *opposite with all of the evil, destruction and chaos, it's HELL!*

I'm not claiming to know everything, in fact, it's just the opposite. The more I go down this road, the more confusing it gets. *Maybe someday it will all become clear.* I haven't studied all of the worlds religions or their origins, *but have you noticed there seems to be so many similarities?* My ultimate ambition is to have peace in my home and love in my heart. I need to works towards something I feel is a worthwhile ideal. *Unity. Love. Enlightenment.* Right now, I'm not feeling that love, *anywhere. I'm just looking to recruit some hopeless romantics and logical thinkers. Who's with me?*

An enlightened person doesn't know it all. Enlightenment simply means walking beyond this and all worlds into nirvana, which is beyond knowledge and ignorance.
—Frederick Lenz

I stand behind the wisdom of the Torah; this ancient wisdom is literally embedded in the DNA of our bodies and the Universe. This is probably the only thing I can actually claim as fact in this book: *Everything that has ever happened, will happen, or could happen, is written in the Torah. It is the Divine's Playbook.* Even just yesterday I saw a video with Gregg Braden, the famous scientist and author, on YouTube talking about the Torah Code: "It is believed to be a Manuel for the quantum possibilities that are available within the Divine Matrix…this Manuel that holds the consequences and the outcome for every possible choice that we could ever make in our lives." *I don't think Gregg Braden is even Jewish, is he? It doesn't matter.* Imagine, my name, your name, everything that has ever happened or will happen or *could* happen is right there in the Torah.

The rule is, that all that was, all that is, and all that will be until the end of time is included in the Torah from the first word to the last.
—Genius of Vilna

There are really only two paths in life: service of one-self, or service to others. There aren't any other choices, it's really that simple. I dedicated my life to serve God years ago, I need to make a difference in the world. To walk the spiritual path meant I chose a life of service to others. I know my soul had agreed to this before I came down into this body. I hate hypocrites, and I know some people that claim they are "religious", yet all they do is serve *themselves.* Hopefully one day they will realize the error of their ways. *But that's not my problem. I can lead a horse to water, but I can't make him drink it.*

I continued down my spiritual path of co-creating with God *to manifest the life I desired. With God as my co-pilot,* I knew that I could have whatever I desired. So long as what I wanted wasn't hurting anyone, it was for the highest good of all, and I wasn't interfering with anyone's *free will.* I knew I could manifest *anything,* so long as I stayed grounded, humble, and *grateful to God.*

Judaism is against using divination as it states in Deuteronomy 18:10: "There shall not be found among you...a diviner of times." I assume that's because *we decide and determine our own destiny.* If we "knew" something was going to happen (even if we were being mislead), it *could end up as a self fulfilling prophecy. It came to pass...because you believed it.* Also, the integrity of the diviner was in question, the possibility of a going to see an evil fortune teller could *change one's destiny, and it wouldn't be good.*

Unfortunately for me, I find tarot cards *fascinating. Always a rebel.* I couldn't put my finger on where this obsession came from. I desired to learn the meanings of each of the tarot cards, and some decks have beautiful illustrations. I spent a lot of time playing around with them, but felt a little guilty about it. *Somehow I never felt guilt from breaking the Mormon rules. But this is a religion*

I had chosen, and I took it seriously. Although, not enough to not go get a tarot card reading. And do you know what happened? Everything she told me wasn't going to happen, I set about to make happen. And everything she said was going to happen, that I didn't want it to, I worked to make it not happen. *Have I mentioned I'm stubborn? Why would I trust this woman's tarot cards over my own intuition? I couldn't.*

One day I came across this Instagram account called @ torah.tarot. The account parallels the similarities between the Torah and tarot cards. The theory of the person that runs this account is that tarot cards sprang up as a *way* of studying Torah when it was *illegal* to study it in the middle ages. *Funny, they just switched up the letters.* There are even Hebrew letters on the original tarot cards from the 1500s. The cards have evolved over the centuries, but I read every post of his and it totally resonates. I believe there's a high probability that tarot cards were invented as a stealthy way of studying the Torah, as to study it in the 1500s meant only one thing: *death.*

The highest form of ignorance is when you reject something you don't know anything about.
—Wayne Dyer

Of course, whomever was in power in the Middle Ages would make studying the Torah illegal, because *it is literally the Manuel on how to create the life you desire.* If any evil king wanted to stay in power, he'd have to outlaw the Torah. And kill his own brother because, you know, his brother might kill him first and take power. *Geez! The Middle Ages sounded like a blast.*

I wondered how many people had been put to death for studying the Torah or for celebrating Jewish holidays. *Oh, did you think the killing of Jews was confined to just the Holocaust? No honey, this goes way back.* It makes sense that those in power would forbid studying Torah, they had to keep *the Manuel on how to create the life you desire* a secret and that we are *all* made in God's image and therefore have *all* the creative powers that He has.

I had chosen the to walk the Spiritual path a long time ago, but now I was fully committed. The Spiritual path meant I had to leave all judgements and prejudices at the door. It requires intense dedication to the path and self reflection and inner healing. It is *hard work. But now it is no longer difficult for me to admit I am wrong about something.* I had removed my ego, and now I am able to freely apologize when I have been misguided. *I eventually learned how to forgive quickly and love unconditionally.*

I could find God through prayer, meditation, and talking a really *hard look at myself in the mirror.* I did honest self reflection. I asked for guidance from my spirit guides, who are always available whenever I need them. However, I learned that my spirit guides cannot *interfere* with my free will. I had to *ask* for them to intervene on my behalf. *When I figured this out, things started to get really interesting. Cue the climax turning point!*

I had to ponder what else us was keeping us divided. Politics, race, masculine vs. feminine, rich vs. poor, royalty vs. common folks, *it all had to go*. When I came across the information that hierarchy is complete *bullshit, that* God has never given any king or government the power to *rule over us, I went full on rebel. We are all Divine Spiritually Sovereign Beings with God given Free Will! The evil reign of control and domination is over.*

The Spiritual path meant I was going towards anything that embodied Love, Joy, Peace, Unity, Compassion, Service, Justice and Truth. Anything that was the *opposite:* hate, fear, chaos, division, greed, injustice, lies, deceit and destruction, I was *walking away from. And I will never return. In addition, I will fight against it!*

Individuals seem to have reached their walls and so has the entire human race. Whatever isn't working, isn't life producing, isn't producing love for ourselves or others, is going to have to go now. Or, literally, there will bear hell to pay.[8]
—Marianne Williamson

There's something else I'm pondering about Christianity: *is it possible that it's allegorical?* Has anyone ever noticed the parallels of Christianity to Astrology? God's only son (sun), the 12 disciples (12 zodiac signs). Maybe Mary *was* a Virgin after all, a Virgo, the astrological sign represented by the Virgin? The "three Kings" (the three stars in Orion's belt) are called *that exact same name! Interesting. How amusing are the musings of my own mind. It's crazy up in here!*

Look, if every possibility is already written in the Torah, I would bet it's already "written in the stars" too. *Astrology! I'd make a mental note to look into astrology.* God created the

8. Marianne Williamson, *Healing the Soul of America. Reclaiming Our Voices as Spiritual Citizens* (Simon & Schuster, 2014).

whole Universe, the Stars included. The more information I came across, the more *I realized that I didn't know anything.* I think anyone who is so sure of themselves, that they know exactly what is going on, *actually knows the least and has most likely been brainwashed.*

The problem with the world is that intelligent people are full of doubts, while the stupid ones are full of confidence.
—Charles Bukowski

My sister had given me an autographed copy of Chani Nicholas' "You Were Born For This", an astrology book "for radical self acceptance". I devoured every word and found it *fascinating.* Next, I ordered Gahl Eden Sasson's astrology of 2023 book "Traversing the Bridge". Gail is an Israeli, and has proclaimed himself to be the "Cosmic Navigator". He combines astrology with Kabbalah, psychology and mysticism…that's right up my alley! Next, I would need to get an astrologer to read my chart, because this whole thing had piqued my curiously.

I have go back and address this concept of the Messiah, because both Christianity and Judaism have this tenet. *I've already warned you that I went all Biblical.* Christians believe Jesus was the Messiah, but he did *not* fulfill the Judaic prophecy, and they *knew* he didn't. So, Christians are saying he will "come again" and then he will fulfill this prophecy. Say w*hat? Come again?* Judaism's philosophy on the Messiah is that no one knows who He is, or when He will "come". Because if we knew everything in advance, it would defeat the whole purpose. *And it wouldn't be as much fun, that's where the surprise comes in! For fun. God has a sense of humor, no doubt.*

The Jewish concept of Moshiach (Messiah) seems more logical to me than the Christian version. The Messianic era will be ushered in by a Jewish leader, a direct descendant of King David. Moshiach means the "Anointed One", and His coming into power as a great leader will usher in Ultimate Redemption. It will be a time of peace, prosperity, wisdom, and the resurrection of the dead. He will rebuild the Holy Temple in Jerusalem. It will be a time of peace and abundance, and there will be *no more wars. The earth will be filled with the knowledge of God.* Now wonder Jews are always saying: "Moschiach NOW"! *Can we make Him come sooner, rather than later?*

Moshiach is not just for the redemption of Jews, *it's for all of humanity. We are all in this together.* Now how He "comes" is up for debate. *Will he be born? Will he rise from the dead and be resurrected, like Jesus supposedly did?* I'd like to think He's going to fly down from the heavens on a white winged Pegasus carrying Archangel Michael's sword of Truth and Justice. *Or maybe He will just materialize in a perfect body wearing stylish clothing, like the characters in Gary R. Renard's book "The Disappearance of the Universe"?* Will He will be transporting Himself, when the time is right, in a Golden Merkaba transportation vehicle, *like the one Ezekiel saw in his vision? I'm having a lot of fun thinking about all the possibilities.* But what I do know from studying Judaism, is that when He does come, it will leave no doubt in anyone's mind, whether Jew or Gentile, that He is the Anointed. He's a righteous *leader,* a King of royal blood who walks with God.

I'm not trying to downplay Jesus' important role on this earth. He is probably an Ascended Master or an enlightened being, sent here to earth to bring in love and light. Jesus' message of "Do unto others as you would do unto yourself" has been completely *misinterpreted. What He was referring to is that when you hurt someone else, you're actually just hurting yourself.* We are all connected and whatever you put out there, will most surely come back to you. It's the basic Law of Karma, *what you reap is what you sow.*

I believe there is more to this Jesus story than we initially thought. I've heard theories that Jesus traveled to India, and that was where he learned esoteric wisdom. I've also came across a documentary where a researcher claims that Jesus didn't die on the cross, he actually moved to Japan where he got married, had children and lived out his life. This researcher *actually went to Japan* and visited his supposed grave, and none of the locals there have ever questioned the validity of Jesus being buried there. *You don't have to believe something just because your parents do. I'm giving you permission to think for yourself.*

When I first read Neale Donald Walsh's book "Conversations with God", I could not believe I had allowed myself to get duped into thinking God was somehow going to punish us all for our sins. *I don't think it works like that. You can do anything you want, but be prepared to face the consequences. Because your karma is coming, whether you like it or not.*

Even quantum physics is proving that we are all connected with quantum entanglement. This rather new scientific phenomenon states that once two particles come in contact with one another, they can be moved to the other side of the universe, and if a change happens to one particle, the other particle is also changed. *Fascinating!*

Jesus was explaining to the world that we all have the power to *create our own reality. Love* is the answer to everything, it is the only *real* thing out there. Fear is something we create in our own minds. *Fear is an acronym: False Evidence Appearing Real.*

Before the Messiah gets here, I have to inform you that we might be in for a little more chaos and destruction. There's this prophecy of an Anti-christ, and he suddenly *appears* out of nowhere. Mormonism and Judaism doesn't talk much about this, and I'm in agreement with this philosophy. *Let's focus on the positive.* But rest assured, *if everyone is blindly following someone, I won't be.*

If you're waiting for the rapture, I've got some news for you; *I don't think it's like what we've been told. I doubt the righteous will all of a sudden go to Heaven.* I think the rapture will be more like a graduation from the 3rd Dimension to the 5th Dimension. Those who have accessed their own *Divinity* within *themselves and others,* have realized that we are all One, and have raised their consciousness and vibration higher, *will get to move forward to a New Earth. This takes work though. Don 't just sit there, go find God! You're running out of time!* Anyone who *hasn't done the inner work* will probably reincarnate somewhere else that's earth like, *and will keep repeating those karmic cycles until they learn. I'll keep doing the work, no more karmic cycles for me.* I don't know about you, but I'm ready to rid the earth of the evil and self serving people.

But first in order to evolve and go to this New Earth, you've got to let go out your attachment to the material world, *even if it's only figuratively speaking.* I think only those who have chosen *service to others* will get to stay, everyone else might get shipped off to another planet, that's just my guess. *I've watched a lot of YouTube videos on this subject, so I think that makes me the expert. Not everyone is going where I'm going, but I guess not everyone wants to.*

It is my belief that n*o one* is coming to save us, not some politicians, military personnel, or even Moshiach Himself. If you're planning on saying "I accept Jesus as my personal Savior" at the last minute, I don't think *that* will save you in the hour of Reckoning. We need to realize our own Divine power *within* us, and start using it for the good of humanity. We need to *unite together in peace* and *pray to God. This is what will usher in the Messianic era of peace and prosperity. I think we are active participants in this, the Messiah is waiting for us! Cast out your fear, and do it right now!*

I'm not going to let fear of the end of the world or all this coming destruction get in the way of my ascension. *No one makes it out alive anyway.* Losing Sammy gave me the gift of living *each day* as if it was my *last, because it just might be.* No one really knows when their time is up; our physical bodies will die, that we all know for sure. *It's what you do while you were still living that can made a difference.* I'm embracing all the Divine *Love* and *Unity* of God's consciousness. *Life is too short not to, I should know that.*

CHAPTER 6

The Dark Night of the Soul

Trying to ascend is hard work, I'm not going to lie to you. The spiritual awakening process painful; it's dark and depressing. It's literally going *through hell.* It's very lonely, *suddenly I could barely relate to anyone.* But now that I'm almost on the other side, I can tell you that it's worth it. *Not that I'd want to do it again, once is enough.* But it's that *fire* of hell that *transformed me*, and I had no other choice than to let it. The whole purpose of the pain is to learn how to *transmute* it into something greater than yourself.

If you're going through hell, keep going.
—Winston Churchill

My Dark Night of the Soul started in 2007 when I went through a traumatic break up. I'm not going to get into the whole dramatic story, as I promised myself years ago I wouldn't relive it anymore. *I am no longer a victim, I now take responsibility for my part in it.*

However, there is one particular story I feel compelled to share. We had been fighting brutally for two long years. We didn't see eye to eye, and we both wanted to go down different paths. I had been praying to God every day, pleading to Him to help us stop the arguing and for Him to restore peace to our relationship. One day this situation had brought me to my knees, *again*. I didn't know what else to do, so I began to fervently pray to God. *This has always been my solution to every problem.*

Christians pray kneeling down to show humility to God, but Jews are supposed to pray standing up. I was already on my knees anyway; *I was literally desperate.* As I began to pray something occurred to me, maybe I was asking God for the *wrong* thing? I knew God had heard my prayers, but He wasn't giving me what I wanted. So I reframed my request. I asked God: *If I am meant to stay in this relationship, give me the strength to do that. If we are meant to part ways, give me the strength to do that.*

The very next day, a miracle happened: a path was cleared, showing me the way out. It was a very clear message, I needed to leave. Where there was once only a brick wall, *now a door had appeared, and it was flung wide opened.* I knew it was a sign from God that I was meant to leave and go down my own path. It was heartbreaking, but I couldn't ignore the signs and I knew there was a different kind of life I was meant to lead.

The next *disastrous upheaval* occurred at the end of 2011, when I had to check myself into the hospital emergency room because of a massive pain in my gut. It was so intense that I couldn't function and do the most mundane tasks. I was filled with *dread; I knew something was horribly wrong.* I was diagnosed with Crohn's disease and was given all kinds of medication. However, whatever the doctors were giving me wasn't making me better. *In fact, I started feeling worse.* They had me on a liquid diet because I kept needing colonoscopies. The doctors couldn't figure out why I wasn't improving.

The pain was so excruciating that I couldn't sleep, all I did was *moan.* I had a roommate that needed an emergency surgery for an ectopic pregnancy. Supposedly those are extremely painful, and it can *kill you.* Yet she was sleeping while I clutched my gut and tried my best not to wake her up. *It wasn't easy.* I ended up being in the hospital for *fourteen days.* The truth is they had sent me home after two days, and I spent New Years' Eve ringing in 2012 *vomiting out what little was left in my stomach. So I had to go back to the emergency room.* After a week I had priests coming into my hospital room to give me my last rites. *How did I get on the "dying all alone" list? Was I really going to die? It certainly felt like it.* Then hospital volunteers came to visit me… *I was definitely on a list. Oh my God..maybe this was it, I'm going to die. Did the doctors know something that they weren't telling me?* The doctors said the ulcers in my digestive tract were "impressive", and not in a good way. The medications didn't help at all. *In fact, I kept feeling worse as the days went by.*

I was grateful that my stepmom came to care for my sons, but I had no one to care for me. *I laid there all alone, in a state of complete panic and misery.* I began to feel this wave of hopelessness come over me, *maybe I was going to die. At least I wouldn't be in so much pain if I was dead.* The doctor had given me a lecture about the dangers of getting addicted to the pain medicine, so I tried going without it for several days. I only ended up making myself more desolate. *It was a really terrible time to lecture me about addiction. If I was dying, let me be comfortable while doing it.* Every day the doctor would come in and check up on me and then leave. *This went on for days. I was seriously over the bullshit,* so one day when the doctor came in, I had questions for him. I asked him: *when I was going to get better? Wasn't there anything he could give me to improve my situation? Was I just supposed to lay here waiting to die?*

After *begging* for a solution other than steroids, the doctor put me on an intravenous immunosuppressant biologic medication. He was reluctant to do so because once I started this medicine, *I could never go off of it.* He said it wouldn't work if I tried to start taking it again. *I felt so desperate and didn't know what to do.* I asked my stepmom for advice, and she didn't know what to tell me. I had to make the decision myself, even though I wasn't in the head space to make important decisions. But I couldn't lay there and *do nothing! !* I was only 37 years old, *I wasn't ready to die.*

While panicking and in pain, I hadn't had time to do my research on this medication. I found out later it was designed to *suppress* my own immune system. Crohn's disease is an auto immune disorder; your body *turns against itself.* Now get this: the medicine is made from synthesized *rat DNA.* I was going to inject another animals' DNA into my bloodstream? *What kind of archaic treatment was this? Only, I didn't know this at the time.* Every doctor recommends it, and there are millions of people on this drug. However, it didn't help me feel better.

I was in the hospital for several more days and nothing was happening, even after the infusion of rat stuff. I felt worse and there was no talk of what was supposed to occur next, and my stepmom and I were way past the point of her telling me how to live my life. In this helpless state, I *had to make a decision. I wanted to go home.* So I announced to the doctor the next time he came in that I was checking myself out of the hospital. I had prepped my stepmom to back me up, because my decision was *final. I wasn't getting better lying around with other sick people in an atmosphere of death and dying. Besides, the food was terrible.* I told him I had a better chance of healing at home. Hospitals aren't prisons, but for some reason, *they tried to stop me. I don't even think I signed out, I just took off. My stepmom drove the getaway car!* I had been in the hospital for *fourteen days.*

Once I got home, I felt relived to be in my own comfortable bed again. I could eat actual real food, not the absolute *shit* they served me in the hospital, when they were *allowing* me to eat. Dr. Strauss, my healer after my youngest son's birth, had retired. So I found a different acupuncturist. This little Chinese guy named Dr. Li *is the one who put me back together. He barely spoke English, but understood what I needed.* He gets sole credit for me being alive today, not *conventional doctors and traditional medicine.* I went a few times a week to get acupuncture and took his herbal remedies exactly the way he instructed. Eventually, I felt better, like myself again. Except, I was skinnier then I had been in high school. *What was so fucked up was that people kept telling me how great I looked.* I would reply back: "Well, I just got out of the hospital and almost died, but thanks." *Our society is so twisted...looking sickly skinny is what looks good? It didn't feel good.*

This was the *second time* in my life that a 5,000 year old ancient Chinese technique had helped me to heal, *when modern science didn't have a fucking clue.* You'd think that if the body is turning on itself, maybe making it weaker by suppressing the immune system wasn't the best idea? *Just a thought.* Never *once* did any doctor ask me what I was eating or how my stress levels were. They never asked what my emotional state was when I was diagnosed with Crohn's disease. I'd find out later *just how important this component was.* At the time of diagnosis, my emotional state was a *wreak.*

Now I go and visit my acupuncturist Michelle Belanger every month like clockwork. I would go more often if I could afford it, but it's not covered by health insurance. I'm not going to wait until I land in the hospital again! My monthly appointments are an energetic tune-up, and are necessary to keep up with the stress of my life. While I can't see my energetic body, *I know about it.* Making sure it is healthy is a *very big* part of staying alive. My self care routine is solid these days, it keeps me healthy and sane.

Next up in my dark night of the soul: the dreaded *C word, cancer.* I had had this nodule on my thyroid for years, I had it checked years earlier and the doctor said it was fine. Yet I had this nagging feeling that something wasn't *right. So* I went to the doctor, *like a good girl,* and had a biopsy. It came back "suspicious"; the doctor couldn't tell me if it was cancer or not. I went for a second opinion to another doctor, *and he said the same thing.* They both said the only way to find out if it was cancerous was to have my thyroid *removed* and sent to a lab. *Conventional medicine always promotes expensive surgeries, keep this in mind.*

I had a huge, momentous decision to make:. *Should I remove my thyroid or not?* If I removed it and it was cancerous, it would save my life. If it wasn't cancer, *I would have removed a perfectly functional thyroid, and* I would need to be on medication for the rest of my life. I grappled with this important decision, again, *all on my own.* I literally did not have one person to turn to. *I felt lost, vulnerable and helpless. Bloody hell! What was I going to do?* But I knew I could always count on *God. It has always been this way.* I asked God for an answer about what I should do, and I *got one.*

It's strange how Spirit gives me messages. Sometimes they show me a scene from a movie. Other times it's from a book, like when I found *Many Lives, Many Masters* on my bookshelf. Sometimes it's a song that is randomly playing on Pandora, *only I know it's not random*. The answer I was looking for came from a line on a Netflix show "Orange is the New Black".

It was 2017 and everyone was talking about this show. I wasn't all that interested in seeing it, it's about women in prison. It sounded bleak and depressing. *Who wants to watch a show about being in prison?* But someone told me it was *so good* that I had to see it. One night I was bored, so I switched it on.

I never made it past episode 1, somehow my television shut down right in the beginning of the episode. But not before the character, played by Jason Biggs, proposes to his girlfriend (who apparently is the one who ends up in jail). She asked if the ring was his mother's? He said, "No, it was my aunt's. She died of thyroid cancer."

Oh! People die of thyroid cancer. The show being abruptly *cut off right after he said this was my confirmation. I already knew it was cancerous, that's why I had this nagging feeling.* I scheduled the surgery the next day and…it was cancer.

Here's the thing: one of the *side effects* of that intravenous immunosuppressive drug *is cancer. This is no small detail, yet no one told me.* It was only later that I found out this fun fact. It's right there on the website, but you'd have to be able to read words in microscopic print. I don't think the human eye is even able to see something written so small, *I had to get a magnifying glass. But it's there on the website.* Because of this, the pharmaceutical companies can never be held liable. I also noticed that a voice over actor says it in the commercials, *but really, really, really fast. You'd miss it if you're not paying attention.*

Somehow this super important information *never got to me before I was put on a drug that I'd "never able to go off of it". For fuck's sake!* Why hadn't I been informed about this? This medication made from rat DNA *is the most viable solution that science could come up with? Jesus Christ almighty. Something is not right here.*

After my thyroidectomy I gained 20 pounds in *ten days.* I wasn't eating like a pig, my diet was exactly the same. But my body was completely thrown off without a thyroid, which controls metabolism and energy. So in addition to gaining weight, *now I struggled to even get out of bed. This could not be happening!* The thyroid hormone prescription I was given by the doctor was a T4 medicine, but my brain had to figure out how to turn T4 into T3, which is the active thyroid hormone that gives you energy and regulates your metabolism. No one told me about the T1 and T2 hormones the thyroid produces, I was clueless about those. W*hy couldn't I figure out some things were missing when the doctor only talked about T3 and T4?* My pituitary gland needed to do synthesize T4 into T3 so I could have energy. However, my brain hadn't caught on and I couldn't get my body back into a state of equilibrium.

Every six weeks I went to get blood drawn, and the medicine dosage went up and down, *like a yo-yo. I was either too tired to get out of bed or I couldn't sleep*. The doctor gave me an extra pill of T3, but that only made me angry and *hungry. This is just fucking great.* My modeling career came to a screeching halt, *nothing in my life was going right.* It didn't matter though, I could barely get out of bed anyway. My son wanted a puppy and thought my post surgery period was the *perfect time* to get one, which I had to house train. *Seriously?*

I forgot to mention to the second worst side effect of the immunosuppressive drug: *complete and total lack of short term memory.* I used to be able to *remember everything* that happened ten or twenty years ago. It was one of my most amazing attributes. *I knew it was the medication,* because every two months when I went to the hospital to have the infusion, I couldn't remember which building I was supposed to go in. *I was a walking zombie...wow, this is fun. So glad I signed up for this.*

After the thyroid cancer was removed, I had to take a pill of radioactive iodine to dissolve any thyroid cells left so that the cancer wouldn't come back. That wasn't so bad, but I had to be isolated for a week so as not to harm others. I couldn't understand how putting something radioactive in my body was going to help me, *but this is mainstream science and everyone seems to agree on it without question. Let's put something in our bodies that's radioactive. Yeah, that's a great idea!*

What pissed me off was that everyone kept saying: "Oh thyroid cancer is the best cancer to have". *I wanted to smack the smirk right off their face.* It actually ended up being *true,* and I'm assuming it's because you can live without a thyroid and I wouldn't need chemotherapy. *But is there really a good cancer to have? They all seem to suck.* I chose not to identify as a cancer survivor. *I'm very careful what I label myself, it could be a self fulfilling prophecy.*

The removal of my thyroid threw my body completely out of whack, and it wasn't just the weight gain. After the thyroidectomy, my whole body broke out with psoriasis, *which is another auto immune condition.* I was *covered* in red scaly patches that looked *horrifying!* It was even on my scalp! I headed to the dermatologist, and her solution was *again, steroids! Is this the best treatment they've come up with, steroids* for *everything?* The medication does reduce inflammation in the body, but not without the most dire side effects. *It should only be used as a quick fix, not the solution to the problem.* It was summer in Miami, and I had to walk around wearing long pants, long sleeves, and socks and shoes because it was the worst on my feet.

One day, *nine months later,* I went to my gastroenterologist to have my bi-monthly infusion of rat DNA meds and showed the doctor my skin. She said: "Oh, yea, that specific medicine can cause rashes in some people." She said it like it was no big deal. *I had already shown* that same doctor my skin at my last appointment, *and the one before that. She didn't think to tell me that useful information then? This shit was getting crazy*! I guess she hadn't thought it might be related because I had tolerated this medication well for so many years. In the dead heat of summer in Miami, *I'm sweating my ass off, and this was not a big deal? Is everyone smoking crack and I just don't know about it?*

So my doctor switched me to a different intravenous immunosuppressant biologic, this one made from mouse DNA. *Wow, I felt much better about being on this new medication. At least I could inject it myself.* This medicine had the same side effects, one of them being *cancer.* Do you know how much this medication costs? *$20,000 a pop. Not a paltry amount for a tiny syringe of clear liquid.* But I'll come back to this later, it's important information. At least my skin cleared up and I could move on with my life.

The psoriasis did eventually go away, but it had killed my career and my self esteem. I spent most days hiding away in my apartment unable to face the world. I couldn't even go on dates, *I was too embarrassed.* Explaining all my health issues and why I wouldn't get naked didn't seem like a great first date conversation. *I didn't go on a date for five years.* I was too tired to think about anyway. *Besides, I'm convinced that Miami is the worst place on planet to be single and date.*

Then I began to have pain in every joint in my body. *At this point, I'm still in my 30s.* It was getting so hard to move around, just bending my knees to pick up the boys' toys lead to *excruciating pain.* I was sent to a rheumatologist to have some X-rays and was diagnosed with arthritis, *another auto immune condition. The doctor's solution: another prescription. The lunacy was intensifying. Somebody help me!*

At this time I was under the care of so many doctors, none of which communicated with each other, all of them pushing more meds. I was taking so many God damn pills that it made my head spin. *This would not end well.* Of course, none of these doctors asked me what I was eating, *what mental state I was in, or what my stress levels were.*

For the next act in my dark night of the soul, a birth control device punctured my uterus and I needed to have an emergency hysterectomy. But first, I had to find a doctor that would perform it! I had gone to different doctor, not the one who had put in the device, and he did a test. He filled my uterus with dye and then took and X-ray. It was clear that there was a *hole* in my uterus, because he could see the dye seeping out in the X-ray. *I could see it too, what the hell was this? When I started to freak out, he backtracked and told me I was fine. How was I fine?* He was obviously covering his ass and since I was a new patient, he probably didn't want to deal with me. But I saw the results of the x-ray, and *there was a hole in my uterus. Cue the panic and spiraling out of control! I was in so much pain my head was spinning.*

I knew there was something terribly wrong because I had been bleeding for months, besides being in *pain.* At one point I went to emergency room because there were blood *clots* coming out, *worse than what had come out post birth. I was completely hysterical!* The doctors looked at me with pity like I was trying to get pain pills. *Were they serious? Did they not see the blood clots? Wasn't I already on enough medications? Fuck them and their medications, I could handle the pain.*

I went to yet *another* doctor and told him the whole story. He said I needed to go back to the original doctor who had put in the device, *and that's when I burst into tears.* I never wanted to see that doctor, *ever again.* I had to beg him to him to help me. Thank God he took pity on me, he could see I was in pain. But don't underestimate the lengths doctors will go to protect other doctors. *Maybe they have some kind of secret code that we don't know about. People are definitely smoking crack and I don't know about it.*

The hysterectomy was the *most painful* surgery I have ever had, and I've had many. This time my dad come down to take care of my boys, because clearly, I needed some help. I had informed my doctor that I had an attorney and was suing the Pharmaceutical company. The attorney had arranged for my uterus to be preserved for the lawsuit, and I informed my surgeon. He came in to my hospital room post surgery to inform me that indeed, the birth control device punctured a hole in my uterus. *The little metal coil was sticking out and I had surgery in the nick of time...*it could have traveled to other parts of my body. *Who knows what kind of damage that could've caused?* The doctor told me that I should call my attorney to secure the organ. He said: "Things have a way of getting lost in this hospital". *Yea, I bet they do. I have so much trust in hospitals now, thanks for that.*

I had my first surgery at 12 years old; something about my kidneys shriveling up and not functioning properly. At this point in my life, I am so used to being in pain, like it's normal, *it's kind of crazy to think about.* I decided to take control of my situation and educate *myself,* instead of just believing what the doctors were saying. *It was very clear to me that modern medicine was making my deteriorating health even worse.*

What I discovered is *mind blowing and very sad.* Drug companies spend twice as much money on advertising and marketing then they do on researching and developing drugs. Training doctors to be a drug pusher starts in medical school, where would-be doctors spend hours learning which medications to prescribe for what. *And why do you think you need a doctor to write a prescription for you? Well, Big Pharma needs to know who to send a kick back to.*

It gets even more bleak: doctors spend about four hours total of training about dietary protocols. They learn very little, if anything, about nutrition. *Yet it is nutrition that can heal us! Doctors don't know about this? How is this even possible or probable? What kind of quackery is going on here?*

I had to educate *myself* on what to put in my body. The first thing I cut out was diet coke. The sweetener in it is a *toxic chemical, it can cause cancer, and I was drinking at least four a day. How are they even allowed to keep selling this stuff?* I also stopped drinking tap water. They (not sure who they are or who came up with this) put fluoride in our water supply. Fluoride is supposed to help strengthen teeth, but it should *never be ingested. It is a neurotoxin! We have been lied to and are being poisoned for our entire lives.*

Bottled water could be *even more atrocious, if that's possible.* I won't even get into how these plastic bottles are destroying the planet, I'm going to focus on how it can affect our bodies. First of all, most of the time you're paying for filtered tap water. *Evian spelled backwards is naive.* Then *the more ominous one,* the lining of the plastic bottle emits something into the water that *disrupts your hormones. This is not good news.* The other day I was scrolling through Instagram, and on both People magazine and Fox News' accounts was a story of a guy that *died* of a brain eating amoeba after rinsing his nasal cavity out with tap water. *The weirdest shit happens down here. Only in Flori-duh.*

Juice is pure sugar. They remove the fiber which your body needs. It is beneficial, it's what keeps you full. It turns out that cow's milk is probably the *worst thing* humans can put in their body, besides sugar. The phrase "Milk, it does a body good" is a total *fabricated lie; it's a marketing and advertising strategy to make more money! Why is it always about the money? I can't take this anymore!* I haven't even gotten to foods yet, this is only the horrifying reality of liquids.

Our food should be our medicine and
our medicine should be our food.
—Hippocrates

It goes downhill from there, like a boulder that picks up speed and crushes you dead. The sugar in juice is at least fructose, it's a natural sugar. *Regular white sugar is more addictive than cocaine.* What happens when you ingest it is your blood sugar levels *spike, and then it crashes, and your body is going to crave more sugar.* The more sugar you consume, the higher chance you have for diabetes and obesity. *Obesity is the real pandemic in America! There are more complications from consuming sugar than just diabetes; there's heart attack, stroke....the list goes on and on.*

Sugar also feeds the *bad bacteria* in your gut, which only makes you more sick, in addition to being fat. Don't even get me started on high fructose corn syrup! "Sugar" isn't even one of the words in the title, but it's an artificial sugar *made from toxic chemicals, and it's in everything!! Argh!* There are literally dozens of sugars in practically everything under 56 *different* names. *So sneaky. Besides High Fructose corn syrup, t*here's sucrose, fructose, D-ribose, galactose, dextrin, dextrose, ethyl maltol, lactose, maltodextrin...the list goes on. *I had to educate myself because I like living.*

I had to unlearn and forget about everything I had ever been told. It's all a lie. I couldn't turn to doctors or my family for advice, I had go and obtain all of this knowledge myself. To make matters worse, it's information that's not readily available, most has been censored. *I had to dig for this information. Food companies hide it in order to sell you more shit. Profit over our well being...isn't this lovely?*

We have a very, very serious problem. If you like being healthy, then please pay attention. First of all, there are literally thousands of *toxic chemicals* in the American food supply that *are banned in Europe.* I couldn't even find the exact number. *So we're being poisoned and they're not? Maybe I should move to Europe.* According to the Guardian: "The US often waits until the harm is done and the EU tries to prevent it to a certain extent. It often seems the US favors the market over protection. Unlike the EU, the US does not have agencies like the EFSA that offer independent scientific evaluation of new chemicals brought to the market. And while the EU has consistently updated its methods and processes for evaluating new chemicals, some experts say the US system, set up more than half a century ago, needs updating." *Sounds like there are multiple things in America that need updating. Land of the "free", where you definitely need to be brave…just to eat. Now I'm definitely moving to Europe.*

Some American breads contain potassium bromate, because it strengths the dough. It's in literally hundreds of food products. Yet it's banned in Europe, China and India because it's suspected to be a carcinogen (something that causes cancer). *There's more.* Titanium dioxide, brominated vegetable oil, azodicarbonamide, and propylparaban are all *banned in Europe,* yet Americans are eating it. Titanium dioxide is a whitening agent, so I guess *whiter is better in America? Is America really that racist that we even need our food to be whiter? Wow. The racism runs so deep here that people are willing to poison themselves to be "whiter"? This is spiraling out of control. I can't wrap my head around this.* The most toxic, preservative filled food product is probably *breakfast cereal.* The same stuff that comes in a colorful box with cartoon characters on it and is *marketed for children.* Sometimes they even put a little toy in there to make sure your kid *eats it.*

If I really wanted to be healthy, I'd have to stop eating anything packaged. Or at the very least, read every single ingredient on the side of the box with a magnifying glass and then Google what it was and how it could affect my body. *Who has the time for this?* The FDA claims that it "monitors, evaluators and regulates substances added to food". However, I do not believe that, but I'll get to why I don't trust the FDA later.

I also discovered that our health is *directly related* to our gut lining. Dr. Amy Myers, whose supplements I often take, was diagnosed with Grave's disease while in medical school. Grave's disease is an autoimmune condition where the thyroid *over produces hormones.* It causes anxiety, irritability and often the patients eyes bulge out. She said: "If you had told me back then that it started in my gut, I wouldn't have believed you". *This woman was in medical school, and she didn't know this? What kind of fuckery is this?* Yet Hippocrates said, who knows how many years ago, "All disease starts in the gut". *Is anyone paying attention?* The gut lining is even responsible for our mood and bad gut health is linked to depression. *Heal your gut and the body will follow* was good news for me, because it was my gut that was the problem in the first place.

To start, I had to get on a diet that would *allow* my gut, and therefore my body, to heal. *When given the proper environment and the right nutrients, the human body is designed to heal itself.* A friend had recommended Jordan Rubin and his Maker's Diet protocol. Rubin had had his own battle with Crohn's disease, and at one point he was 104 pounds and in a wheelchair. Doctors thought he was going to die and had virtually given up on him. *The doctors were really going to give up on him? Why, because their medication didn't work, and might have even made his condition more awful?*

Although Jordan was determined to live, and thank God for that! He tried over 70 different alternative treatments until he found the best one: a California nutritionist told him he wasn't healthy because he *wasn't eating the way God had intended him to eat.* So Jordan sought after the answers *in the Bible, of all places. Funny how I always end up back here, to the Bible. Our Maker-God-get it?* He changed his diet to what they were eating in biblical times: raw, organically grown whole grains, fruits and vegetables, fermented diary, and grass fed beef and poultry. He added in a high quality probiotic for good measure. *So simple.*

The simplest explanation is usually the best one.
—Occam's razor

I decided to do some research to find out how the health system got so fucked up in the first place. I came upon a YouTube video entitled "The Big Secret-Full Medical Documentary". The chaos all began in 1865 when John D. Rockefeller purchased an oil company and gained control of the entire oil industry by buying up smaller oil companies. He now had the power to control the all the oil production and distribution in the United States. *This is how John D. Rockefeller became the richest man in the world.*

The documentary goes on to say: "At the beginning of the 20th century, the Rockefeller Foundation turned its attention to the acquisition of pharmaceutical companies. They started buying them up in order to profit from their patented drugs. However, in 1912, vitamins were discovered." It goes on to talk about how certain vitamin deficiencies cause health conditions rather than diseases. For example, rickets isn't a disease, *it's a vitamin D deficiency.* This was not good news for pharmaceutical companies because vitamins cannot be patented. *So how was Rockefeller going to make a huge profit on his drugs? He wasn't rich enough already?* He found a way to control and influence doctors and what they prescribe. This was the beginning of methodical takeover which led to a profit driven system promoting pharmaceutical drug sales and profitable surgery over curative medical practices. "Basically, the long term management of diseases was found to be more profitable than efforts to cure diseases." *This is the truth, but only if you want to believe this documentary.*

It went on and gets more disturbing: "In 1910, the Carnegie Foundation decided to focus on reforming health care and commissioned Abraham Flexner to study medical schools in the United States. Even though Flexner had no medical training, he continued his research by visiting every medical school in the U.S at the time. The Flexner report was published in 1910, and it criticized most of the medical schools and called for "higher standards, more hands on clinical work and more research." "The Rockefeller Foundation seized on this opportunity to promote their own agenda. They used their influence to help pass legislation putting the American Medical Association, *a private institution*, in charge of overseeing medical training and practices…they used campaign donations and lobbyists to further their agenda in exchange for large campaign contributions, legislators gave the Rockefeller Foundation just what they wanted. Unfortunately, the AMA was heavily influenced by the Rockefeller Foundation...*so they promoted allopathic medicine to the point that it became the only approved form of medicine taught in the U.S.*

Consequently, doctors began prescribing the Rockefeller's patented medicines to manage instead of cure diseases...Medical schools were under intense pressure to conform to the wishes of the Rockefeller Foundation and they began awarding large grants to medical schools that taught allopathic medicine. Schools that still embraced alternative forms of medicine could not compete financially were forced to shut down. In the end, half of the medical schools were closed." So basically we now have a health "care" system that chooses profit *over our health! They are literally lying right to our faces and we are dying!* If something doesn't change soon, our children will have a shorter lifespan than we do. *This situation is absolutely horrific.*

The documentary goes on to say that Rockefeller medicine also removed preventive medicine, *because it wasn't in their best interest to inform patients how to prevent diseases. That's a bad business model, right? Why inform people how to avoid buying their medicine?* This is a gross *violation* of the hippocratic oath, where new physicians swear to uphold specific ethical standards and not to do the patient any harm or injustice. *Yet, this is exactly what is happening!* I don't think all doctors are evil people, but some have been misinformed and we are being *deceived.* And we are paying the high price of our *lives. Where is the outrage?* If you are a scientist or a doctor reading this, *start paying attention to the dissents among your colleagues and peers. If anything is labeled as quackery...please go investigate. Don't be afraid to stand alone! We need to trust you again, all of our lives depend on it.*

A patient cured is a customer lost.
—John Roulac

Don't get me wrong, I'm not some airy fairy hippie that doesn't shave my armpits and exclusivity uses essential oils for any ailment. I'm very aware that antibiotics can save your life if you have a severe bacterial infection. Accutane, even with the bad side effects, was the only thing that finally cured my decades long battle with cystic acne. Xanax is a life saver when I am spiraling out of control from a panic attack. I'm grateful that pharmaceutical companies make thyroid medication, because if I don't take it, I will most certainly die. *But at what point do we say enough is enough?*

Taking a pill for everything has become what's considered "normal". The worst thing about this "normal" situation is what happened after Sammy died. Everyone around me kept encouraging me, *pressuring me even,* to take an anti-depressant. Besides an old school sleeping pill, *I just couldn't do it.* SSRIs are a class of drug called "selective serotonin reuptake inhibitors" (*say what?)* Serotonin is a brain chemical, so that means the drug somehow messes with it. *It's not a very scientific explanation, but it's the best I could come up with.*

By this time in my life I didn't have enough trust in doctors or science to take a pill that could mess with my brain chemicals! *Wasn't my brain fucked up enough already?* People would say to me: "It's ok to ask for some help." and "Don't be ashamed of this, that's what these medications are for". Except...*wasn't I supposed to feel this way? My son had just died!* Am I the only one who that thinks giving a depressed person a pill that could give the possible side effect of suicidal thoughts is a *really terrible idea? Are you kidding me? Oh my God, wake me up when this is over.*

The other day I was at a dinner party at my neighbors' house. I was sitting next to a woman that volunteers for an organization that brings awareness to mental health issues. *So I had to ask her:* "How does a psychiatrist determine which patient actually *needs* medication because of a chemical imbalance, and which ones just need therapy for trauma? I mean, there's no blood or pee test...you can't do a MRI or CAT scan to find out if someone is a bipolar malignant narcissist...*can you?*" She shook her head, "No, you can't." I kept looking at her inquiringly for an answer. She paused, and then said: "It's not so much a science, it's more of an art". For the first time in my life, *I was speechless. I wasn't even sure what to say.* The only thing I was thinking was: *I won't be visiting any "museums" where these "artists" "masterpieces" are displayed. I've learned my lesson, these days I stay far away from the loony bin.*

I'll give you my cure for depression and anxiety in one short paragraph. Depression is *guilt and shame* about the past. *But I can't change that,* so I may as well let it go. Anxiety is *fear of what may happen in the future.* I'm not there yet, so *why worry about it?* Of course, I'm smart to take precautions, but besides that, *I try and stay in the present moment.* If I ever feel sad or anxious, *I switch up the energy.* My favorite things that do that are: going outside for a walk, taking a hot Epsom salt bath, playing a meditation video on YouTube, taking long and deep breaths, going to the gym or calling up a friend I know will make me laugh. I avoid anyone who is envious and tries to compete with me. I steer clear of people who make me second guess my own intuition or discourage me from following my heart. *I avoid rude and nasty people like the plague. Basically, I stay away from assholes. I think it's a better solution than taking that pill.*

In addition to doctors not informing patients about preventive medicine, *they don't cure diseases.* They just prescribe toxic chemicals in order to *mask the symptoms. If they cured a patient, they would lose billions, maybe trillions of dollars!* The toxic chemical drugs in turn only makes the patients *more sick!* The toxicity of the drugs was creating *entirely new diseases*, and yet doctors just call them "side effects". *But don't trust me, I'm not a doctor or a scientist. I'm just a crazy person trying to not go crazier.*

This video went on to say that millions of people have been prescribed a class of drugs called statins. These drugs are supposed to lower cholesterol and thereby prevent heart attacks. While statins do lower cholesterol, they *do not prevent heart attacks. And the side effects are catastrophic.* First of all, cholesterol is key to overall health because it is so important to the cells, *especially to the brain. They are messing with the brain…again? I'm starting to see a pattern here.* The brain has 25% of the body's cholesterol, it is needed for the brain to function. The way they got so many millions of people on statins was by lowering the standard of what was considered to be a normal level, thereby creating new customers to buy that shit. *Trickery. It's Evil.* I have slightly higher levels of cholesterol, and my doctor (who is not my doctor anymore) put me on a statin. I couldn't raise my arms, they felt like lead. *I stopped taking it after only three days.*

It gets more disturbing: "Lower cholesterol levels are associated with an increased chance of death, increased chance of cancer, higher percentage of birth defects, peripheral neuropathy, short temper and aggressive behavior, kidney failure, and dementia. Alzheimer's was virtually non-existent until right around 1940, then it started to show up. Then after 1980 it skyrocketed…it rose from obscurity to become the sixth, fifth, or fourth leading cause of death."

Another doctor goes on to say that donating blood once or twice a year can decrease your risk of heart attack and stroke by 75-80%! *But no doctor will tell you this. If this information got out, what would happen to the sales of statin medications? Do you see where I'm going with this?* "Cholesterol is so important, every cell wall in the body is made from cholesterol, it makes the cells waterproof. Cholesterol is extremely important for your health, all of your sex hormones are made from it. If you don't have enough cholesterol…not only does your brain dry up and you get Alzheimer's, but your sex hormones dry up too…causing erectile dysfunction for men…and women get hot flashed for years…unlike our grandmothers who got hot flashes for a few months. *Alzheimer's disease* is *a physician caused disease!" This is a quote from this documentary.*

You don't have to believe me, do your own research and make your own conclusions. *It's your body, your life, after all. If you don't care that you can't get it up, then why should I?* Everything I learned only made me more sick to my stomach. Any doctor that goes *against* the mainstream agenda of *profit from allopathic medicine* gets crucified, mocked, and outcast. *Those are the only doctors that I listen to now, they have risked their careers and reputations to inform us of the Big Lie of our modern health "care" system.*

THEN I CAME ACROSS ANOTHER DOCUMENTARY ENTITLED "Burzynski: The Cancer Cure Cover-up", and the opening scene is a shocking and absolutely *heartbreaking* story. A father is testifying in court about his daughter who died at four years old. The little girl had developed a highly malignant brain tumor that had spread to her lower spine... doctors told the parents they had only two options: take her home and let her die, or give her massive doses of chemotherapy and radiation simultaneously. They chose to follow the doctors orders and gave her chemo and radiation which burned her skull so bad that she had second degree burns and her hair never grew back. After sixth months, she survived the treatments yet she still had cancer.

The parents of the little girl refused to give up and started researching. They found Dr. Brzezinski and used his treatment, a non-toxic medicine he called antioneoplastin. *Her cancer disappeared.* When she died, the autopsy showed that she had *no cancer,* and the *cause of death was neurological necrosis. Her brain had fallen apart from the radiation and chemotherapy. This is so heartbreaking!* As a parent who has lost a child, I can understand the pain. I wouldn't wish that pain on my *worst enemy! But this little girl's death could have been prevented! I can't stop crying.*

Dr. Brzezenski had made a profound discovery: he found a strain of peptides in human blood and urine that had never been recorded before in biomedical research. His curiosity led him to discover that people who were inflicted with cancer seemed to lack these peptides, while those free of cancer had an abundance of these peptides.

Dr. Brzezinski decided to chemically extracted these peptides from the blood and urine of healthy donors and began administering them to patients with cancer. Legally Dr. Brzezenski would only be allowed to treat his patients within the state of Texas, he could not introduce anti-neoplastons into inter state commerce. It goes on to say: "However, once word began to spread that Dr. Brzezinski was successfully treating what was once considered terminal, incurable cancer patients, people began traveling from all over the country to receive his treatment....Much of the medical and hospital industry operates on a very closed shop, and if you have ideas that in one way or another might jeopardize that economic base you fall into disfavor very quickly."

In 1984, Dr. Brzezinski's patients were being approached by agents sent to them by the Texas Board of Medical Examiners. They were trying to convince them to file complaints against the doctor. He was called to the Texas Board of Medical Examiners and they began investigating him, *even though no patients had filed any complaints. I mean, they were alive because of him! Why would they report him?* The board requested him to send in medical records that would be reviewed by an expert oncologist. The doctor never heard back from them, so he assumed the board was satisfied of his results.

Two years later, the Texas Medical Board of Medical Examiners came back to Dr. Brzezinski claiming that the cases that he had submitted were not successful and claimed he was violating a law (that supposedly didn't exist). He was told this was grounds for the board revoking and suspending his medical license. While the board had no case, they filed a complain anyway in 1990. They filed a second complaint in 1992. Because of this, sixty of his patients petitioned the board to stop harassing their doctor, *which was promptly ignored. They even attempted to strike the petitions from the record.*

Yet *somehow* in 1993, the case went to trial. There was *overwhelming* evidence that his treatment helped, and sometimes even cured the patients. Yet the State of Texas proceeded with their case against Dr. Brzezinski. They wanted to stop him from healing patients with a terminal illness. *Why would they try and stop a doctor who was just trying to save lives? Nothing makes sense anymore.*

The state of Texas acknowledged that his medicine could be helping a patient who was terminally ill, yet the Texas Medical Board decided to take the doctor to an even higher district court. They wanted to revoke the doctor's license based on the fact that his drugs have never been "approved". "It was eventually realized, *even by the mainstream press*, that the Food and Drug Administration had been pressuring the Texas Medical Board to continue trying to take away the doctor's medical license. *Now do you understand why I don't trust the FDA?*

To make a long story short, the FDA continued to raid the doctor's clinic and this witch hunt lasted for *ten years.* Did it ever cross their minds that while they raged an all out *war* with the doctor *people were dying?* On November 20, 1995, Dr Brzezinski was charged with 75 counts of violating federal law and fraud. If convicted, the doctor would spend up to 290 years in prison and would have to pay an 18.5 million dollar fine. *That's a really harsh sentence for a guy that's saving lives, don't you think?* This madness cost the doctor two million dollars and *60 million of our taxpayer dollars! I never consented to using my taxpayer dollars for this, did you?* Why should I trust any agency that is in it for *profit? I can't and I won't.*

Suddenly everything that I had been taught like: "You have to follow your doctor's orders" was complete bullshit and an absolute fraudulent *scheme.* I had been brainwashed *since birth. Which in my mind that meant: what else are they lying to us about?* I went from a trusting, naive girl to an outright *enraged* woman. *If you're not angry at this injustice, then you haven't been paying attention.*

But this story gets even *more* interesting, *but not in a good way.* Dr. Wilhelm Reich (1897-1957), an Austrian psychiatrist, invented an "organe accumulator" which consisted of alternating layers of organic and inorganic materials. This produced a significant amount of bioelectric energy which has a healing effect. He got to work curing many people of cancer, until the FDA had him arrested. *I wonder on what grounds the FDA could arrest him? Did anyone even know the FDA can arrest people?* He died in prison in 1957. *So apparently, the FDA is in on this scam to kill us while making us pay billions while they do it. Which leads me to yet another question: Are the insurance companies in on this too? Is profit really more important than human life?*

This is urgent, we need an overhaul of our health system before *more people die. We should not take gross injustice lying down!* We are talking about is *people's lives! Big Pharma is getting away with murder! We need to stop this.*

I had heard about this book "The Truth-310 hidden cures "they" hoped you'd never discover" by Dr. Fred Pescatore. So *of course* I wanted to get copy. I went to every online book store and couldn't find it. I even went to Dr. Pescatore's website, and every other book he had written was there, *but not the one I was looking for. Isn't that strange? Am I stuck in the upside down world on "Stranger Things"?* By this point nothing was shocking me, but I was determined to *find that book.* I ended up buying it used on Ebay. *When there is a will, there is a way.*

I read another book "You Can Heal Your Life" by Louise Hay. This woman actually cured *herself* of cancer using the power of her *mind.* She realized her cancer had come from trauma experienced during childhood, and used positive thought patterns, affirmations, visualization, psychotherapy and nutritional cleansing. *Within six months, she was cancer free.* This woman was absolutely *amazing,* I highly suggest this book. She has categorized every diseases' origin back to lack of self love, self loathe, or holding onto to anger and being unforgiving. *Fascinating.* She built a whole healing empire around her methods.

My massage therapist recommended another book "Dying to be Me" by Anita Moorjani (which is published by Hay House, the publishing company founded by Louise Hay). Now, this woman fought cancer for four years and *actually died and came back.* She realized *while on the other side,* that her cancer came from her *lack of self worth.* She had been pushed and pulled by religious and cultural customs since she was a little girl. Upon regain consciousness, her cancer *disappeared* and *she gave herself the permission to be herself. The doctors were amazed and called it "spontaneous remission". I call it a miracle. I only had to give myself the permission to myself to be healthy?* I was already doing that, so I was one step ahead of the game. Once I fully understood where all of this was going, I felt like I found some missing buried treasure. *This is absolutely incredible and so simple.*

I had to know more, I had made an amazing discovery! I came upon the work of Dr. Bruce H. Lipton. He discovered the field of *epigenetics.* Dr. Lipton left his tenured position at a prestigious university when he discovered that our genes actually *do not determine our health. We are not doomed to get a certain disease because of our genetics.* He had to make a choice; continue teaching something that he knew wasn't true, or *walk away to test his theories. He took a chance, and I'm glad he did.* Now the field of Epigentics is pretty mainstream, but only because Dr. Lipton was brave enough *to stand up for what he believed was right.* He took a chance at being ridiculed and *outcast by his peers* because well, *it was the right thing to do. It's called having integrity, everyone should try it.*

His book "The Biology of Belief" was mind blowing, it forever changed how I think about my own thinking. "Stunning new scientific discoveries about biochemical effects of the brain's functioning show that all the cells of your body are affected by your thoughts." *My body hears everything I'm thinking whether it was true or not. So I might as well make those thoughts be about being young, healthy, and sexy!*

I'm currently reading "Becoming Supernatural-How Common People Are Doing The Uncommon" by Dr. Joe Dispenza. Joe was in the hospital in excruciating pain from multiple spinal fractures. He vowed that if he ever walked again, he'd devote his life to studying mind-body medicine so others may find healing too. Dr. Dispenza was up and walking *in less than twelve weeks,* and he and a team of scientists have been studying neuroplasticity, epigenetics, and mind-body medicine ever since. *Give me a few months, I'll be immortal.*

So I did a full swap out, a complete 180 degree turn. I went from a woman that was always sick and in the hospital, *to a full on goddess who only visualizes a perfect, pain free, healthy body.* That's my goal at least, I'm taking baby steps. I'm allowed to be a work in progress and a masterpiece at the same time.

I think aging in general, is *optional.* Every day cells in our body die and are replaced by new ones. For example, the inner intestinal lining completely replaces itself every 5-7 days. Other areas of the body take longer to regenerate, but it's still happening. The gut lining is the area that regenerates the fastest…*do you see now why gut health is so important?* If you want to heal your gut, it will only take a week if you give it the right nutrients and conditions.

I wanted to find out how long it takes the *whole body* to regenerate, so I did some research. Scientists at Weizmann Institute of Science in Rehovot, Israel have "pinned down the speed and extent of this turnover. About 330 billion cells are replaced *daily,* equivalent to about 1% of all our cells. In 80 to 100 days, 30 trillion will have replenished-the equivalent of a new you." *I had to reread that last sentence. So you mean to tell me that every 100 days I'm a whole new person? How fascinating.*

I loved the idea of the "new you" thing. My cells were regenerating spontaneously, I didn't have to work at that. All I had to do was keep my thoughts positive and focused on my health and wellness and keep practicing gratitude. Now I look in the mirror everyday day and say; "Hello, beautiful! You look young, gorgeous and *healthy* today! You are at your perfect weight and are so *fit!* You seem to be aging *backwards,* good for you!" I feel like the little engine that could…*I think I can, I think I can.*

I knew that the majority of my health issues were caused by my emotional state. Trauma had gotten trapped in my body and if I didn't get out, *it was going to kill me. If Big Pharma didn't kill me first.* I knew that the *power of my thoughts* was the key to having a healthy body. I fueled my body with healthy organic foods, stayed away from toxic preservatives and yet *another* prescription drug, *if I could.* I was going to ignore conventional medicine's advice, *following it had only landed me in the hospital.*

To be honest, it took the introduction of the Covid "vaccine" to *really wake me up.* Now it doesn't matter what side of the fence you're on. The pro-vaccine people are *deathly* afraid of the unjabbed, while the anti-vaxers are deathly *afraid* of what the vaccine would do to them. Whichever side you're on, both are trapped in a state of fear! *Fear is the real enemy here, it keeps you in a low vibrational state which just causes more problems. Fear* spews *hatred* that is *toxic,* and arguing with others about their opinion of the vaccine would do nothing for my own health, *so I didn't bother.*

I remembered that our thoughts and beliefs are the *main source* of our well being. That's why the placebo effect works so well. I think scientists discovered this by accident. When testing a new drug, they would give one group of test subjects the drug, and the other group a pill with inert ingredients. They discovered that some of the patients in the control group improved just as well as the other group taking the drug. *Their symptoms improved because they thought they were taking the medication.* It turns out *thinking something will help you will actually help you.* Let's all get our minds straightened out, shall we?

Despite the intense *pressure* from practicality *everyone and their mother,* I didn't feel the need to get the Covid vaccine, nor did I feel the need to *explain to anyone why* I refused it. I had already *had* Covid in October of 2020 and for me, it wasn't that bad. Even a year later when I went to get the blood test to fly overseas, I still had the antibodies for it. I couldn't understand why everyone, including *my own family, was aggravating me so much to get that damn thing! As far as I was concerned, I was already immunized.* How were they *afraid* of me being "unvaccinated"? That somehow I might be putting everyone else's health at risk? *It was disempowering and complete bullshit. I would never put the blame of my health on someone else.*

I still can't understand why it's called a "vaccine" in the first place. I'm vaccinated, my boys are vaccinated, but I made sure to find a pediatrician that used vaccines that were free of the toxic chemicals like thimerosal. Thimerosal is basically mercury, which is very poisonous. It's used to *preserve* the vaccine, *because if they had to throw it away they'd lose money! It's all about money, when is it not about money? This is sickening.* There's a theory that this neurotoxin in children's vaccines is what may be causing so many neurological problems. *I wasn't taking that chance with my boys, why would I risk it?*

I'm not a doctor or a scientist, but I do have some common sense. The purpose of a vaccine is to inoculate a person with a virus that you can *only get once,* like the chicken pox. I remember getting the chicken pox as a kid, my parents were relived I had it young and "got it over with". Apparently, the older you are when you get chicken pox, the more dangerous it can be. But after being infected and healing, my body had the built in antibody defense against the chicken pox and *I would never get it again.*

However, the flu is a virus you can get over and over again. There are so many different strains, and it can mutate. One time many years ago, my former doctor somehow convinced my to get the flu vaccine. *That winter I got the worst flu of my life.* Not only did it not *prevent* me from getting the flu, *it made it worse! I vowed to never get a stupid flu vaccine ever again.*

The most unsettling thing about the Covid-19 "vaccine" was this: I couldn't imagine injecting myself with a substance that could supposedly change *my DNA. I already knew that God had made us perfect.* Our bodies, if given the right conditions, are *designed* to *heal* themselves. Obviously, the most important component was *our thoughts and beliefs regarding our health.* If I had that vaccine, I felt it would be like saying that *I didn't have faith in God, that I had more faith in a scientist.* I put my faith only in God! *Besides, how could I trust Big Pharma when I already knew that they put profit above my well being?*

I spent a considerable amount of time wondering and worrying about this stupid Covid-19 vaccine. I couldn't understand the logic behind it. The only reason I even gave it so much thought was because of my boys, I had to beg them not to take it. My older son, who is serving in the Israeli army, had to get a Covid test every time he went back to base. My younger son was *so mad* at me that I wouldn't let him get it and he had to miss a basketball tournament in LA. They where they were requiring all the kids to show vaccination cards. *I was gripped in fear about the possibility of losing another child and I was having a complete melt down.*

Lucky for me, his anger towards me waned when he actually contracted Covid-19 and couldn't go anyway. I gave him ivermectin and he was fine within 24 hours. Although, he was pretty pissed he couldn't taste his food for a few months. So what was all this hype about? *Why such pressure to get a vaccine, which is not really a vaccine? And If it's not a vaccine, then what is it?*

I do have theory about it, *of course,* I've spent hours thinking about it. *This happens often because I have to come up with something that makes sense.* I believe that whatever they're supposedly putting in that vaccine is specifically designed to *slow down,* or even completely halt, *the ascension process. They want us to stay asleep!* The other medications they're giving us probably do that as well. I lost my memory almost entirely when I was on that intravenous immunosuppressive medication. Statins are literally the *cause* of Alzheimer's disease. *They don't want us to discover the power of our own Divine given creative abilities, they would prefer to keep programing us to be slaves while slowing killing us and making trillions of dollars in the process.*

Personally, *I'm out.* This shit has gone on *long enough, it's time to wrap up this buffoonery!* People are having spiritual awakenings all around the globe, i*t's about time!* The Earth is also evolving, it is a conscious sentient being. The only thing constant in life is change, and if we all don't get on board with changing and evolving along with the earth, we may just get *left behind. I'm not joking about this, I'm serious.* The urgency is just to *start* self reflecting and doing the inner work…or get left behind.

THESE PHARMACEUTICAL COMPANIES MAKE *BILLIONS OR trillions of dollars.* The richer they get, the more out of luck the regular folks are because now their wealth can *buy them more power. This is the greatest injustice to mankind in the history of the entire planet. How much longer are we all going to let them continue with this mass genocide?*

Even though I was afraid, *I made decision to pull the plug on the intravenous immunosuppressant biologic.* My body, my choice. *How much longer was I going to inject another animal's DNA into my body*? How many more times would I go through cancer before I would wake up to what was happening? I was scared, but I knew I *had to do it.*

I found a good Integrative doctor, and made an appointment to go see him. Integrative medicine doctors take into account *all* the systems of the body as well as the diet, stress and emotional state of the patient. They are *real doctors,* they go through medical school. While they can write prescriptions, they often suggest natural remedies before prescribing a toxic drug. *But here's the catch: Integrative Doctors are not covered by any health insurance plans. Why do you think this is the case?* It just confirmed for me what I already suspected, *the insurance companies might be in on the scam as well.* I recently switched my thyroid medication to the natural one, *and discovered my health insurance doesn't cover it.*

To be healthy in America, you need to be well informed. You need to *dig* for this information, it's not readily available and is often censored. Second, you have to *have money, and lots of it!* Integrative Doctors, acupuncture, chiropractors, herbal remedies, and high quality vitamins and supplements are *not cheap. Organic foods cost more money too. Does that sound like the "American Dream" to you?* The Declaration of Independence declares: we are "endowed by the Creator with certain unalienable rights, that among these are Life, Liberty, and the pursuit of Happiness". We are being *robbed of our lives,* lied to for profit, and this does *not make me happy.* The only happy ones are the people lining their pockets off of our sickness, death and misery. *This bullshit has gone on long enough.*

The entire world is *ass backwards* and maliciously *poisoned.* Yet they package it up all neat and pretty and then *make you buy it. That's how you get to be "a part of society"?* This way you won't be an outcast? *Are you fucking kidding me? Is everyone on crazy pills?* I don't want to be a part of this kind of society. It sounds too wacko, *even for me.*

So I went off the medication I had been on for seven long years. At first, I was super careful with my diet. I didn't eat any gluten, sugar, and dairy or drink any alcohol. The doctor told me to drink Cat's Claw tea and take certain supplements. I was frightened and wondered what would happen if I got sick again and needed medication. I was already told I could *never* go off of this medication or it "wouldn't work" if I went back on it. The explanation the doctor gave me for this was flimsy.

When I went to see my gastroenterologist, she was *angry with me. She demanded to know what gave me the right to just go off of my medication. Excuse me?* Her anger took me off guard, but I calmly explained I did it under a doctor's supervision. *Are we like children, we all need supervision?* I told her I felt great and that I'd get back to her if I needed anything. *I haven't had to go back. Although, I'm looking forward to my colonoscopy coming up to see if my theories have been right.*

Now I see why I had to be *on the medication for life:* I was a pharmaceutical "cash cow" and they would do any thing and everything in their power to *keep me in fear and paying. This medication costs $20,000 for each infusion, and I took it every two months!* When I let my diet slide a bit and was eating pizza and drinking wine, do you know what happened? *Absolutely nothing. I'm fine.* I realized that every disease and ailment I've ever had in my life could be traced back to some sort of trauma or negative belief, thought pattern or emotion. Every time I landed in the hospital or doctors office, *my emotional life was in complete chaos and turmoil. My hypochondria had spiraled out of control and the result was…illness.* I'm done being scammed and *deceived,* nothing gets by me. I vow I will *not rest until something changes in the health "care" industry!*

My lawsuit for that hole in my uterus took five long years to settle and they threw me a few bucks. It was sad and depressing, *just awful.* This paltry amount was supposed to make up for months of *pain and suffering and losing a bodily organ?* I had spoken with the person who is in charge of distributing the funds for the class action lawsuit, because I had flown into a rage while on the phone with my attorney.

She was very nice person and listened to my rant. When I was finished, she proceeded to tell me the most *heartbreaking* stories. Children being born with severe deformities and the family getting only a few thousand dollars. The child would need constant medical attention and around the clock care *for the rest of their lives.* And the drug that caused the deformity *wasn't even taken off the market! I felt like such a fool! I was ashamed of my behavior* and for thinking that they owed me something. I had voluntarily put in the device, *against my better judgment. The alarm was going off in my head, and I ignored it.* I was acting like such a diva! *God, please forgive me.*

Once I discovered that pretty much everything I've ever been told was a lie, *I started questioning everything else. What else are they lying about in order to make a profit*? I first noticed something else was *off, like really off,* was when a certain man announced he was running for President of the United State of America. This man wasn't a normal politician, he was a businessman. For some odd reason, this announcement sent practically *everyone* reporting the news into a tailspin! *The outrage and hatred, everyone was up in arms...what was this all about?*

Every news channel I turned to was *blasting* this guy with such *hatred, and he hadn't even had a chance to open his mouth!* I couldn't believe it. I wondered: *what the hell is going on?* How could all these news reporters start hating him, *out of nowhere? Was I living in the Twilight Zone?*

I am registered to vote as an Independent, I refuse to take a side. Bringing up this issue is not about politics, it's about the *insanity* of what was happening. I vote for the candidate that I think will do the best job running the country. Politics, like religion, is a trick they use to *divide* us. *This is just so stupid already.*

I couldn't understand what was happening. No one had ever said anything negative about this guy running for President, although he does have quite a big ego. He had lost everything, made it back again, and had one of these great comeback stories. He made cameo appearances as himself in movies. He was funny, and he never seemed to take himself too seriously. He even did a Visa commercial mocking himself. *I liked that about him. People that are always so serious are no fun to be around.* I had to stop watching the news *because I got angry, and not at the guy running for President, but the mockery of it all!*

If you try and address something that changes the status quo of a political system you better be prepared to be crucified.
—John McAfee

The next year Sammy died. I thought my dark not of the soul couldn't get any more disastrous, *but it did.* Next up, the pandemic and lockdown. I went from being a joyous mother of three boys, to being all *alone.* While I had been looking forward to having an empty nest so I could travel more, this loneliness and isolation came too soon for me.

At first, I was happy that everyone else was locked away in their homes, because now they joined me in my miserable situation. I had been hiding away in my apartment for a some time, just trying to get through each day. Sammy had only been gone a year, and I was still in a state of shock and denial. Grief gripped my *heart and soul,* and I was refusing to let it go. *I couldn't, I wasn't ready. It felt like if I let my grief go, I was letting Sammy go too.* I couldn't understand my neighbors though. They were wearing masks, face shields, plastic gloves, and *looked like they were about to have a nervous breakdown.* This was before they started making *everyone wear masks everywhere we went.* Since I wasn't watching the news anymore, I didn't have any idea what I was supposed to be afraid of on any particular day.

I was happy to have the excuse to stay home all day, but after a while, it became *too much!* I love my alone time, but I was starting *to lose what little of my mind I had left. Why was everyone was running around in a hazmat suit looking like they were about to have an heart attack? Did some radioactive material get leaked somewhere and I just didn't know about it? Wait...this is over a strain of the flu?*

So, besides the pharmaceutical companies lying and killing us, *the basic bitch news channels might be lying to us too?* I wondered if they'd kill us as well. *My Lord. This realization set my head on fire.* I couldn't understand why most people didn't see it, they are literally telling you what to focus on and it's all bullshit. *They are trying to shove fear down our throats! Was what they were talking about even true?* By now I was super pissed, and I wasn't having anymore of it.

On every news channel there was a story of some horrific school shooting, *but I was wondering what was really going on. Why did they keep repeating the same stories, were they hiding something?* I think the "news" was the smoke and mirrors so I wouldn't notice what the hell was *really* happening. *Only I wasn't asleep anymore, my bullshit detector is not broken.*

Maybe the story on the news was to distract everyone from the fact that CIA documents had just been declassified? Most of these documents are redacted, so they're *still hiding something, but we'll never* hear any announcement about it. *It's all smoke and mirrors, are we not smart enough to know the truth?* I remember in 1994, there was a big story on the news about the very first cloned animal, a sheep named Dolly. It was a pretty big deal. Then just like that.. *nothing. Not one more word on the news in all these years about cloning.* Did they expect me to believe that cloning just stopped because they weren't telling people about it? I bet there are billionaires that have a spare clone lying around in case they need it. *I'm no fool. What else are they hiding from us? God, is this the end of the world?*

If you're brave enough to leave behind everything familiar and comforting and set out on a truth seeking journey either internally or externally, and if you are truly willing to regard everything that happens to you on that journey as a clue

and accept everyone you meet along the way as a teacher and...face and forgive some of the most difficult realities about yourself, then the truth will not be withheld from you.[9]
—Elizabeth Gilbert

I began my journey deep down the rabbit hole. The whole world was shut down due to a flu, what else was I going to do? I don't really identify as a "conspiracy theorist", I'm more of a truth seeker. *But if there was story, I was going to read it.* My curiosity has always gotten me in trouble. It didn't matter to me if it was true or not, *at least it was entertaining. There was nothing else to do, at least they let us have an internet connection.*

The stuff I was reading was some *crazy shit*, but a lot of it *made sense*. It sounded more logical than the bullshit they were trying to spoon feed me. *Some of it was so dark, it made me sick to my stomach. Could this really be true? That thought sent a shiver down my spine.*

Once you eliminate the impossible, whatever remains, no matter how improbable must be the truth.
—Arthur Conan Doyle

The more things I read, the more I realized I didn't know anything. I had to wipe my mind clean of everything I had

9. Elizabeth Gilbert, *Eat, Pray, Love. One Woman's Search for Everything Across Italy, India and Indonesia* (Penguin, 2006).

been programmed to believe, because none of it was true. *In fact, everything in the world was backwards-literally. Any time I had trouble figuring out the truth, I would just think: well, what is the opposite of that? That's probably the truth.* At certain point, I decided to believe that *all of these conspiracy theories were true, just to save myself the time and aggravation.* I had never believed that JFK was murdered by a "magic bullet" anyway.

I literally spent *months* trying to figure out if JKF Jr., Princess Diana and Elvis were really still alive. Who or what was the "cabal", or "deep state", and why did they kept lying to us? Who was running the show here? Did we really land on the moon? I had to wonder, was the world actually flat? Was 9/11 an inside job? Is the world really run by a Satanic cult? *What is going on here? You've had these questions too, don't lie.* By this time everyone was so divided, people seemed to be demanding that everyone take side. They wanted to know: *Are you a crazy conspiracy theorist, or a more logical person that thinks children should be able to decide what gender they would like to be?* I couldn't stand on the side of the liberals, they had their heads so far up their asses all they could see was their own shit. But these MAGA "freedom fighter" people...they didn't even live in the same country that I did. They lived in this place called Merica. Plus, they were *super Christian, like beating me on my head until I accepted Jesus Christ,* and it was a total turn off. *So some Christians are getting violent too, like some Muslims? This situation has gotten out of control.*

Me being *me,* I decided I couldn't stand with either group. I was never one to follow the crowd anyway. I'd go forge my own path, *which was far away from all these nut-*

cases. I'd have to formulate and hypothesize *my own theories. Truthfully, I've never been more sane.*

It was the part about the adrenochrome that stopped me in my tracks. I called up my sister to inform her about what I had read. She scoffed and told me it couldn't possibly be true, it was incomprehensible to think a human could even do such a thing. *That was my thought too,* and was glad for her input. While I was going down the MAGA "freedom fighter" hole, she was sitting at home in Manhattan watching CNN. This was great for me because sometimes I needed to be pulled out of that rabbit hole. Yet, this feeling of uneasiness persisted. *Then...it turned into nausea.*

It reminded me of then Kashrut Laws from the Torah. My sister had done a conversion too, but in a Reform congregation and they do not keep kosher. The consumption of blood is *utterly forbidden.* There is quite a lengthy process to ensure that it is not consumed, even rendering parts of a cow unkosher because of this. There is a way that an animal is supposed to be killed for it to even be kosher. The procedure used to kill an animal is called shechitah. The shochet cuts the animals throat, quickly and skillfully, *and the animal loses consciousness and dies immediately with no suffering.* The Torah specifically forbids consuming an animal that *has suffered torture and died a cruel death.*

Then I remembered the Noahide law to "never eat the limb of an animal while it is still alive". Now I was convinced that someone probably had *thought about doing it, and was most likely already doing it. Otherwise, why would God have to specifically prohibit it? It's right there in the Torah.* I was coming up with my own conclusions and it was getting out of control, my head can go *so many places.*

So, there's a possibly that the devil has been controlling the planet, for a really long time? Well…Satan hasn't met me yet. That's when I began to craft my plan to outwit the devil himself. You don't think I can do it? *Hold my beer.*

Although, I couldn't wrap my head around the idea of the world being flat, I'd have to save that postulating for "Flat Earth Dave". The dude actually set out to *prove the theory wrong,* and discovered maybe it wasn't. *You would have to ask him about that.* There is still the fact that a third building collapsed in NYC on September 11th, and it wasn't even hit by an "airplane". Let's not forget that no one was telling us where that 2.3 trillion dollars went that was missing from the Treasury Department. Donald Rumsfeld had announced it on live TV just the day before. Then, there's the eerie fact that now, after September 11, 2001, *the government can legally spy on us. Isn't that convenient?* Once I saw the documentary "The Conspiracy Theory of Everything", it started to make more sense. I'm not saying I believed all of it, but it was *more logical than the history books.*

Here's my problem with their narrative: In 2001, most people had cell phones, *but none of them had the capability of filming videos.* Only a select few people just *happened* to be in the vicinity with VHS camcorders in their hands. In the footage I've seen, there are no airplanes. The technology of CGI (computer generated images) was already being used in movies, *so someone could have easily added in an airplane.* Also, someone could have *removed* the airplane, so there's that. Apparently, *most of the people that filmed this event are already dead.* There were many "ear" witnesses that heard multiple popping noises before the towers fell. Plus, I saw the testimony of a structural engineer that claims the towers couldn't have fallen had it not been for pre-placed explosives that were detonated. *He says it would've been impossible.*

Most of these things I've seen and read have *disappeared from the internet. Why do you think that is?* I think we are way past the point of 9/11 being a "theory". A conspiracy is a very intricate plot that takes years to plan, and many co-conspirators *to cover it up.* There are many people out there that know what is going on. Please, come forward, because I'd like to know the truth! Maybe if *everyone comes out with what they know at the same time, it might be enough to throw them off. They can't 'suicide" you all at once, it's too momentous of a task.*

If we understand the mechanism and motives of the group mind, it is now possible to control and regiment the masses according to our will without them knowing it.
—Edward Bennays

At a certain juncture in my spiritual awakening, I decided to just assume every movie I'd ever seen was real, like Alex Jones said. I had to save myself the time and frustration. I now had a fresh perspective: *everything was complete bullshit. From there, I could start over, and I felt relived.* We live in a world where conspiracy theories make more sense than what they were telling us to believe.

I'll take one "conspiracy theory" as an example, and go into depth about it. Let's examine the moon landing. Some people say we never went to the moon, it was all faked. One guy says it's impossible to travel to the moon, because we are living in a fixed firmament (he's probably friends with Flat Earth Dave). Yet another "scientist" claims we wouldn't be able to stand on the moon, because it's made of plasma. Then there's the supposed death bed confession of the famous movie director Stanley Kubrick, saying that his best "masterpiece" was a faked moon landing. He hadn't been allowed to talk about but, since he was dying... Of course that "confession" could have been faked with computers. But there is still this issue of the original live footage of the "moon landing": at one point the *flag started to wave, whereas it hadn't before.* The moon doesn't have a gravitational force, *so why would the flag suddenly start waving? Oh my.* There are rumors that there are man (or alien) made physical structures on the moon. Some are ancient, others newer... and the faked footage filmed from a studio was *just in case,* and I'm assuming they may have needed it. *What did they see up there? Oh my God, I can't think straight!* I decided that I would never be going to the moon, *just in case. Houston... we have problem. If all of this was designed to make us dizzy and confused, then mission accomplished.*

I got really into the alternative news sources, but it started to be downright ridiculous. I was on stupid Telegram for nine months trying to decide which accounts were "real", and which ones were "deep state fakes", designed to throw everyone off and make us look like crazy people. *Clearly, we were all going a bit mad. It was getting sickening.* The fact remains that something is *not right* in the world today, a*nd I'm determined to find out what that is.*

The worst part was that the country was *more divided than ever! How was this helping? Actually, I think that was the whole point.* Have you ever thought about what was *really going on* while they're telling you what to be afraid of and who to hate? *Insanity. I wasn't having any part of it.*When I first read about the "conspiracy theory" of the evil Draconian "reptilian" aliens, the ones that are supposedly "controlling the earth for eons", I almost *choked on a sip of coffee.* It sounded like a really bad sci-fi movie, one that I would *never* pay money to see. It sounded so *outlandish,* and anyone who spoke about looked like a *crazy person.*

Then I heard people saying: "They are already here among us", I almost *lost my cool. This was not a good situation.* Look, I'm all for Making America Great Again, but I am really supposed to believe the "white hats", some computer *hackers,* are "winning" this spiritual war? Good Lord. Unless they are hacking the *Divine Matrix,* we are *all doomed.* But the topic of this Draconian bullshit kept coming up in my face, *despite my scoffing at it.* So I was forced to investigate the whole malignant thing, and use my *logic* to come up with something that made sense in my head. Otherwise, *I'd never be able to sleep again. I needed my to formulate my own theory.*

I starting digging for the truth. I read all sorts of nonsense, but none of these stories were adding up. So, I took the most obvious and unambiguous theories and put them all together, like pieces of a puzzle. My puzzle doesn't look like anything yet, *I'm still in the hypothetical phase.* Although, I don't think it matters what the real story is, there's more of a pressing concern of: *what are we going to do about it? Are the manics really in charge here?*

Here's my theory: Extraterrestrial means "not from planet earth". But, *what if some aliens* aren't actually another planet, but from *another dimension? Are they demons from hell?* I say *most likely.* If that's the case, then they don't have bodies. That's where humans come in, *they need us to survive.* Of course, some aliens are from a different planet. The universe is infinite and it would be foolish and egotistical to believe that we are the only life form in this vast universe.

There is this rumor going around: in the 1940s president Franklin D. Roosevelt signed a deal with the evil Draconian reptilian aliens in exchange for advanced anti-gravity technology. They say that they keep that stuff at none other than Area 51. In exchange for this technology, the government allegedly allowed the Dracos to abduct humans, and use them for experiments or for their own evil purposes. *Holy fucking hell on earth! If this story is true, it's like the blind leading the blind.*

Apparently, the Nazis had this same agreement and have the same technology. Oh and by the way, supposedly Hitler never died like we were told. He probably just went to Argentina with a bunch of other Nazis. *Operation Paperclip: officials put a paperclip on their files in order to pass them through. You really think people would let them just slip away when they had all this advanced knowledge and technology? You do? That knowledge could help them win more wars. Oh joy.* Allegedly, the Nazis are now based in Antarctica *with the Dracos. This is Hell. On. Earth!!!!*

But I remember being a kid in the 80s. I'd be sitting there munching on my toxic, preservative filled cereal, and looking at the faces of all those missing children on the side of the milk carton. I would wonder: *where are all of these kids going? Why were there so many of them disappearing at an alarming rapid pace? It haunts me to this day.*

As it turns out, I think our own government is staging alien abductions to continuing to perpetuate this insane theory of "aliens" in order to *cover up* the fact that the *real aliens are actually demons, and they might be the ones in charge of this running this shit show!* Life as an Earthling really is a *horror movie.* There are so many real live accounts of people who have been "abducted by aliens". Out of the 22 things that they *all mention,* 20 of those things are the *exact same things* that happen at Satanic rituals. *Oh! My! GOD!* I can only hope and *pray* I am wrong about this. *Could demons really be in charge, since before biblical times, disguised as a Satanic cult?*

I had to break this all down into bite sized chucks. I was starting to feel like a nutcase and I was barely sleeping, *this was too much.* If the Dracos are demons from hell, then that means they *need a human host* to do evil. I believe they're associated with the reptilian, because they highjack the human *reptilian brain.* They have to attach to someone. I've had an entity attachment myself, so I know it's a possibility. When my shaman removed it for me, I asked her what it was. She said: "Well…we really don't talk about it." *For the first time in my life, I didn't ask anymore questions. My life was starting to feel like an actual sci-fi movie.* I told her that maybe she was right, I didn't want to know. *I accepted that answer and didn't probe further. Seriously God, I wouldn't mind being able to sleep again.*

So maybe they already are *among us.* A demon might be attached to your everyday evil and greedy sociopath, psychopath and narcissist. My theory is that if these people give in the the "demon in their head" one too many times… *it takes over. I'm not saying every narcissist is a shape shifting Draco, don't twist my words.* What I am saying is that if you know someone who's behavior is erratic; *they lie, cheat and steal without any seeming remorse, they might have an "attachment."*

Just ask Leslie Wexner, the billionaire dude who owns Victoria's Secret and was Jeffrey Epstein's mentor. He's been talking about his "dybbuk", which loosely translates to demon, for years. He's quoted in the New York Times: "I have a demon in my head that tells me what to do." *Gulp, that's not good.* He's quoted in various other news articles as well, and it's expanded upon in Whitney Webb's book "One Nation Under Blackmail". Disclaimer: I have not read this book, nor do I plan on reading it. *It's way too dark for me.* I listened to a podcast where Whitney was interviewed. She's young but very intelligent, and her work is throughly researched. *She gives references for all her information* and there's so much information that there are *two volumes.* She even encourages people to go fact check her story, but *I'll take her word for it.* My God, I guess some people like Wexner are past the point of needing a therapist, *they need a God damn exorcist! How do I keep earth from becoming hell? Maybe I needed some holy water? Hold on, I need to go burn some more sage.*

Here's how the whole blackmail thing got started, according to Whitney Webb. In the 1930s, the mob got a photo of J. Edgar Hoover sucking a guy's dick. Hoover was the *director of the FBI for 37 years,* but he was apparently owned by the mob. *He didn't want that photo getting out.* Fast forward to more recent times, Epstein flew many notable and influential people to his own personal island for supposed "drug filled parties and orgies". Only...the real reason they were there was probably so Epstein could film them and *blackmail them too. Then, he would own them and they'd have to do whatever he wanted.* Although, one guy sucking another guy's dick isn't a big deal these days, *so Epstein would have to up the stakes. Allegedly, there was non-consensual sex and even violence with minors aka children. If this is true, the world really is going to hell.*

Here's the scary thing, no one can just shut themselves away inside their homes and expect to not be attacked by a demon. This is a *spiritual war,* and demons don't have bodies. They can get to you wherever you are. I'm not trying *to scare the living shit out of anyone, I'm scared enough for all of us.* I'm just bringing awareness to the situation. *Obviously,* I *have a solution* to this problem, I think I know how to beat these demons. *Otherwise, I wouldn't have brought it up.* But I'll get to that later.

I decided to pull the plug on Telegram and everything "conspiracy" related. *As far as I'm concerned, this is reality now, not some crazy theory.* I threw Telegram and all that other nonsense away, I had better things to do then worry myself sick about the evil on planet earth. *But I wasn't going to pretend it didn't exist either.* I put all that shit into the same grave I put the mainstream media in, I'd deal with it later. It's tucked away, for now, in my "it's all bullshit" file. I was really kind of pissed at myself for wasting time and wanted those nine months of my life back. What a crock of shit. *Seriously Rebecca?*

I figured my time could be better spent on things more uplifting that kept my vibration high. I needed to continue with my Ascension plan, and reading all that dark shit wasn't helping me. Besides, *they use fear as a weapon of control. So long as we are afraid, we in in a low vibration and cannot ascend. I still wanted the truth though.* I figured I'd have a better chance of discovering the truth if I learned how to astral travel, read the Akashic records, and do remote viewing. *I will find out the truth myself.*

Plus, I wanted to know this esoteric information that they purposely kept hidden. I came to the conclusion that it might be the topic of my next book. *Once I figure it all out, the world will never be the same.* The book could be about my journey into the occult and I'd reveal all of its secrets. *Oh man, I really am quite the weirdo.*

This was much more than a basic spiritual awakening, I was *slowly going mad!* I was waking up to the fact that literally *everything* they've been telling us was invented, *made up out of thin air.* At the very least, they're telling us half truths. *There's more, obviously. Did you think my rant was over?*

There's this rumor going around that the "war" in Afghanistan was a front, our own government just needed to protect their poppy fields they use to make heroin. Also, there's a very high probability that the CIA is actually running the drug cartels. The movie American Made with Tom Cruise didn't just pop up *out of nowhere.* I think this is the devil's way to get around his problem of us having free will. Once you've seen the movie, *now it's in your consciousness.* Since you're *not actually objecting to it*, you're just thinking, *well was an interesting movie, you're kinda sorta agreeing to it. Well, I'm not agreeing with this!* The CIA can't allegedly run drugs and make a profit from it! The very people they are peddling it to are already at a socioeconomic *disadvantage, and they're dying!*

To add insult to injury, we might be paying for this CIA operation *from our very own tax dollars. There is a very good reason they're called Spooks: they're scary.* To make matters worse, apparently the government thinks they don't have to disclose this information about where our tax dollars might be going "for reasons of national security". *Looks to me like the only thing we might need protection from is our own government.*

Then there's the human trafficking problem that the government might *allegedly* be involved in, *if not running themselves*. I'm not buying the narrative that Avicii died, apparently of a drug overdose. I don't believe this because it was right after he wrote the song and filmed a music video "For a Better Day". *The song is about saving children from human trafficking. Do you really think he just made that story up... for the song?* And everyone believes the narrative that Avicii died of a drug overdose because...*he's a DJ?* DJs know how to party sure, but there are plenty that are still alive. He might be dead, and it could be from drugs, *but I'll bet money that whoever is making a profit from human trafficking made him that way. Go watch the music video on YouTube and get back to me.*

Also, I'm not buying the "suicide" narrative of a certain famous handbag designer and celebrity chef, that just doesn't add up either. I've already told my boys that if I end up dead and it's ruled a "suicide", *that they had better investigate. Because I would never kill myself. I found out later that it was empathetically true.* I would never commit suicide, *even when pushed to do so.*

Then there's this *super shady* information that the United States might actually be a corporation and they allegedly think they own us as a commodity by way of our Social Security number. There's *a high probability that they are making money off of us as a commodity, trading on a black stock market somewhere under the radar.* Have you ever wondered why they start sending you checks at age 65, and *where that money comes from?* I have already started practicing my speech, just in case: "No, I am not REBECCA JANE BROCK in all capital letters, *you do not own me!* I am Rebecca Jane Brock, a Divine and Sovereign being! I will keep using my *God given Free Will to do whatever I want, so long as I'm not hurting anyone! End of discussion!* I think this is a solid plan.

Here's the thing: I didn't have any inside Information, I have no idea what's really going on. *But I will tell you the old adage that "dead men tell no tales" is entirely fabricated, because I'm hearing those tales right now.* I only know that I am *responsible for my own life,* and that my thoughts were creating my reality. I chose instead to focus on what I could control, *which was only myself. I am in charge of my own destiny!* I have to constantly turn my thoughts back to my own progress of spiritual evolution because all this was so distracting. I also can't ignore it either. I'll figure something out and get back to you.

Strange times are these in which we live when
old and young are taught falsehoods in school.
And the one man that dares to tell the truth is
called lunatic and a fool.
—Plato

My Dark Night of the Soul continued...*it was dragging me through hell.* I had booked an astrology reading because I figured an astrologer could give me insights about my life, I certainly *needed some direction.* He told me that in January of 2021 the "nodes of fate" would switch signs in my 5th and 11th house. I asked him what he meant by that, I know next to nothing about astrology. He said it meant that my 5th house of romance and creativity would *expand,* and my 11th house of friendships and social circles would *contract. I really dug the idea that my house of romance and creativity would be expanding.* He said it might not be easy to lose friends, but it was a good thing. *If people exited my life, it was because these people weren't real friends to begin with,* and I had to agree with him. The only thing was, I didn't expect it to be that difficult and *extreme.*

The first friend that I had to let go of I had considered a *best* friend. We had spent a lot of time together and told each other our dreams and ambitions. About a year and a half after Sammy died, she asked me why I felt so "entitled" that I didn't have to work? I had just quit my job writing for a magazine I had been working for, and my modeling career was still near non-existent after my health issues. Most days I had a hard time just getting out of bed. I couldn't believe how *mean* her comment was, and *it came at the absolute worst possible time, I could barely make it through each day. What's worse was that this wasn't the first time she had said something mean.* But I gave her a second chance.

I was absolutely crushed, I couldn't wrap my head around how she could be *so cruel.* Maybe it was because she was comparing our lives as single moms, and it was *toxic.* But she was comparing apples to oranges, we are *not the same!* I had to learn how to stop *caring about people* so much, *but how was I supposed to do that?* I felt like that was impossible. *My true nature is loving and I couldn't change that.*

I had to really sit there and ponder about why I was so offended by her offhanded remark. Clearly, she was projecting onto me, *that I could see.* She had only recently begun to do commercial modeling. *Yes, she was definitely in competition with me, without me being in competition with her.* Although, the real reason I felt violated by her cutting words was because of something from my childhood. My stepmother had given me the nickname "Queenie", and I could never understand why she called me that. I'm assuming it's because people are very intimidated by someone that doesn't *need* anyone else, even if it is just a child. *I truly thought I was minding my own business. But if the crown fits, I may as well wear it.*

My stepmom was the first one to slap the "vain" label on me too. *Personally, I don't know a single person that prefers to be ugly as opposed to being attractive.* Is being into fashion and wanting to wear a cute outfit a sin? *I thought dressing well was a form of good manners.*

I wrote Mean Girl a letter *apologizing*, because I had been triggered. I gave her an honest explanation as to why I felt that way. Her response: "Apology accepted." I was literally *stunned*, I couldn't pick my jaw up from off the floor. *Did she really just say that?* I mean, I wasn't raised that way, *but I guess she was.* When someone apologizes to me, even when they were being the mean one, my response would be: "Omg, no, I'm so sorry too." And we'd go back to being friends again. *But I had had enough!* From that moment on, I simply couldn't allow people back into my life that didn't have good intentions and didn't 100% *have my back. It hurt like hell, but I learned a very valuable lesson. The first time...shame on her. But the second time...shame on me! I should've known better.* I still give people second chances, *but a third? No way.*

When someone shows you who they are,
believe them the first time.[10]
—Maya Angelou

10. Maya Angelou, *I Know Why the Caged Bird Sings* (Random House, 1969).

The next close girlfriend that exited my life was by her own choice. She didn't like my political views, as they were *diametrically opposed to hers.* It's funny though, because we hadn't spoken about politics in *months* at the time she announced to me she was no longer interested in being friends. *One day she just woke up and decided she didn't want to look at my face because of the way that I viewed the world?* What's even weirder, I was never once was angry *at her* for her political opinions, *nor did I even try and change her mind. But I guess this wasn't a two way street.*

The next friend to fly the coo-coo's nest I'll call Gossip Woman. I had been a "close" friend of hers for at least a decade. Every few years, she would pick a woman to target and directed all her gossip towards her *to destroy her.* She made sure everyone else in this friend group knew what "crime" she had committed, and *made everyone else in her cliche put her in "exile" too. Are we still in high school?*

One year on my birthday, I had invited an "exile" to my birthday dinner. *Apparently, I hadn't gotten the "memo" that we were supposed to all hate this woman and turn our back on her.* She had never been anything but a friend to me. But Gossip Woman *flew* into a *rage,* and demanded I tell her how and why I would invite this woman to my birthday dinner? *Was she really serious about this?*

Well, I was disappointed in *myself,* because it took me 14 long months to actually speak my truth to her. I felt she was misguided and I had to tell her: *She had no right to decide who I invited to my birthday dinner!* Just come, or don't, *but shut the fuck up about it. Just sit on the other side of the table and keep your trap shut.* Why did she make *my birthday about her?* She was the type of person who always made *such a big deal* of her own birthday, and *it was nauseating.*

One year I was out of town to visit my son on *his birthday*, and I had to hear about it, that I missed her birthday party, for the next three years. *It was pure insanity. Did Gossip Woman really think that her birthday was more important than my son's? Unbelievable.*

Gossip doesn't even bother me anymore, I'm so used to it. In fact, it is quite beneficial for me, it is *free PR*. It doesn't matter if the rumor is true or not, *now everyone knows my name.* Did these people spreading rumors about me even realize t*hat they were the ones actually making me famous?* Whenever I hear a vicious rumor, I automatically assume that the person spinning that tale is *covering up the fact that that is exactly what they are doing, and projecting it onto the rumor victim. Boom!* Problem solved. *It's so obvious.*

Gossip Woman had ruined our friendship, and she ruined my birthday. Not that I ever make a big deal about my birthday. The only person that I would expect to make a big deal about it is maybe my boys any *guy I'm fucking. But that's a different story, I'm not going there.* She had made me feel like a deflated ballon, *all the air had been sucked right out of me.* I guess I shouldn't be able to have some joy and laughter and not be bothered, *even on my own birthday.*

But I knew that when I expressed my feelings to her, *I was doomed to be an exile. And so it was, she made sure of it.* I'm probably being viciously gossiped about *right now*. If any of you ladies are reading this book, *you must realize that you could be next.* I truly thought that if any of the other women were my real friends, I'd hear from them. *But so far...crickets.*

By this point I am no longer anyone's pawn and I don't give a flying fuck about being part of any group. Group mentality is so *basic bitch* anyway, and *I am not basic.* Funny thing though: according to social media Mean Girl and Gossip Woman seem to be "besties" now. There's this saying: *Birds of a feather, flock together. I guess that's the God's honest truth. The saying had to come from somewhere.*

There were *three* more woman that exited my life, mostly because I called them out on their bullshit. *I was no longer in the mood to deal with this.* I could see right through their manipulative tactics they used to make their insecure ass feel better about themselves. *Seriously, if you're insecure around me, then you need help.* I do nothing but lift people up, point out greatness, and encourage them to follow their dreams. I make people laugh and feel good about themselves. *Is there a help line for insecure women? If not, maybe I needed to start one.* There is a serious epidemic going on with people doubting themselves. How was their distorted way of thinking, that hating on someone else, *was somehow going to improve their life?* I was done being the people pleasing, funny, party girl clown that made everyone laugh, *and they knew it.* I won't even go into those stories, because they're more frivolous and shallow than the first three, and *it's a waste of my breath.*

You are the sum of who you
surround yourself with.
—Jim Rohn

I am just an authentic, loving and giving person. *But clearly, not everyone deserves to have access to my life.* I vowed that from now on, I'd reserve my stellar advice and positive energy for those that deserved it. These people were *draining my energy, like vampires.* I only had so much energy to give. I knew it was better to direct my positive life force towards my own life. I could use it for healing, improving myself, and for accomplishing my life goals and ambitions. I'm pretty sure they all thought they were "teaching me a lesson" by isolating me from the group. *But in fact, they all did me a huge favor.*

I discovered that it's impossible to stay in a high vibration and think positive thoughts when you're surrounded by hateful, negative people and *gossip*. My frequency always *dropped too low* around these people. *This is not being snobby, it's reality.* I couldn't even share my dreams and ambitions with them, they would automatically try to make me doubt myself, *which never worked. Better luck next time.* I was wasting my time hanging around such low vibe people. These people weren't on my team, *they didn't want to see me win! So why was I spending time with them? My time is worth money!*

Solitude made all their useless chatter they tried to fill my head with come to a screeching halt. *In solitude, I discovered that only my beliefs and opinions mattered, and I never doubted myself again.* I had been given the *gift* of foresight, and these bitches couldn't even past their nose. I *saw the vision of the potential of my life, and it was absolutely glorious! I was going to hold on tight to my vision, and never let go. Even if that meant I had to stand alone.*

Most people think that when they are giving me advice I never *asked* for, that they're actually helping me. But mostly, they were projecting their own fears and insecurities onto me. *I was on to them and I didn't have time for that.* If they wanted to believe that abundance wasn't their birthright, then that was *their choice, but it wasn't mine.* Anyone that was jealous of my life *didn't understand the basics of the Law of Attraction*. If they were envious of something I had, they were *pushing it away from themselves. One can never have anything if they're not happy for others having it first.* Dumb bitches. These people didn't understand that there was no need for jealousy, there is enough abundance in the Universe for everyone. *Not to mention envy is a low vibration.*

The next act in my very own little horror film entitled "The Dark Night of the Soul" was being forced to move. My landlord had sold my apartment and I had to find somewhere else to live, and *fast*. That dumb ass broker, the dude that managed the unit, was literally knocking on my door every God damn day! *He wanted me gone. As if I could find an apartment overnight? I couldn't believe it!* Now I was being thrown out of the only safe space I had known for the last 12 years. *This was spiraling out of control, it was too much for me to handle.* But everyone in the building was being bought out, they were going to tear the building down. I had no control over my desperate emotions. *I was drowning in my own tears, I didn't think my life could get any worse or that I had any tears left to cry out.*

If I hadn't made you uncomfortable,
you never would have moved.
—God

Maybe moving was the best thing for me, as I still lived where Sammy had died. But it was so hard for me to let go, that was the place where all my memories of him were. My youngest son never wanted to be at my house, and I felt abandoned. He used the excuse that my apartment was too small, and during the lockdown he was doing school online. It made sense, and I couldn't blame him. If I were him I*'d avoid me too* at that time, *I was a miserable dump of a mess.* What I know for sure is that when the Universe is nudging you to *go somewhere else* and you *ignore it,* it's going to have to *force you* to go! *That's just the way it goes.* I had to start accepting that change was the only thing constant in life. I would have to figure a way out of this dark hole *before it swallowed me alive.*

Once I got settled into the new place, I had high hopes for the future. I decided to *do something* to change my life and go in a different direction. I'm usually quite the optimist, but lately I had been unable to take care of simple basic things. I was in the *grip* of grief, it had this *intense hold on me and I couldn't seem to shake it.* I *missed Sammy so much!* My heart ached tremendously, and there was nothing that could take the pain away. I wasn't willing to settle in romance just to *have someone*, I had waited too long to do that. *I couldn't just keep drinking more wine, that only made the situation worse. Something had to change!*

I was determined to do something, *to go somewhere.* I figured throwing myself into my career would be just the thing I could do to distract myself from my misery. I kicked my ass into high gear and got my real estate license. It was pretty easy, once I understood that they were purposely trying to trick you into picking the wrong answer on the test. *I'm not easy to manipulate anymore.* For a few months, it seemed like everything was going to be alright. My older son had gotten stuck back home in the U.S. because of the "pandemic". This was great for me because I had him helping us move, he's so tall and strong! I am very blessed. I turned my focus back to my daily gratitude again, and I told myself that *everything was going to be fine.*

One should *never say;* "*I've hit rock bottom! It can't get any worse!" Because, it almost always does get more pathetic.* I wished life had a seatbelt so I could've strapped myself in before this next act. I had a new apartment and a new career, and I was working hard. *But things seemed to keep falling apart.* My hair was falling out and I couldn't sleep. I was losing money and clients, even though I was giving this new career *all my energy.* I kept gaining weight, and everything I tried to do about it failed. *Even after a three day water and bone broth fast, the scale hadn't gone down, not even half a pound.* My romantic life was next to nothing, every date I went on was worse than the last. Also, I was seeing broken glass *everywhere,* even in my house. *What the actual fuck was going on?*

I even felt this sense of impending *doom,* like something terrible was about to happen. It occurred to be that I might be "cursed" or some shit, *was that a real thing?* So I Googled "How to know if you've been "cursed". *Wouldn't you know,* I had all the symptoms of a curse, a "hex", or whatever you call it, *right down to the broken glass. God damn it!* What did I ever do to *deserve* this? Why was I being *cursed? Was it all in my head? It wasn't.*

Sometimes the most evolved souls
take the most challenging paths.
—Dr. Brian Weiss

I found out that someone, or some people, entities or *demons, wanted me dead.* Two days before I was going to leave for Israel to visit my oldest son, I get this call from my doctor's office. The lady who ran the office had this *edge* in her voice. It was the *same edge* that my doorman had had when he called me the night Sammy died. *My blood ran cold,* and I could feel my heart beginning to pound in my chest. *I wondered what her problem was.* She wanted me to come in and do another round of ketamine. I had done it twice in 2020, and it does help with depression.

But I told the lady I was fine, I didn't think I needed to do ketamine again. She told me she'd give me a *major* discount, and the shit was expensive, so I thought, *why the hell not?* Ketamine is pretty trippy, but it did help me see things differently and it had stopped my obsessive thinking for a while.

So I headed down to the doctor's office and when I got there, everyone seemed *so concerned. They all asked me if I was suicidal. Seriously people?* I said, no, of course not! I told them I had a lot going on and I was a bit overwhelmed. I was leaving the country in a couple of hours, and traveling can be stressful, *but I'm not suicidal. I have never been suicidal, my God!*

So here's the scoop on this situation. The guy, who's job it is to observe the patients under ketamine, let's call him Dave. Dave came into the treatment room and told me that he was doing some research into how ketamine had helped people connect to the other side of the veil. It was his own little unsupervised and unapproved "experiment", and he seemed very proud about it. I told him that his idea sounded great, I thought it was pretty interesting. I was already connecting to Sammy, and I thought if others could connect with their deceased love ones too, it might help them with their grief. Then he asked me *again* if I was having suicidal thoughts. *Dave, I already told you, the answer is no. I am not suicidal.* Now all the nurses were in the room and asking me the same question. *What the hell was going on?*

Then Dave *got really serious and everyone in the room got quiet.* I wondered if everyone had lost their mind. My eyes widened and I said: "What?" I tried not to act too crazy, because they all thought I was suicidal and I certainly didn't want to make things worse. *Maybe doing ketamine again was a bad idea.* Dave told me that another patient had been talking to Sammy while under ketamine and he had filmed it. Interesting! I made a joke and said that Sammy had better at least come and say hi to me if she had a full on conversation with him. Everyone in the room was absolutely convinced she was talking to my son, *so who was I to question it? I could communicate with him too, so I thought it was no big deal. Sammy was always very friendly, it didn't surprise me if he was reaching out to others.* Dave put the needle in my arm, and I happily went down the K hole.

When the treatment was finished, they brought this woman into my room, the woman who had supposedly been talking to Sammy. She was dressed in all black, her hair was jet black, in the whole of her, *there was not a stitch of color.* She said she going through a divorce and plagued by her own demons, so that's why she was doing ketamine. She asked me if I had ever heard of Wiccans. I said sure, I have, but I told her I didn't really know that much about it. *She told me she was one, a witch, and even admitted to doing black magic.* She told me about the time she summoned up a demon in a mirror to break up with a cheating boyfriend. I laughed and said, "That's the most creative way I've ever heard of to break up with a cheater!" We laughed and I thought *she seemed nice.* She explained that she doesn't do black magic anymore, because she didn't think it was right and now she's a mother. Wait, *what? Obviously, I was still high on ketamine.* She explained that Sammy was really worried about me. I told her that he shouldn't be worried about me, I was *fine. Besides, I explained to her I was already in communication with him.* We laughed some more, then she gave me her phone number. Then I drove home and jumped on a plane to Israel.

But there was something that didn't sit right with me about this whole situation, and *my intuition went off like a bell shattering alarm in my head.* First of all, I hadn't *asked* to meet this woman. There are strict HIPAA laws with regards to privacy of patients and their information. Also, I was *high on a drug.* Weren't there any laws regarding that? *But it was more than that.* I had an eerie feeling that just wouldn't go away, a*nd I always trust my gut.*

When got back from Israel, I marched right down to the doctors office and demanded that Dave show me the videos. He took me into a room and sat me down and asked me *again,* did I have thoughts about killing myself? *No! I don't! Then, the nurse gave me a valium.Obviously, I was all keyed up, but NOT suicidal!* I told Dave that if she really was talking to Sammy, then I wanted to see those videos. I couldn't understand what was going on. *Why wasn't he letting me see those videos? Apparently, he had a bunch of them.* This was the doctors office from *hell, and trust me when I tell you, I have never been back.*

Dave sent me a clip, and then instructed me to watch it when I got home. My head was spinning with questions, *I had so many questions.* I had no choice but to agree, and rushed home watch the video. I kept wondering why he wouldn't let me watch it there at the office the whole way home.

What I saw in that video *shocked me straight to my core.* I literally felt *all the blood* drain from my body, there was nothing left. My knees buckled beneath me, and *I fell to the floor in a crumpled mess.* I had a complete nervous breakdown, so much so that I made myself sick and couldn't get out of bed for three weeks.

The video was very *dramatic..* When I first pressed play, the opening scene was this woman, the Black witch, calling for Dave! Dave. Where was Dave? *Hey Dave? She said his name several times.* Congratulations *Dave,* she just appointed you the director and executive producer of her cute little film entitled "Let's push Rebecca over the edge". Then she screamed out: "*Oh no! She's going to jump! She's going to throw herself off the balcony! She's going to kill herself!*" There was panic in her voice. *What the hell was going on? I had never had any thoughts of throwing myself off my balcony!*

Then the woman started *bawling, she was sobbing actually.* She said: "She thinks it's all her fault! She thinks it's all her fault." *I had never thought Sammy's death was my fault. Where was this coming from?* Then she said something and *I knew she could not be talking to Sammy.* Whoever she was talking to was suggesting she find me a witch. *A witch? Why the hell would I need a witch? Sammy has such a pure neshamah, and has great faith in Hashem. He would never say that.* There was more to her shit show film, but I stopped it *right there. My blood had run cold, and a shiver went down my spine. What. The. Actual. FUCK!!!!*

Once I calmed down and was able to breathe again, I Googled her name. Luckily, she had given me her first and last name. She's an actress, and not a very good one at that. I went back and watched the clip again, through the a lens of an actor. *I was correct, she's a terrible actress. I could've done this act better.* From the internet I learned that she been on one season of one of those Real Housewives reality television shows.

First of all I have to explain, *any actor that's honed in their craft knows that we don't do reality shows. Serious actors* stay far away from that scene of made up shit. *It's not even exciting or interesting to watch. It's where has been actors who never amounted anything go to get some attention and make extra cash.* But she had gotten kicked off the show after one season because another cast mate's husband got really sick. *They blamed her and her black magic for him being ill. Well, she admitted to me she had done black magic.*

I saw a clip on the internet from the show the season she was on it. The other cast mates were making fun of this woman's choice of names for her kids. I guess because they were weird names, and she didn't seem happy about being teased. I'm sure it was all just for the drama of the show, yet she took it so personally. I watched the clip Dave sent me again after having new information and it all looked so *staged, like a God damn reality show. My life is a reality show now? Are there cameras filming me right now? I'd prefer my life to be a great movie, not some reality nonsense.*

I did not know this woman, I had never met her in my *life.* And she definitely wasn't talking to Sammy, he would never say the things that she claims he was saying. After this incident, I got so *sick* that I thought I might *die,* and it's not a coincidence that I had stumbled upon that story of the husband getting super sick. *Yet here I am motherfucker, I'm still breathing!* Fuck *you! I want to live! Who was this person, and who wanted me dead? Her demons? Had someone hired her to stage this performance?*

I recounted the people I told about the ketamine and how it helped me. *Shit, it was practically everyone I knew!* I was trying to be helpful, as usual. But I opened my big mouth too much and all it did was give away precious personal information about myself, and now it was *being used against me! Why would anyone want me dead? My head was spinning,* I felt like I was going to pass out and never wake up. This was getting way more creepy than those stupid conspiracy theories! This was *my own life on the line, and I was determined to live!* I wanted to thrive even, and I wanted to have love and a*bundance, finally!! I have been waiting for so long! Why was this happening? I cried out to God for help.*

Help and answers came, and fast too. I was shown exactly who did it and why. Downloads were coming in hot and heavy now, and *I learned the truth and it broke my heart.* I had so desperately wanted to see the good in all people, *but it's just not there sometimes. Pure evil now had a face,* and I never wanted to see their face or hear their name ever again. I knew who it was because this person *had known my destiny before I did! Do people really have nothing better to do with their time than to look into someone else's destiny?* It reminded me of another person, many years ago, that had *also* wanted me to kill myself. So much so that this person *gave me* a *loaded gun.* The thought that these people might be teamed up *against me almost pushed my over the edge.* I removed that thought from my mind immediately, and I told myself to be grateful that none of these people had tried to murder me. *I was still standing! I had a pulse. Fuck them! No one is going to take me down!*

God also showed me why this black magic "curse" or whatever you call it, was able to affect me. *I was trapped in a very low vibrational energy of grief. I was shown that I needed to raise my frequency up to a higher level and keep it there.* Being in a higher frequency would protect me from the adverse side effects of these "spells", and from any negative energy. *Also, I had to stop thinking about it, I was giving it more energy. This was harder than I thought.* My thoughts about it was what was giving it more life. *I still couldn't believe a human would do such a thing, and I had been nothing but nice and helpful to these people! Maybe the entity attachment had taken over...*

I had to change my beliefs that it could harm me. I started grounding myself daily by walking on the earth with bare feet. I took hot epsom salt baths *daily* to cleanse my aura and energetic body of their negativity. I burned sage, palo Santo, and incense. I kept adding things to my rituals *to protect myself*, the best one was to mentally say: *Return to sender-* over and over again. But mostly, I just fervently *prayed to God. Please God, show me the way out of this. God answered my prayers, a*nd I knew that I was protected. "Black magic" wouldn't be able to touch me if I could stay in a high vibration.

Despite my attempts to try and not obsess over this drama, I was clearly *disturbed and traumatized.* I couldn't shake this feeling that Sammy might have been affected by a black magic curse as well. He was telling me something about a "confusion spell", although I couldn't figure out why anyone would want him to be confused. *However, he was certainly wasn't thinking straight the night he died. Was it possible he had discovered a dark secret he shouldn't know about?* Sammy was always very perceptive and had an inquiring mind, like I do. I remember he used to go through all of my things. He wanted to know what everything was, what it was used for, and how it worked. *I hoped to God that it wasn't true, despite the fact that I was getting the same message over and over again.*

Remember how I said I was going to tell you how we beat the demons? *The secret is to raise your vibration, and keep your frequency high. Remember, fear is the lowest of vibrations, and it is used as a weapon of control.* There is a simple scale and you can find it anywhere on the internet. There are emotions and thoughts that will keep you in a low vibration, making you vulnerable to everything from narcissists and black magic, to *demons. The lower your vibration is, the easier it is to manipulate you.* These dense emotions like fear, grief, anger, jealousy, apathy and even pride, will have you on a lower vibration. These days I give myself permission to get sad every once in a while, but I know I can't stay there for too long. The tables start to turn to a higher frequency with emotions and thoughts of courage, love, unity, neutrality and joy all the way up to *enlightenment. If I could just get up there to enlightenment and stay there, I knew I would become untouchable.*

I still had so many question about how this could even happen. The Black Witch had given me her phone number, so I dialed her up. I demanded information from her. Had someone paid her to stage this? *Did someone put her up to this? Who wanted me to kill myself? Who wanted me dead?* I already knew, of course, but I still found it hard to believe and wanted concrete evidence. I told her I'd find out either way, my lawyer and the police would be questioning her. *I was bluffing, but I wasn't lying.* I had spoken with an attorney. He told me my boys would have a case, *had I thrown myself off the balcony.* I had gone to the police. I showed them the video and all about the debacle at the doctor's office. The officer told me: "This sounds like a spiritual attack. You should pray for her." *Excuse me?*

The Black witch swore to me up and down that no one had put her up to it. She explained that she was dealing with her own demons, paying the price for things she had done in the past. Her voice was shaking, and I believed her. *I'm not easy to lie to.* My stance softened and suddenly, *I felt sorry for her.* I felt we had connected, maybe in a past life we were great friends. But right now she was dealing with *receiving back whatever she had put out. She had no way around it, she had to accept her karma.*

The witch gave me some advice, she told me I needed to learn how to protect myself. She said I should sprinkle some salt around the perimeter of my balcony and in front of my door. I thanked her for this information, and told her I could do that. I already had some salt in my house and I figured it couldn't hurt. Then she said she would try and get in touch with her witch in LA so she could give me more information, I *empathetically declined. A Jewess would never trust a sorcerer.*

I hung up the phone and realized all my anger towards her had vanished. I thought to myself, *maybe I will pray for her, she's definitely going through hell and could use the help.* I hoped she had learned her lesson that whatever she sent out there, *was bound to come back to her.* I asked God: could He at least give her a karmic hall pass for summoning up that demon in the mirror to break up with a cheating boyfriend? *Because I thought that was the best story ever.*

It had taken me years to figure out how to truly forgive someone who had done wrong to me. What I found incredible was that I forgave this person, *the one who had cast the spell for me to throw myself off my balcony*, right away. I was grateful that I had finally seen this person's true colors. I learned a very valuable lesson. I knew I could no longer keep thinking that *all people were good, because some are not. These people were probably overpowered by a demon, they're not even human. I knew this is how humans do inhumane evils towards others.* This was my only solution for something I couldn't accept as reality. My guides made me aware that this situation was *supposed* to happen, designed in such a way so that I could figure out what it was, and how *get rid of it. I had already sent every spell, curse, hex and evil eye right back to them, like a sling shot.*

*Except...*I had a very hard time sending the "go kill yourself" spell back to these people. *How could I possibly do that?* I didn't wish death on anyone, *even if they had wished it upon me.* I just couldn't do it and live with myself, it felt *wrong.* But I had to send that vile energy *somewhere, so I sent that back to God, I figured He would know what to do with it.*

The only problem is, this person *kept going* and casting idiotic spells! By this time I could *feel it,* and I didn't even bother to examine what they were trying to ail me with, I'd just *sling it right back-return to sender. Were these people serious? I couldn't even fathom doing something over and over again that wasn't working. You really hate me that much?* This person's anger was only hurting themselves, *not to mention that it was going to come back around and eventually destroy them. It would not end well for these people, and they only had themselves to blame. Their fate was sealed by their own doing.*

I even felt a "black magic sickness" coming on the other day; it didn't feel like a regular virus, or even the other "get sick" spells. *It came on so hot and heavy, and my heart started to race. This was voodoo death spell, and I saw who it was from…someone I didn't even know!* I got the sense that this person didn't even know what they were doing, they thought it was some kind of game. *Oh my God honey…you have no idea what kind of power you are playing with, but I do.* I was told by my guides to *Send it back! Send it back!* Which I did, while guzzling EmergenC. I popped another Zycam and tried to fall sleep. *But I was disturbed.* I had seen an angry brunette, and I knew who they might be connected to. *Holy fucking hell! How many people were doing some form of black magic out there? I had no idea.* I wasn't getting any more information besides seeing the back of their head. I know my guides don't always tell me everything I want to know, *but maybe I didn't want to know. But I had already sent it back to them, I had no choice, and I knew it would definitely not end well for them.*

When I told a couple of people about the cursing incident, both had snapped back: "Well, I don't believe in black magic". I told them both that that was good idea to believe that way, because the more you believed in it, the more it could affect you. *Believing in it gives it more power. But you better believe there are people out there doing it, don't fool yourself.* Here's the thing, you don't have to buy a cauldron and witch supplies and cook a spell up in your kitchen, or pay some sorcerer over in Europe to do curse someone for you. *Just saying or even thinking: "I hope he burns in hell", over and over again, can curse someone. Everything is energy and intention.* Now, I am very careful of my thoughts and words because *I know whatever I put out there, will eventually come back to me.* I'd like only love and positivity to come back to me, thank you very much.

In the morning after the voodoo incident, I felt much

better, but my mind was still in a fog. *I didn't even know who this person was or why they wanted me to die. The other people who had done the spells I actually knew, and quite well. This was a complete stranger!* I had to add another hater to my already long list. *What the hell people?* I had to inquire with my guides what was going on. I was told: *You're protected, there's nothing more you need to do. They've been warned, if they continue, they will be removed.* This sounded *morbid, but it wasn't my decree.* I was told to keep going and focusing on my life purpose. I just had muster up the strength. *By this time, I had plenty of that.*

I couldn't imagine why this person had thought a *go kill yourself* spell would even work on me. I instantly *knew* after having that past life memory that *suicide was something we weren't supposed to do*! *It's quite possibly the worst sin, there were the most dire consequences.* It's like skipping out half way through a test and not finishing the exam. Your teacher is going to force you to take it again, so you might as well sit there and finish it. *Suicide was the worst thing you could do to yourself. You'll just reincarnate and come right back, and most likely in even worse circumstances as a punishment.* You didn't *learn* what you were here to learn, so karmic cycles will keep *repeating* until you figure out how to *break free* from them. *I had learned this lesson already, and I will not be repeating it. Besides, I had a mission to fulfill. It is what has kept me going!*

I WAS SO TIRED OF ALL THIS *SHIT* THAT *I HAD TO DECLARE to myself that my dark night of the soul was over!* I was going to have to end this shit show *myself.* I had done all the shadow work, it was time to finish this because *I had had enough!* My entire self worth did not come from any external source. It came from the Divine spark *within* me. What started out as an ember, *when put through hell, became a fiery inferno blaze!* I decided to use that fire, and I *burned up any and all karmic ties and cycles. I set ablaze any soul contracts that didn't serve my higher purpose.* I threw any ancestral curses and trauma from this life *or any past life* into that fire as well. *I wanted to write my own destiny! I took my power back, this was my life. I am the one in control!*

I've got my own kind of "magic" that I call *manifesting* because: *logic.* Imagine, I discovered I could do *magic,* simply because *people had tried to use it against me.* Otherwise, I might not have ever discovered this fun fact. I didn't even need to learn Kabbalah or cast some sort of spell like the Wiccans do. I didn't have to sell my soul to Satan, join a secret society, or summon up any demons either.

No would would ever dare call me a "witch". That moniker implies working with the devil, *and I answer only to God.* It smacks of smug and greedy *manipulation,* and I already knew that what I reaped is what I'd be sowing. Manipulation is a play from the devil's handbook entitled "How to Fuck Shit Up and Make Everything Backwards". My Manuel for living is God's way.

I feel sorry for anyone who has sold their soul to the devil. The cold hard truth is that the devil can't give anyone power that they don't *already have.* But that's the great *deception, and that's what demons do, they deceive people.* I'm not surprised. Of course, the devil's way is taking a lazy short cut. *Sure, you might get fame and fortune, but at what cost?* The moment everyone else realizes that they have the *power* to create the life they desire, *the demons little game is over.* It's going to take dedication and hard work, but trust me, it's worth it. *Hello demons! Your time of ruling the world has come to an end. I'm officially dethroning you.*

The word "magic" has gotten a bad reputation over the years, and I'm pretty sure it's because some of it is *manipulation. It's a grievous sin,* no one is supposed to hurt people or interfere with another Divine Being's *Free Will.* This whole "spiritual war" isn't good versus evil, *it's an all out attack on our Free Will!* Darkness in and of itself has no power, *it is simply the absence of light. Evil tricks us into giving our free will away.* I was shown it will not end well for any evil souls that *had tried to harm another or tried to interfere, delay or manipulate someone else's Destiny, because it goes against God's natural laws.* Besides, don't these people have their own destiny to fulfill? I think that's what the apocalypse is all about, *removing these evil fuckers, and I can't wait!*

I knew that this experience what was supposed to happen for me to realize *just how strong I am.* I knew that the Angels protected me and the demons *respected* me, *because I could see right through their deception.* Besides, I had made peace with my own inner demons long ago and *now they work for me.* How could I get rid of all those broken and dirty pieces of myself if *I had already fallen in love* with them? *I couldn't.* But for Light to exist, it needs the Darkness to anchor it. *And there was so much light inside of me that some days I thought it might consume me.*

It's called shadow work, but that's a softer way of saying *I needed to face my demons.* At first I turned my back on my shadow side, I pretended that it didn't exist, *that I wasn't into all this freaky shit.* But my shadow side would not be ignored, and it creeped up on me like a big black shadowy arm like you see in movies.

I had to turn around and *face it and examine my dark side.* I had to understand why it was there and why I felt so ashamed of it. I decided to *embrace my shadow side* for a while, and I went deep down into the nothingness; *I almost lost myself in the darkness.*

The problem with giving into my shadow side was that it never *seemed to be enough.* The demons just kept wanting more and *more; it was never ending.* It was like an eternal black hole of absolute nothingness that just made my desire grow stronger. The demons appetites were never satisfied. *I had to take back the control, this was my life! I get to write how my destiny goes!* I could not let the dark side take me down! What was this…*Star Wars?* May the force be with all of us, I have a feeling we are going to need it. *I had already been through hell, and it was time to go back up to the earth to get some air.*

My voyage to the underworld was like a shamanic journey, yet I knew I couldn't *stay* there. I needed to gather up all those broken pieces of myself and put her back together. I found medicine and *healing* down there, *in the pit of lifelessness. It was like a seed; it needs to be buried in the dirt and surrounded by darkness in order to grow.* I had to die and get shoved into *a grave* in order to be *reborn, there was no other way.*

I uncovered some pretty powerful and useful tools from going to the dark underworld and putting my demons to work for me. But I knew I couldn't stay there, so I decided to *go up and go the other way.* I joined the New Age movement. I went to group meditations, did breath work, and had reiki healers do their thing on me. I bought crystal necklaces and found myself saying "Namaste" all the time. I pretended that I had never given into my shadow side, and that I *didn't have a dark side.* The new age movement has one very huge problem though: *spiritual bypassing.*

Spiritual bypassing was coined by the prominent psychologist John Woodward and he describes it as: "Using spiritual ideals and practices to side step personal and emotional issues. It is basically the avoidance and repression people use to bypass challenging traits such as low self esteem, social isolation, or other emotional issues." It's the land of: *let's ignore evil and pretend it doesn't exist.* It was a place where unicorns were *real, and they shit ice cream*! Every problem could be solved by sprinkling some "love and light" fairy dust at it. *Except, that was a huge mistake too.* That's not how the Universe functioned, I had to keep my darkness. *It was the very thing that anchored and enabled my light to stay and thrive.* Besides, the whole thing was too airy fairy for me. *This was the moment I knew I didn't need to belong anywhere, I was good on my own.*

I've done a lot of bad things in my life, and I cannot promise anyone I won't do them again. But all of my demons are sexual, never violent, greedy or manipulative. *I was never deceitful in the process.* I had done it out of pure *love,* it was never to gain anything or used to get something I wanted. *So was it even a sin? However, I was the one in control now,* I took the wheel of the car of my own life. I hadn't yet met anyone else that I trusted enough to drive *my car, so I took my power back!*

There was something very special about going through hell all by myself, without help from one single person. I got *stronger,* and I found out what I was truly made of. My challenges were not fun or easy, but I can honestly say I'm grateful for each and every experience. I had learned so many valuable lessons, and I was able to gain *mastery over my life. But I'm not going to do that again, not that I'd need to.*

REGARDLESS, THERE WAS ONE DEMON THAT I WOULD need to *cast out* forever. This one monster was the mother of all illusions, he was the Devil and Satan *himself combined: Fear.* I would not let fear ruin my life or hold me back! I trusted in God and had faith in Him, *so fear was unnecessary.* All I had to do was trust my instincts, God would show me where needed to go.

I realized that fear is attached to pain, death, and the material realm. E*xcept, I had already gone through more physical and emotional pain than anyone I had ever met in my life, so what was there to fear?* I already knew I could handle whatever life threw my way. Pain was inevitable, but how much I suffered from it, *that was entirely my choice.* I had to accept and take responsibility for letting the pain get to me, and for *so long! From now on, I would transmute it.*

Even death I did not fear, that was *inevitable.* It is literally the *only thing we can be sure of.* One day it will come, and I am not afraid because I know that I will not cease to exist. I knew that the material world was an *illusion.* I had lost everything and had to start all over again so many times in my life that I lost count. I knew I could do it again, *as many times as was necessary. Material possessions have never been able to buy anyone love or happiness. True love is the real commodity that has value.* I couldn't fear *lack either,* because I knew God always answered my prayers.

I know that we get in life *exactly what we deserve.* I knew I deserved far more than I had, and that one day I'd be able to manifest it.

Yet my needs are always met; I've never been starving or homeless. *God, I am forever grateful!* I now also had this knowledge that was priceless. I had the ability to make to the engine of my life run *on fumes.* I understood that it is *God* that gives us our blessings, and He can certainly take them away again if I needed that lesson. I let go of my attachments to any particular person, place or thing. *If it something not meant for me, holding on to it would only cause me pain.* So the fear was *gone,* and *just in the nick of time.*

Every brick someone threw at me, I used as free material to make my foundation stronger. Every breakup and heartbreak taught me how to fully love myself. All the deception and betrayal taught me how to listen to my intuition more. Even the haters showed me that I couldn't share every detail of my life with people, *not everyone can be trusted.* Every evil eye sent my way only seemed to enhance my appearance *and* my bank account. *Did these people know their shit was only making me stronger?* I knew I was on to something.

I will no longer dance with that devil, fear. As it turns out, I don't even need a dancing partner, *I can dance all by myself.* He had deceived me for the *last time, and he knew it.* I finally understood that he had *no power over me,* nor would he ever again, unless I let him. *I chose instead to make God my dancing partner, my faith is stronger than my fears.* I choose to collaborate with the *Divine.* I knew that was the only way I would not fail in fulfilling my Divine mission. I was amazed at how *good* I can *dance!*

CHAPTER 7

Surrender

My dark night of the soul had lasted for *fifteen years*. It's not that every day was terrible, but overall is was just *shitty*. This dark period of my life completely stripped me of whatever ego I had left. It brought me to my *knees* and humbled me in a way *nothing else could*. But something needed to change, I had to pull myself out of this mess! *There was no one around that was going to save me.*

But I knew it all had a purpose. I needed to *grow up*, and re-mother myself, that's what was missing from my childhood. I already knew how to mother, so that part was going to be easy. But I had to learn some very harsh lessons along the way. Even though I didn't know where I was going, *I knew I had to keep moving forward.* I had stepped *way* outside of my comfort zone, and *there was no going back*. A Spiritual Awakening is irreversible. Once I saw the *truth* of the nature of our reality, I couldn't go back to sleep. *It's just not possible. I saw my future, and I couldn't unsee it.* I *knew* I couldn't even turn around and look at the past because I could *miss* my future, *and my future looked so bright!* But first, I needed to get myself out of this mess.

Instead of letting this grief break me down, I let it *break me open*. The crack was already there in my heart, I could feel the pain. Now, all I had to do was *surrender. Then, the most amazing thing happened...my mind was blown wide open too*! I was given more information and I saw that *there's a possibility that I might be living this life and all my past lives simultaneously.* This Divine Matrix was where we all are connected *in every dimension.* This was exciting idea, yet scary. *I wondered what another version of me might be doing in another dimension.* The juxtapose of emotions felt strange to me, but *tantalizing* as well. *I just had to hold tight to my vision and never stop believing.*

I realized that in order to climb out of this dark hole, I needed to get rid of all this trauma I was carrying around, *it was a burden.* The grief, heartbreak and loss, the broken down feeling from being deceived and betrayed *felt so heavy, and it needed to go. It was so dark, thick and dense, and it was too laborious to carry it around all the time.* The weight of the burdens was *slowing me down.* I had already integrated my own personal darkness because I knew it needed to be there, but I was heading towards the *Light!* I knew had to release this heavy weight and surrender it to God. *I was so tired of trying to swim upstream.* Maybe I was supposed to just sit back, relax, and let the river take me where I needed to go? *God, let me go get my unicorn floaty first.* I was so sick of this fear based time-space box I felt trapped in. *God, get me out of here!*

The Lion's gate is one of the seven open gates that leads to the Old city in Jerusalem. The Lion's Gate is also a *portal,* an energetic phenomenon that combines ancient astrology, cosmology and numerology. It's a very specific celestial alignment that is the *perfect time to manifest.* It happens every year on August 8th and is called the Lion's Gate because it happens during Leo season (the astrological sign of Leo is a Lion). *Oh... the things you can learn from the internet.* I wasn't exactly trying to manifest anything, I just needed to lighten my load. *It was hard to stay positive and manifest while carrying around so many burdens.* My feelings towards the situation wasn't going to somehow turn back time.

I decided that this was the perfect time to get *rid* of everything that was *weighing me down and keeping me stuck.* I wrote it down in my journal, *six whole pages of it.* I released it *and surrendered it to God.* I let go of all the anger for being lied to, manipulated and deceived. I surrendered all the sadness for not being chosen by any certain man. I emancipated all of my fears of what the future held. *I unchained myself from anything and everything that was not serving my higher purpose.*

When I woke up the next day, everything felt *different.* There was something happening in my life that can only be described as *magic.* I was meeting new people, opportunities were coming to *me! I didn't have to go searching for it.* It all just seemed to flow, I didn't have to struggle anymore. I had gotten so used to the struggle, *but maybe it didn't need to be that way. I had completely surrendered to God. My life was His now, I would do whatever He asked me to do.* I embraced the mystery and excitement of the unknown. I didn't have to have everything figured out right now, *but I knew one day it would all make sense.*

A FEW DAYS LATER ON THE FULL MOON, I MET *HIM*. HE walked through the door and I felt and heard this *whoosh.* I momentarily stopped breathing and my *heart skipped a few beats.* I never believed in love at first sight until *that moment.* It wasn't what he looked like, although he is quite possibly the most handsome, stunning man I have ever met in my life. It was more like *a soul recognition. Hello…there you are! I've been looking for you.* And I already knew his name, because I had seen it on the production call sheet. *What's crazy is I wasn't even trying to manifest a guy! Yet there he was…*

He is absolutely gorgeous, almost perfect. I'll call him Starboy, although it's obvious that's not his real name. But I was given a glimpse of his possible destiny, and *saw he was famous!* I had seen his acting skills more than once. He was good, but something was missing. He is very intelligent and he took his acting career very seriously. *But maybe that was his problem, he was overthinking it?*

We started hanging out. I was stunned and *dazzled* by his unique range of characters he could portray. *Besides, he is so damn hot.* His look is so *versatile,* he could play dozens of different roles. He speaks like *six* different languages. If one day he didn't shave, he could be a latin gangster or a dude from the Middle East. If he put on a pair of glasses, he could be a computer nerd or a wolf on wall street. When he was speaking another language, *he could play a completely different character!* If he was clean shaven he could be a heart throb in a rom com or an FBI agent/cop/military guy. I told him that when he started to get lead roles he should choose a role that was *the complete opposite* of what he had just played, and that he would work in Hollywood *forever.* I had already been type cast as the "trophy wife", "mom", or "sexy secretary", *so I amazed by this.*

But it was the "act" of his life that he was giving *an all star performance*! I couldn't understand why he was putting so much energy into this act or what he was getting out of it. As psychic as I had become, I couldn't figure out what he was hiding or why. *Please, take off the mask. I already know you anyway.* Maybe I should've focused on a future career as a talent scout instead of *being so boy crazy.*

We hung out a few more times, and it seemed like we could talk for days and days and still have a million things to talk about. *Then, he just vanished into thin air*. I'd love to say my heart wasn't broken because my heart was already broken after losing Sammy. But the truth is, *it crushed me*. My heart went from having a huge crack in it to *breaking into a million pieces. I had just found you again after so many lifetimes, where did you go?* My heart was a pile of mush and I didn't know how to fix it.

I couldn't understand why this kept happening to me! *I didn't want to close off my heart to love, but God, why did it always get broken?* I had to keep loving and believing God would bring me the right man in His Divine timing. Although, I wasn't sure if I would make through another heartbreak. *I had to make sure that God knew that I had reached my maximum boiling point.*

I wanted to pull up to Starboy's house in a rocket ship, dressed to then nines, high heels and all and say to him; "Hey! You are so hot and *perfect,* are you even *real?* The chemistry between us is so *intense!* It's not just that, we have some many things in common. I feel like I could talk to you for a million hours, and we'd still have things to talk about. I want to *know* you, yet my soul already does *know* you. *I realize that doesn't make sense!* Want to go for a ride? I've got this bright shining Star calling my name from the other side of the Universe. It's light years away, but I know a wormhole shortcut, we'll be there in seconds! *This is weird, I know, right?*

Hey, if you prefer I can turn this spaceship into a magic carpet, *would that be more fun for you?* How about a chariot from Roman times? A Golden Light Merkabah? *Do you know what that is? Never mind!* Hop in, it will be the greatest *adventure!* Don't worry, we'll come back to Earth, we're meant to." Of course, I can't create a magic carpet with my mind, *or can I?*

But I didn't have one moment to pay attention to what this situation with Starboy is or was, because of what was happening to my *body.* I may have given up all of my grief to God in the mental plane, *but it still needed to come out of my body.* I had all this trauma *trapped* in there, all the way back from childhood! I was having what can be called a kundalini awakening, although the label is not important. I had read somewhere that sex can trigger it, but I had never experienced anything like this. I had to *purge* the trauma from my body and my soul.

I had to check in with my guides, *I wasn't even trying to manifest a romantic partner when I met Starboy. I was working on my career!* I had spent 22 years putting myself second and raising my boys. *Now was my time to shine!* I wanted a romantic partner, sure, but first I wanted to manifest some resources. I wanted, no *needed,* to travel and see the world. I had a bucket list a mile long, there were so many places I needed to see and experience. I wanted enough abundance so that I could *help people, especially children!* I wasn't even focused on finding romance at that moment, *but then I remembered when my guides explained to me how powerful my thoughts were; I was unintentionally manifesting at all times, so I may as well be intentional about it. I was actually manifesting at every moment, with every thought, word and action.*

But I was working on manifesting a suitable career for myself now that the role of mother was coming to an end. I had put myself on the back burner for *so many years,* and I was eager to get back to *building my empire.* Of course, collaboration with someone else would help me get there faster. *How had I missed that fact? Why was I resisting it? Maybe it was because he vanished into thin air.*

The only thing I could do was keep following my intuition and I was instructed to *keep moving forward. You've said that before, I got it!* I used my manifesting skills I had developed thus far to try and make my dreams my reality. *I had to take inspired action!* So I was doing literally *everything* that I knew how to do. I was writing, acting, modeling, and helping people find new homes with my real estate license. *I was throwing so much shit against the wall, something had to stick!* Being a mother has an income of zero, and I hadn't even had a chance *to save any money,* it all went to the boys and their well being.

Here I was trying to play "catch up", everyone else my age was enjoying a fruitful and satisfying career, and I had to start from *nothing. Good thing my ego was already gone and I am no stranger to working hard.* I loved and was passionate about everything I was doing. The writing helped me to heal, acting enabled me to express myself and release my emotions. Modeling is easy, I had been doing it for years. And since I had already dedicated my life to service of others, it felt rewarding to help someone find a new place to call home. The home is so *personal,* it's a sacred space, *and people need to feel safe.* Real estate is a career that will never be obsolete; everyone needs a roof over their head.

I was burning the candle from multiple ends, and I knew I couldn't keep up this pace or I'd burn out. I was working all day and into the night, and I knew I'd need to *prioritize.* I had to be honest with myself: *What would I be doing if didn't need to worry about starving*? The answer came quickly: I'd just write, act and travel the world. I can write from anywhere inspiring, and writing is what I'm truly passionate about, I *had to follow my heart.* The heart has coherence like the brain, and the more broken my heart was, my brain followed. *I saw even more potentials, and I was ecstatic about the future! Except…I still wanted my Divine Masculine. Where was he already?*

A SPIRITUAL AWAKENING IS NOT SEXY AS IT SOUNDS, IT'S lonely, *painful* and *irreversible.* I had to get this shit *out* of my body so I could vibrate at a *higher frequency.* The only thing I could do besides working was try to release the trapped trauma. So I would run, walk, stretch and *dance.* I sobbed, moaned, and *breathed.* I stretched and did yoga, and over meditated myself to the point of oblivion. *I had to keep moving, if I stopped it would be more painful and I'd be sad about yet another heartbreak.*

I had bought a dry skin brush when I read on Goop or somewhere that it helps the lymphatic system, but I had only used it a few times. *Out of nowhere,* I had to use it every God damn day *like my life depended on it.* I had enough knowledge from all of my health issues to understand that my health was solely my responsibility, and negative emotions stuck in my body could *kill me. I wasn't ready to die yet!*

But I couldn't *wait* for Starboy to get his shit together, I was not going to sit around and get tripped up on him. I had learned this lesson so many years ago when the man I had manifested didn't want anything to do with me. *It took me a while to get over a guy that had never even asked me out. He never even called me or sent me a text.*

I think this is where most people get stuck when manifesting a partner. There is Destiny and Fate, but you can't forget about *Free Will!* This other person has to choose you *too.* The element of free will means that there are *infinite possibilities,* and the outcome depends on the choices we, and the other people, make.

I couldn't get my heart set on any one person, *I already knew that.* I did not want to wait for *anyone!* If a man didn't choose me, the Wheel of Destiny would turn, the Universe would shuffle the deck and *another* card would pop out. *Isn't this game fun?* But first, I had to put back the other card into the deck. If I didn't like the hand I had been dealt, I could always give it back. Although, I wasn't going to get dealt a new card until I *completely let go of the other card.*

Here was my problem: *I was already in love with Starboy.* It didn't matter if he chose me or not, *I knew he would always have a part of my heart.* What's a hopeless romantic like me going to do about that? *He would have to choose me too, like I had chosen him, or I'd just manifest someone else. I had already put the card back in the deck... waiting for it to reshuffle...*

This is when it occurred to me that Starboy might be my "twin flame". First before I explain what I know about this, I have to tell you *I do not like the label,* or any label for that matter. The term "Twin Flame" gives the illusion that there is only one person *on the planet* that I was meant to end up with, and *I already knew that wasn't true.* It wasn't even a possibility that if he didn't chose me that I was meant to end up all alone. Besides, I had known people that used a "twin Flame" as an excuse to sleep with a married man, sit around waiting around for years, or stay in an abusive relationship. There are many people who don't believe in "twin flames", but apparently not everyone is on that "journey". Crappy Childhood Fairy on YouTube says that people that believe in twin flames have intense childhood trauma, and *that's entirely possible. My personal verdict on this subject isn't out yet.*

I'm going to tell you what I have read about the twin flame phenomenon. I have this information because, as embarrassed I am to say this, I thought it was another guy for a long time. *Cue the eye roll.* I've read books, articles, watched videos, and did clearing karma meditations. Once I even paid for personal coaching regarding this topic.

Anyway, some people say that twin flames are the *same soul* split into two different bodies. *This sounds so far fetched.* If anything, we are all one soul, *God,* split into many bodies. What resonated more with me was when I heard someone say '*these two share the same core soul frequency." Getting warmer.*

So the journey I was talking about is real, but this is not a happily ever after fairy tale romance. *But...wouldn't that be nice?* What happens when you meet this person is they mirror *back to you* everything about *yourself that you don't like and needs to be fixed.* The coming together serves as a catalyst *for an awakening* and it brings up any core wounds that have yet to be healed. *I can attest to that. I had woundings that came up that I thought I had healed long ago!*

So, the unawakened one "runs" while the other one "chases". What the runner doesn't realize is that they are only running away from themselves. You can't forever run away from your own reflection in the mirror. I*t's extremely intense, and mine was so intense a blood vessel burst in my right eye when we had sex. Crazy!* Then there is supposedly a separation period, and this is where most people get stuck. *The separation is filled with the pain of heartbreak, sadness, and loneliness. I can attest that this is true too.*

Supposedly, Divine Union happens only when the awakened one *balances out both their masculine and feminine qualities* and learns how to unconditionally *love themselves, so much so that they actually don't need a partner and they stop chasing. Wasn't I already there? I didn't need a man, but I definitely wanted one.* After the initial meeting, the separation period is where each person can get their shit together before things can get cozy again. I can see how one can stayed trapped in their heartbreak during separation; it was only the most intense sexual chemistry and spiritual connection *I had ever encountered in my life…no big deal.*

Sometimes, there are stark differences between these two souls, like age gaps, being from wildly different cultures, or being raising in opposing socioeconomic backgrounds. I already knew the purpose of that. *Could we both face our fears and fulfill the soul contract no matter what anyone else thought of it?* I am the older one, which made me hesitate, *but only for a moment. Age is just a number. Besides, I'm a Capricorn rising, we age in reverse!* If we didn't come into union, it wouldn't be because of my doubts and fears. *I had already decided that fear would not hold me back ever again.* It remains to be seen if he will come with me where I'm going, *or if I will even want him to.*

The real purpose of the Divine Union is because of the shared Divine Mission and life purpose that only those two can fulfill *together.* I was shown exactly *what that mission was. I saw bigger picture, I saw it all, the whole enchilada. Damn!* It's no wonder these witchy diviners were tripping over themselves to put me in a grave, *they were jealous! My Divine mission was kind of a big deal. It was a little scary too.* But I had been called by *God, how could I say no?* I felt like *Joan of Arc-I have been called by God to do this!* It was *sheer insanity,* yet it was the only time in my life where things seemed to *click into place. But, what was he doing…had I scared him?*

Possibly, I was scaring the shit out of myself right about now. He did realize that not making a decision is also… *a decision, right?* I was going to have to proceed with the mission because, well, *I had already said yes.* But I couldn't slap a label on the situation, nor would I identify with anyone else's journey. I already knew that it was my thoughts and beliefs around it that would *make or break it.* That, and *whatever choice he made. I know what I saw, and I couldn't ignore the vision.*

I WAS INSTRUCTED BY MY GUIDES TO PUT STARBOY BACK in the deck. I felt like a little child whose favorite toy had been taken away, and I pouted for a little too long. But since I had already made the mistake of holding on to an idea of a certain man and it had led to me sabotaging other relationships, I knew I couldn't make that mistake again. Maybe he was just meant to be the catalyst to kick my awakening into high gear? Or maybe he was supposed to be my co-star or co-collaborator, not my co-pilot? That was an *interesting* thought. *I can't see the future, no one can.*

What I can see are the *possibilities,* and more options keep presenting themselves everyday.

I saw Starboy a few more times *as friends.* I figured I should at least try to salvage a friendship. Maybe we could collaborate, but I wasn't sure. One thing I know is that meeting him *is when I finally started writing this book. Apparently, I was supposed to give Starboy a specific message from beyond the veil, and then release him to do his own healing.* So I did. *Sheesh!* No wonder I was still single! I was that woman who said: "Hey, my spirit guides want me to give you this message-so here it is!" and then I sent that man home so I could get some sleep. *I bet he was pretty freaked out and thinks I'm a wacko.*

But fuck him and everyone else, *I was freaked out!* My life had gotten so damn *witchy* by this point, and *there was absolutely nothing I could do about it. I had already surrendered, and I just had to go with it.* I had stepped into the *unknown,* and had embraced the *magic.* I realized that my guides weren't telling me certain things on purpose, because it might have changed my actions if I had known the truth. *But they'd inform me after the fact.* I was meant to give him the message. But the truth is, I was going about creating my own destiny, it didn't matter what anyone else thought about what I was doing, or if he came along with me.

However, I still had this nagging feeling about Starboy. It was probably because we had a psychic connection. *Or maybe I really am crazy?* Once the link was in place, it couldn't be broken. I felt this feeling of *despair* coming from him, and I didn't know why. From the time I had spent with him, our lives definitely mirrored the other. Maybe he had curses put on him too? *I have zero evidence of this, of course. Maybe I was paranoid from smoking too much weed?* He really had never shown me his *real self, but he also hadn't given me any reason not to trust him.* I couldn't understand why something so short lived, with a younger guy, *could throw me for a loop! Who was I even?* He broke my heart, not that it wasn't already broken. *There had to be more to this story.*

A FEW DAYS LATER, I HAD ANOTHER READING BOOKED with my astrologer. I told him about Starboy and asked for his advice because I was mystified as to how this man had gotten to me. Since my first session I had regularly booked another one with him, just to check in with the stars to see if I was heading in the right direction. He asked if I knew Starboy's birthday and place of birth? I did.

My astrologer said, "Wow, his sun is right on top of your north node." I said: "What does that mean, exactly?" *I told him to explain astrology to me like he would a five year old.* "Well", he continued, "He is someone that is meant to come into your life for you to realize or remember your life's purpose." *Wow. Ok... he had done just that!* After my reading, I pulled out my vision board I had made over a decade ago, and it was all there! *I had forgotten all about my life purpose until I met Starboy!* So maybe that was the whole reason I met him, to rediscover my life's purpose.

To think, I had almost settled for a hum drum life as a divorcee real estate agent. Everyone and their mother has a real estate license here in Florida. It's almost a joke, anyone can do this job. I wasn't making the best use of the *gifts* I had been given. And have you seen how they dress real estate agents in the movies? *The bad hairstyles and frumpy suits are not my style.* I'll keep my real estate license though, I plan on investing in real estate *one day very soon. Besides, I happen to be really good at the job, so there's that.*

ALTHOUGH I STILL HAD THAT BRIGHT SHINING STAR that was calling my name. I knew I had to get there, I just wasn't sure *how.* I knew if I followed my intuition and let God lead me, the way would be shown to me when the time was right. I trusted in Divine Timing, because I knew that if the time wasn't right, it wasn't going to work out for the highest good of all involved.

Instead of getting depressed about yet another heartbreak, I threw myself into manifesting. I was getting the hang of it, it's like *magic!* All I had to do was state my intentions out loud, there couldn't be any doubt in my mind when I was speaking. Then I would write it down, I'd be specific, yet general. For example, when I had described my dream home, I would state the location it would be near, how big it might be, and what it might look like, but it wasn't any specific place. I couldn't be attached to anything specific, or even attach to the way I was going to get it, or *how* it was supposed to manifest into my world. Then I acted *as if* it had already manifested, I had to *feel* the emotions of already being in my dream home. I was surprised how quickly I got my dream home. I *felt* the *gratitude of being in my new home, before I even got there.* I will admit that when I spoke this particular manifestation into existence, the idea was in the back of my mind that it was sometime *in the future,* a few years from that moment. *Except... it showed up only a few months later. I wondered if I could start manifesting what I wanted faster?*

I was getting pretty good at this manifesting! I was getting more downloads, and they were coming in *fast and furious*. I have to admit, sometimes the truth is really heartbreaking. I had to remind myself that *I wanted to know*. Now I know why witches are associated with brooms, and it's not because they're out there flying around on them. It's because *cleaning my apartment* was the single activity that brought in the most clarification. *If I needed an answer, I just started cleaning. I'm OCD anyway, so it all works out. However, I'm not a witch. Also, I prefer to use a vacuum.*

One day I decided to just let it all go and give that task of manifesting to God. *He already knew what I wanted and needed, so why was I trying so hard?* I'm sure He knew He would have to bring in those things in order for me to fulfill my mission. Besides, maybe I wasn't dreaming *big enough?* Maybe God had something planned for my life that was more *enormous* than I originally thought? I hoped it would all make sense soon, but for now I was just *going with the flow. Which by the way, isn't an easy thing for me to do.*

I knew I needed to be a little more specific on what I wanted in a romantic partner. I knew that it wasn't the right time for a life partner, *or he would be here.* But I had to do something to hurry it up and *make it the right time, I had waited long enough.* I felt like I had earned my stripes for getting my heart broken so many times. *Is there some kind of award for that type of thing?* I decided I had to get clear about what I wanted in a partner *now. I really didn't know when he would show up, and I was always unconsciously manifesting. It was better to be prepared and state my intentions clearly.*

I wanted a man who could *manifest* like I could. He was as *sure* of *me* as I was of *him*. I could tell him *anything*, he was my best friend. He was not only my lover, he was my business partner or co-collaborator. *We had the same life vision and we had some sort of mission to fulfill together.* This man will have already chosen *service to others,* like I had. Even though he could manifest anything he wanted, he wasn't so attached to the material world and he kept his ego in check. He didn't go too fast, he took the time to get to know me. *He didn't just disappear either*. Whatever he said, *he meant it* and he always followed through on his word. He was a good communicator, he was romantic and a *giver,* like I was! He had integrity and confidence; he was passionate about what he did for a living. He was someone who would support me and understand me emotionally, physically, mentally and spiritually, and I would do the same for him. I wanted *the Emperor!*

This Emperor in the traditional tarot deck is a *boss,* he's *In Charge.* He is a man who steps up to the plate and is responsible, reliable and logical. In "Tarot for Beginners" by Meg Hayertz, she describes the character: "While the Emperor's counterpart, the Empress, overflows with creative ideas and nurtures possibility, the Emperor deems which ideas are most viable and effective, and carries them out. The Emperor plans, delegates, structures, and carries out projects." *Gulp. I could use a structured and logical partner, no doubt.*

My Emperor would also be loyal and have self discipline. He wouldn't play mind games or try to manipulate or control me. We would both be committed, yet feel completely *free* to be our authentic selves. He may be the one leading, *but I was the one pointing the way, and he did not question my judgement.* I have been here before, *we go towards the Light! The darkness exists, it has to be there, we've already integrated the shadow within ourselves, and now we are going towards Light. We are staying on this path of love, peace, joy, unity, compassion, service, truth and justice!* I have been single for so long, *I wasn't going to settle now!* Here I was, standing in my Divine Feminine *power,* not needing a partner. It seemed like every time my heart got broken, *my standards went up, instead of down.* I could take care of myself, and fill up my own cup. I didn't need someone to take care of me or "save" me. I wanted nothing less than my *Divine Masculine.*

The Divine Masculine's mission is to *protect,* while the Divine Feminine *creates.* But somewhere along the line in today's modern world the wires got crossed and *everything got so fucked up,* and the Divine Feminine needed to learn how to *protect and defend herself!* It's no wonder there are so many tired and *angry* women out there, *this is exhausting!* Who was going to step up and restore the balance? I wanted nothing less than the *Emperor!*

THE EMPRESS IN THE TRADITIONAL TAROT DECK REPRESENTS the *Divine Feminine.* She is the mother and a master at manifesting. She can "birth" anything she wants, from any other realm, into her physical existence. The Empress is the psychic High Priestess *afte*r she has birthed her creation. She embodies *all four* queens of the tarot deck. She's the Queen of Wands, fire element; she's confident, creative and *ambitious.* She's the Queen of Cups, water element; she's loving, nurturing, kind and *intuitive.* The Empress is also the Queen of Swords, air element; she's intelligent, quick witted and *logical.* She's the Queen of Pentacles, earth element; she's grounded, stable and *abundant.*

The Empress has a fifth element that she embodies: *Spirit*. She is the ultimate *Divine Feminine boss. She's got it all,* beauty, brains, passion, and intelligence. She's chosen to collaborate with *God, and everything she wants comes to her*. She just sits on her throne and *manifests! All I needed to do was call in the Emperor!*

I THINK I ALREADY KNEW THE EMPEROR! COULD HE HAVE been right in front of my face this whole time? Maybe it wasn't the right time? Maybe I wasn't ready? Was it possible that I wasn't shown who the Emperor was until I put the card back and the Universe shuffled the deck? *I always have so many questions.* I knew it wasn't the right time, or he would be here already. *But maybe I still had some things to heal? I'd have to get on top of that, right away.*

Of course, Starboy could step up and become the Emperor, *he has free will.* I'm sure the Emperor was doing what I was doing, wrapping up old karmic cycles and healing. He needed to *take action, and I knew* this Emperor had already heard me calling him. I even felt his presence so strongly in my bedroom the other day. Was he doing remote viewing? I wondered if he was some kind of wizard. If he didn't heed the call, the Wheel of Destiny would turn, the Universe would shuffle the deck *again. In my world anything can happen, the possibilities are infinite!*

I still wanted to know why my guides had lead me to believe my destined soulmate was *someone else*. That's when I found the YouTube channel, Crappy Childhood Fairy, that I mentioned earlier. I love this chick, she gives it to you straight, with no bullshit. She had mentioned that the fantasy of thinking someone you don't know is your soulmate comes from childhood trauma. There's even a term for it: Limerance. *Shit! This childhood trauma was ruining my life!*

From that moment on, I did not question what my guides were telling me, *they know what they are doing.* Maybe I wasn't given all the answers all at once, but they told me what I needed to know and when I needed to know it. I knew I would have all my questions answered if I kept myself grounded and proceeded with truth and integrity. *I was told to focus on my life purpose, and that the Emperor would step up or I'd meet him along the way. Got it.*

Maybe the Emperor was still in his Dark Night of the Soul. I hope he would snap out of it soon! My Dark Night of the Soul ended when I decided it was over. I realize bad shit is going to happen, people die, there's evil, and sometimes the guy I didn't vote for gets to move into the White House. *Yada, yada.* But I didn't have to let any of it *affect* me. I wasn't about to knit myself a hat that looked like a pussy and stomp around the city all mad and shit, that's just wasted energy. I was putting all my energy into creating a life that I was giddy about, a life full of *love and abundance!* I had wrapped up my dark night of the soul because I was just so sick of it, and I think *the Emperor could do that too.*

I had so much knowledge about romantic relationships, *and yet I kept failing at them.* My writing career literally started by a string of *really bad* dates. *This is not a joke, I'm serious.* I entered the dating scene at 32 after my divorce, and I was unbelievably naive. I hadn't dated that much before I got married, I met my former husband at 19 years old. *Also, I live in Miami Beach, FL, The World's Worst Place to be Single™.*

I'm pretty sure I made every dating mistake a woman could make, *I could write a whole book on the subject.* I was never one to play games, it all seemed so fake and contrived, and I wasn't very good at it. *If I genuinely like a guy, he will definitely know.* Which completely leaves out the mystery and isn't how you're supposed to "get" a guy, *but I don't give a shit about that.* I have to always be myself and I wear my heart on my sleeve. I am not afraid to be the first to reach out and say Hi, *I'm not shy or a wallflower. I can flirt shamelessly, and I have a lot of fun doing it.* However, I had to draw the line *somewhere.* I *would not be the one to ask a guy out on date.* That's the man's job, *men are supposed to lead.* I have to be true to my feminine nature…*I rarely wear pants.* I'm really glad I made this decision years ago and stuck with it, if I had not I probably would've tracked down Mr. Limerance and made a complete fool out of myself. *To be honest, that's probably what he was expecting.* Rejection is God's protection. *Dodged a bullet.*

There was one guy in particular that threw me off, I'll call him Mr. Shady. He treated me like *shit,* but for some odd reason, *I just couldn't quit him.* Trust me, I tried to multiple times. *Alright, maybe it was more like dozens of times, but who's counting?* We had the same dark and twisted sense of humor. Before we even met, we would rag on each other's Facebook posts in the comments section. *This was years ago, Facebook was cool back then.* This went on for months, and people probably were wondering what was going on. *I was wondering that myself.*

But he fell *way* short of the standards I had for a life partner, and he knew it. *He didn't seem to care though, he was like a cold, weird robot.* So I kept telling him it was over and would go on dates with other men, because I knew we would never end up together. But the shit that these men did on dates, their behavior, was *mind blowing! I wondered if other women were having the same experiences?*

The worst dates I ever went on were with a guy I'll call Mr. High and Mighty. We met at an event through a mutual friend. She giggled and told me he had sold his company for hundreds of millions of dollars. I didn't give a shit about that, but he *was* exactly my "type", Ivy league educated, intelligent and nerdy Jewish guy. I guess I'm a sapiosexual person, not that I like labels. *Only...I shouldn't have immediately thought he was intelligent just because he went to an Ivy League school.*

For our first date he wanted to make it a "group thing" because he had some friends in town. I was fine with that idea, it took the pressure off of the whole first date thing. So I invited a couple of girlfriends and we headed down to the SLS in South Beach. The first thing Mr. High and Mighty did was *make fun* of my sober friend. He just wouldn't stop ragging on her for not having an alcoholic beverage. *What kind of person does that?* I was proud of her for getting clean and staying sober, *it's not easy in this town.* I was so happy for her that I was even going to have an extra cocktail myself, in her honor. *She pretended like she didn't hear him. She's smarter than he is, now that I think about it.*

Luckily my other girlfriend stepped in and *took over.* They both went to Harvard, and her wits and intelligence matched, *maybe even surpassed,* his. Except it became apparent that he didn't *believe* she went to Harvard, so he started to question and *test her.* He was asking her about specific buildings on campus and all that jazz, and she snapped back with all *the right* answers. But for some weird reason, *he kept going and tried to prove himself right. Holy shit, was he serious?* Apparently *a*n Ivy League education doesn't buy you any emotional intelligence, social skills, or *tact. Zero, none. Nada.*

But me being me, I decided to go out with him again and give him a second chance. *Doesn't everyone deserve a second chance*? Maybe he was trying too hard to look "cool" in front of his friends, but Lord knows he was way too old to be doing that. Besides, this was the type of guy that didn't have friends, he had *employees.* I couldn't imagine anyone that surrounded him wasn't somehow on his payroll. I only needed to have been sitting next to him for about 42 minutes to realize his company was an absolute *buzzkill, even with that extra cocktail.*

Anyhoo, for the second date we went to some shitty Mexican restaurant up the street from my apartment. We went there because he made *me decide* where we going to eat. *I was already pissed, wasn't the man supposed to make these decisions?* I mean, sure, it's nice if the guy asks for input on what I liked eating, but I hated making the final call. *Wasn't he the man?*

So we're sitting there waiting for the food to arrive and I'm trying to get a WiFi signal on my phone to get more info about something we were talking about. He said: "Hey, I'm good with this kind of thing", and grabbed my phone from my hand. He proceeded to sit there and scroll through my phone for what seemed like forever. I was *flabbergasted,* I could only describe the situation as...*amusing. What was he even looking at?* The camera roll? Past text messages? We were on a *second* date, I hadn't even let him *touch* me. *Yet here he was acting all suspicious, like a jealous boyfriend!* But I have absolutely nothing to hide, so I didn't stop him. *Scroll away you little bitch!*

Then he decided we should play a game where we told each other what body part we hated about ourselves the most. *Pardon me?* I folded my arms across my chest and gave him a glare. I didn't think that sounded like a fun game, and I hoped my body language would convey that message. *But of course he didn't notice, he was too busy looking in my phone.* So I snatched my phone back and said: "You first." He waved his hand to dismiss me, and insisted that I go first.

To be honest, I couldn't understand where he was going with this. I told him: "I really like all my body parts, thank you very much." He told me I was full of shit. *He wore glasses, I assumed he needed to update his prescription...he could see what I looked like, right?* I took another swig of my beer, as this was way too much to deal with while being this sober. *Yet he insisted I come up with a body part of myself I hated.* Was I not going to get to eat if I didn't come up with something? *What the hell was he thinking?* I'm not a stick in the mud but truthfully, I really had to give it some thought. Then I finally said: "Well, I guess the top of my hands look older than I really am." *And he agreed with me.*

I was really trying not to shake my head and roll my eyes. Then I said: "Ok, it's your turn." He claimed he had *never said he was going to share which body part he hated the most about himself.* I couldn't believe it! But then I understood... he *hated all of his body parts. He hated himself.* I already knew that the man with the *most inflated ego was also the most insecure.* The huge ego is an attempt to *cover up this fact.* It was so obvious, and *sad. Whatever.*

I should've left right then and there, but I was hungry. *Sometimes being human is so damn inconvenient!* I ate that shitty Mexican food and since we were sitting outside, he lit up a cigar. As he took a long drag, he informed me that if I ever smoked a cigarette, he would never kiss me. With my mouth agape, my only thought was: *Did I give you the impression I would kiss you?* Then he asked me what kind of underwear I wore. I'm not embarrassed by these type of questions, so I told him I like Hanky Panky. This guy *flew into a rage;* apparently one of his two ex wives liked Hankys, and he *hated them. How could this dude have such strong emotions about something he never had to wear? Or maybe he was wearing them…*

I persisted in my pursuit to defend my Hanky Pankys, because they're comfortable, *God damn it! But he would just not let it go!* I decided right then and there that he would *never* be seeing *my Hankys, like ever. I couldn't even wait for the check, I had to get out of there.* I don't think I even thanked him for dinner like I usually would; I made up some flimsy excuse and got the hell out. *I berated myself the whole way home for not listening to that gut feeling I had about him. Damn it all to hell!*

I was literally about ready to *snap*! *Shit was just about to pop off up in here, and it would not be pretty.* The next day I realized I had to do something about this, so I started an anonymous rant on Facebook called Reasons You're Not Boyfriend Material, and it was based on Mr. Shady and Mr. High and Mighty. This shit was *insane,* and everything went *viral. I couldn't even make this shit up if I tried, I am not that clever.* When I told Mr. Shady, he was unimpressed and seemed unfazed. It was like he had zero emotions and I wondered how he pulled that off. Some people found my posts hilarious, others were downright angry. I even had one jealous woman message me to tell me I would probably never go on another date in my entire life because of it. *But you know what? I didn't give one flying fuck, and I told her that.This stuff was just too juicy and ridiculous, I had to share it. I wanted everyone to know how ludicrous men were behaving these days.* Everyone was telling me I should write a book. Well, here's the book. Even if I never got asked out again, I needed to expose this ridiculousness. *What are men thinking? Can someone explain this to me in plain English, please?*

Yea, it's a man's world, but that's all right
because they're making a total mess of it.
We're chipping away at their control,
taking the parts we want.
—Cher

Then the most interesting thing happened: another miracle. An editor from a local magazine approached me and asked me to write a column for his magazine about dating and relationships in south Florida. His only request: "make it funny." *I am a master at that! And I have a PhD in sarcasm, it's a real thing.* What was weird though, suddenly my inbox was *flooded* with men requesting a date *with me. It was as if the world had turned upside down, it's all backwards.* Well, I knew that already. *Did these guys want to be the next "Reason You're Not Boyfriend Material"?* When I started not giving a shit about dating, that's when I was getting asked out the most. *How ironic. But the real irony is that I owe my entire writing career to a couple of douchebags!*

The shit that men would do was so ridiculous that the only thing I could do was laugh about it. If I couldn't have a sense of humor about it, I knew that my life would suck. I even created this sexy, fun, party girl persona around this debacle and I called her the Savvy Single Girl. Then I realized the moniker was actually keeping me single. This was before I could recognize that monikers and labels were a self fulling prophesy. *Oh well…I'm still single without the nickname…*

I wrote this column for *seven years,* and I threw myself into the subject of figuring out men and relationships. *Because hell, I'm the one that really needed to figure it out*! This childhood trauma had caused me to make the absolute *worst* decisions in relationships. Those choices led to emotional abuse, manipulation and all sorts of nasty shit which led to *more* trauma. I had my heart broken *more times* than I could even count! I read countless books and articles and watched hours of YouTube videos. I had to figure this all out, *otherwise I'd be single forever. What was I missing?*

To be a spiritual warrior, one must have
a broken heart; without a broken heartland
the sense of tenderness and vulnerability,
your warrior ship is untrustworthy.
—Chogyan Trungpa

Although, the more I got into this topic of soulmates, the more I realized that this was *no laughing matter.* Who I choose as my life partner would either make or break *my life.* It was a *really important* decision, and one I would not take lightly. It is quite possibly the most important decision I would ever make in my life! *I knew that, I had already been married, and getting a divorce is not a cake walk.*

After studying twin flames in depth, I had gained some valuable knowledge. This journey was about me really loving *myself,* and choosing *me* above *all others.* It's not *even* about finding or attracting the right partner! *It was journey of self discovery, a coming home to myself.* I was once lost, but now I am found. *I'm home at last, and safe and sound. From that moment on, I knew I would always choose Me.*

But I knew I was meant to have love in my life because my capacity to love was *enormous.* I could love someone that hated me. I could love someone, from afar, who had treated me like shit. I could love someone who just couldn't or wouldn't step up. I could love someone who disappeared, just as things were getting intense. I could even love someone who had tried to *destroy* me, because it showed me how powerful I really was! But they better stay *far away from me,* or I would send my own demons to set boundaries with them. I'm traditionally not a fighter, but there are some things worth fighting for. *And when pushed as far as I had been, I wasn't given a choice, I am no doormat. I am a Spiritual Warrior! You cannot destroy Me! My prayers and connection to the Divine was stronger than anything anyone could throw at me!*

These days I carry around a sword with me wherever I go. It's not a real, physical sword, it's made of my own *light energy.* But I will not hesitate to use it to cut someone off *or out* who wasn't serving my higher purpose. I buried Ms. Nice Girl People Pleaser right there in the *dirt. She was an over giver anyway, and it was not serving me. It left me depleted and I had to stop giving and loving so much if I never got anything in return. I couldn't and wouldn't sacrifice myself ever again.*

It takes a warrior's courage to acknowledge that your point of view matters, that your truth matters, that your gifts matter, and that your presence on this earth matters.[11]
—Debbie Ford

While I knew I could do life on my own, I still wanted to have a partner. I wouldn't let all my experiences cloud my judgment and start believing that *all men were bad and behaved this way.* That is a false and limiting belief, and I don't have time for those. I only needed ONE MAN after all! Besides, I had raised amazing sons, I knew there had to be other great men out there, *I just hadn't met them yet.* I knew that having the right partner would get me to where I wanted to go much faster. The "master mind" principle is number one component in the "Law of Success", one of my favorite books by Napoleon Hill. Two minds working together in the spirit of harmony for a shared purpose was a personal goal of mine, *but I knew I could do it on my own if I had to.*

I had sent Starboy an email with just a sliver of the vision I had seen of my life purpose, to see if maybe it aligned with his. But he never responded. In his defense, this guy got way more than he signed up for. He didn't know his date was a psychic and that *banging me would make me more psychic. Hey, I didn't know that either. Oh man, I'm sorry.* I wasn't sure if he believed in himself or knew what his life purpose was. Although, I'm assuming most people don't know what their life purpose is, *I had only discovered mine recently.*

---

11. Debbie Ford, *Courage: Overcoming Fear and Igniting Self Confidence* (Harper One, 2012).

One day it dawned on me that I had *unconditional love* for this man. I had never felt that except with my sons. That meant he didn't need to do anything or be anyone other than exactly what he was for me to love him. He didn't even have to love me in return or even pay attention to me. I felt like I had just passed the *ultimate test* from the Universe, and I wanted to give myself a trophy and pat myself on the back! *The whole purpose of incarnating on this planet was to learn how to love unconditionally, even amongst all these demons. I had done it, I passed the test!*

I hope the Emperor, whoever he is, wraps thing up and gets here quickly, because we are running out of time! We are heading straight for the *apocalypse, buckle up!* I'm not going to let fear take over when I think about the apocalypse, it's something that's meant to happen, and will be happening *soon.* It's a Jewish and Christian prophecy of an imminent cosmic cataclysm in which God *removes* the ruling powers of evil and raises up the righteous and ushers in the Messianic Era. It's *about time!* I want peace, joy and *prosperity* for *everyone.*

It occurred to me that this spiritual war between the Light and the dark has been going on for *eons.* The apocalypse is where God just steps *in,* He intervenes and then the balance is restored. I could *feel* that it was *any day* now. If you haven't yet chosen the Light and *service to others,* it's not too late. Let the Golden Age of Love, Light and *Ascension* begin!

The only way out of this mess we are in is to *transcend* to the 5th dimension. We are currently in the 3rd dimension, but are dealing with all these entities from the 4th dimension. Apparently the 4th is the largest dimension, so it has the greatest range of frequencies. This is where the Heaven and Hell and Angels and Demons concept comes from. *No wonder it was so hard to transcend beyond it, it was easy to get ourselves trapped in there. The Universe is not black and white and there are way more than fifty shades of grey. My dirty mind is confirmation of that.*

I think God is just waiting on us to figure it all out, *I don't think we are passive observers here.* I believe when enough of us *unite,* and embrace our differences and pray *to* God or the Universe, whatever you want to call it, *to intervene on our behalf then the apocalypse will come. If anyone has any better ideas, I'd love to hear them.* Personally, I can't just sit around and wait for something to happen, I needed to *do something* about it! I couldn't wait to get to the next level and actually start *enjoying* my life.

CHAPTER 8

Healing

True healing is multi-dimensional and there are many layers. It's not just about healing of the body, I couldn't forget about healing my mind and soul as well, it's all interrelated and connected. If I forgot about one area, it would be like hitting up the gym and then stuffing my face at McDonald's.

I continued my daily meditation and prayers, but I added in some extra stuff to see if that worked. I discovered grounding, or earthing, where I walked barefoot on the earth to ground myself. It works great, something about the electromagnetic power the earth had. I starting doing more yoga to move the trauma that was trapped in my body that needed to be released. I couldn't put my finger on it, but yoga *did something* to me that took me to another level. *Those yogis are on to something.*

I discovered that hot epsom salt baths would cleanse my aura. *Now I take one everyday, it's my secret weapon against sorcery.* I kept being reminded that *everything is energy.* While I couldn't see it, I had to work and heal my *Energetic* body too. I started sun gazing because I learned that it helps decalcify the pineal gland, and it increased my psychic abilities. I continued to burn sage and incense to ward off evil spirits, demons and negative energy, and *I do that a lot.*

I use the cycles of the moon to manifest. The "Moonology Diary" by Yasmin Boland has been very useful. The diary uses astrology and tells you what house each new or full moon is own for your sign. *New moons are when you set intentions, full moons are when you release what is no longer serving you.* I continue to use astrology as I find it to be incredibly fascinating and a useful tool. I use tarot and oracles cards to heighten my already sharp intuition. I collect crystals, I love them. Don't ask me how that can heal, but I'm pretty sure they do *something.*

I am a Hermit most days lately, t*his book has taken more of my energy than I had intended it to.* And you have no idea what it took to actually finish writing it, *I felt like I was being increasingly attacked spiritually as the days went on.* I'm assuming the demons don't want me to publish it because it exposes them. *Maybe they could delay me, but no one can stop me!* I am very picky with whom I choose to surround myself with, *my energy is a precious commodity.* Spending time alone in prayer and meditation has helped me to heal and receive the information I am supposed to receive.

Normally I'm a social butterfly, but I needed the alone time to process and recharge my batteries. As an empath I can absorb another's feelings and emotions, and sometimes it's just too much. People try to drain my light, they don't realize they have it within themselves too. *I had to learn this the hard way.* Hopefully one day soon, I can reenter the world, more enlightened and healed. Because, quite frankly, I was losing my mind up in here! Too much isolation wasn't good either. Damn! *It really is all about balance.*

The truth is like a bitter pill that everyone seems to want, but can't seem to swallow. Just because someone doesn't believe it, or refuses to *see* it, doesn't make it any less true. As it turns out, we can't make any mistakes, I don't think there's a hell in the traditional sense. But for every action there is a *consequence. Do whatever you want, but be prepared to face the repercussions.* Free will is the *wild card* that makes this all possible. This physical realm was created just for our soul's spiritual *evolution. Ascension*, or Nirvana as the Buddhists call it, *is the ultimate goal.* Until we reach that level, we are bound to keep repeating this birth, suffering, death and rebirth cycles.

One day I felt that I had come as far as I could with my own healing and needed to get some outside help. I came across this psychologist through Instagram of all places, she used her own kind of therapy called Theta healing. She put me in a meditative state and went about uncovering where I was stuck and where I needed to reprogram my subconscious mind.

I was really surprised to find out that I had done all of the healing from childhood and had accepted my mother's death and my father's emotional absence. I had even healed from Sammy's death, because *I knew he was with me all the time.* At a certain point, I had asked God to just keep the line of communication open with him *all the time.*

What shocked me was that I still had some *major* damage from one particular emotionally manipulative and verbally abusive relationship! Even though I had stopped interacting with him a long time ago, whatever he had said to me had been programmed into my subconscious mind. I had heard: *you're stupid, you're nothing without me, you'll never be successful* and *no one will ever want you*, and it had gotten *in my head*. It didn't matter that my conscious mind didn't believe it, it had been repeated so many times that it affected me. *I had to reprogram my subconscious mind or it would continue to run my life.* Luckily, there are thousands of YouTube videos of meditations and affirmations that could help me. Some of them played all night long, so I started doing it every night, *in addition to my regular meditation.*

I had come across this research article about how psychedelics could cure depression. I had already tried ketamine for depression three times, and it had helped. This article talked about using MDMA and psilocybin (the compound found in magic mushrooms) under the supervision of psychoanalysis and it had helped cure depression. I wondered how I could sign up for one of these clinical trials. *But I didn't have time do to that, so decided I could just micro-dose myself.* I went with the natural version, psilocybin, and it didn't matter to me that it was illegal. I still can't understand why the government would think they have the power to make something *God grew from the earth, without us even having to plant it, illegal.* But this wasn't a problem, *Miami has plenty of drug dealers.*

I knew where to get some mushrooms, and had done it many times. I had straight up tripped my face off while doing LSD when I was younger, but I was much too old for that. In recent years, I had taken very small amounts of mushrooms as part of the "party", and it was always fun.

But this time it wasn't about the party, or even doing it with other people. I wanted to do small amounts and just see what came up. I felt like it could help me reconnect with my soul and I'd be able see if I was on the right path. I knew exactly how I wanted my life to look and feel like, and I had let go of all attachments or expected outcomes and be open to whatever God had planned for me. *But was I on track? Tripping out seemed to be the answer.*

So for the next three months on the weekends, I took small amounts of psilocybin every few hours. *It was wild! Well, now I know why this stuff is illegal! Whatever was occasionally blocking my third eye was permanently removed, and I could see everything clearly.* It's no wonder the government doesn't want people taking this stuff, it's illegal because they don't want anyone becoming enlightened and discovering the truth. *If that were to happen, their feigned power of control would come to an end.*

If you are really comfortable living the lie that we've all been spoon fed and don't wish to know the truth, then you should've stopped reading this memoir. I'm not claiming to know exactly what's going on, but I just imagine that everything we have been led to believe is true is a flat out lie, or half truth at best. *Then I go from there. The first step is to remove the old, untrue beliefs, which was the same things I was removing from my subconscious mind.*

It was around this time that I couldn't get Starboy off my mind. *Well, it was more like I thought about him all the time, I had never stopped.* I knew we had some sort of psychic connection, and I couldn't sleep at night and felt distressed.

Maybe I was picking up on something happening in his life, but I couldn't be sure. I know I had let him go a while back, but I got this feeling that he needed help. I felt this sense of *despair,* and I knew it wasn't coming from me.

I had sent him a text, and later he called me. I asked him how he was doing, and he said he was "fine". He told me his mother was making him go and see a therapist, and I told him that was a good idea. I told him if he felt he needed some help, a therapist was a good place to start. I had spent years in therapy myself. Then he told me he thought something might be wrong with his head and that he needed to get an MRI. *Wait, what?* I told him to get the MRI if he thought he needed one, but I informed him that I thought that he was fine and that he shouldn't worry about it. *I already knew the power the mind had over one's physical health.*

After we ended our conversation, I couldn't help but be *worried* about him. He sounded so confused. He wasn't acting like his normal, intelligent self. Then I remembered the confusion I had had several months before due to some black magic, and *got really nervous.* I felt like the voodoo brunette was somehow connected to him and I got even more freaked out. *We definitely had mirrored lives, and had gone through some of the same things. Maybe he was being manipulated too? Was it possible someone had put some sort of spell on him or have I totally lost my mind?*

I felt his sense of desolation, and I didn't know what to do! I couldn't keep texting him, it felt like I was chasing him and I was too smart for that. Besides, it wasn't like I was hoping for a relationship with him, I had already let that go. I was instructed to release him, and I had.

I did the only thing I knew how to do in times like this: I prayed. I prayed that Starboy would be safe and would be able to free himself from whatever was holding him back. I prayed that he would start believing in himself and find happiness, *even if it wasn't with me. I love him that much.*

I kept walking past my bookshelf and was drawn to a particular book entitled "Communicating With The Archangel Michael For Guidance and Protection" by Richard Webster. This book I had bought a while ago, it didn't just appear there like *Many Lives, Many Masters* had. But I had never opened it. *Now,* it *was calling to me.*

After reading it, I started to invoke Archangel Michael's Divine guidance and protection, for myself and for Starboy. *It felt weird, invoking an Archangel, but I figured it couldn't hurt.* I knew enough about the way then Universe worked and understood that by helping someone else was like helping myself. *We are all connected and what you put out there comes back to you.* I even started lighting a black candle for protection for him and myself, which I had read about on the internet. Although I had already been informed that I was protected, I wasn't sure he was. Then…I didn't know what else I could do for him.

I felt like I had done all I could for Starboy, it was time to turn the focus back to myself and my healing. I was on a mission to become enlightened and to ascend. Ascension is not trying to obtain "sainthood", *I had to keep reminding myself this.* I wouldn't ever stop drinking wine occasionally or suddenly become celibate. While I have tremendous self control, I am a very sexual being and couldn't deny that. *Although I am very picky with whom I bring into my bed.* I think one of the amazing things about being in a physical body is pleasure. I've dealt with so much emotional and physical pain that it was high time I started experiencing real pleasure and *joy.* Whether it's having a delicious meal or getting an amazing massage, I made a commitment to myself to only do things that delighted me. *While I'm in a body I intend to enjoy every single moment. I became the Self Care Queen. Hopefully one day it will include great sex.*

I pretended that I was completely fine, *everything was normal.* But it really wasn't…I was lonely! *God, I am still human, where is the Emperor? What is he so busy doing? I had to* take a hard look in the mirror and ask myself: how was it possible that I was *still single? Was I missing something about myself that I needed to heal before I could manifest him?* There's a high probability that everyone thinks models have charmed romantic lives. *But for me, nothing could've been farther from the truth. Was it what I looked liked?* I realize some people may be intimidated by me, *but I wish they'd get over it already.* People probably make snap assumptions about me once they see my face, *which is biased and unfair. Don't judge a book by it's cover.*

I remember one time when I was a kid, we were all on a roadtrip. My parents *loved* road trips, and my sister and I have been to every single touristy destination in the United States of America, from Yellowstone National Park to Mount Rushmore. We were at this log cabin house, it was supposed to be a Joseph Smith museum or something, and there was an older couple running the place as Mormon missionaries. The gentleman told my step mother: "Your daughter is very beautiful." She snapped right back at him: "*Well,* she's really beautiful *on the inside too.*" I said nothing, but I wondered why she had to say that so *snarky. Was it because I wasn't her actual biological daughter so she couldn't claim that compliment?*

She did stuff like this all the time. I think it was designed to keep me humble, which it did. But I had this feeling she wanted me to be ashamed of what I looked like. Even though I was just a kid, *I didn't fall for that crap.* I was smart enough to know that there were things everyone could do to enhance their appearance…*up to a point.* She is the one who would always say to my sister and I: "You get what you get and you don't get upset". Well, here I am, *not getting upset.*

I always assumed that people's vibration attracted what types of people were drawn to them. I foolishly believed that if I just kept vibrating high, I would eventually meet my perfect match. The truth is, I attracted only *two types: t*he fuckboys, who were proud of that, like Mr. Shady; or the egotistical trophy seekers, like Mr. High and Mighty. *All of the men in between seemed to be too insecure to be with someone like me.* Not many men could handle being with the woman that everyone turned around and stared at when she walked into the room. Sometimes people stared so much, they'd *embarrass themselves.* I'd play the dumb blonde and pretend not to notice. I was saving them *further embarrassment, I'm a nice person.* If any guy in between these two extremes could muster up enough confidence to ask me out, it was only to try and *get me in bed,* nothing else. Again, just another example of how the whole world is askew and ass backwards. *God, where is the Emperor? What is taking him so long?*

What's a girl to do? I was desperate to know: *what was I doing wrong?* Maybe I needed to start being bitchy and learn how to play hard-to-get. *Wait a minute-hold up! I actually am hard to get, it's not a game.* Maybe I was just being impatient. *God, fifteen years isn't long enough to wait?* I guess all I could do was keep doing what I was doing: praying, visualizing, believing and manifesting. *God knew I was getting quite impatient…that was a nice way of putting it*. Maybe I should try manifesting something else for the moment, just to practice? I *was* getting antsy, and *annoyed! I never said I was perfect.*

So I TURNED BACK TO THE TASK AT HAND: ASCENSION, the state of retuning back to God, which is already *inside of us. I think I was already there, wasn't I? Can I skip to the next step now where my life is filled with love and laughter?* I had striped away my ego. *Done.* I could see past the illusion of the material realm. *Check.* None of it is real, we can't take any material possessions with us when we die. Yet there is still evil in the world, people keep killing, lying, cheating and stealing in order to gain more material wealth and power! Their bank account may grow larger, but their spiritual bank account is severely overdrawn. *Was I missing something, skipping a step?*

Enlightenment involved becoming very aware of my own inner divinity. It meant that I could sense when my vibration was low and take steps to vibrate higher. I had released all my fears, I didn't even fear death. I let go of any attachments because I knew the the more tightly I held on to something was the first thing God would take away. I understood that all of my suffering came from my own mind, my thoughts. I could easily detach from these thoughts because they weren't reality and would think more positive thoughts. *Yet here I am, still suffering. I am ready for love! Wasn't I?*

I was still struggling with missing Sammy. I wanted so badly to hug his skinny body and kiss him on the cheek. I missed those times when he would stretch across my bed and tell my *everything*. He was my best friend, he was my *person. Maybe that's what it was, I missed Sammy. I could be patient, couldn't I?* His brothers always had girlfriends but he and I were always single, and we used to make jokes about it. I had put dating on hold to raise my children and deal with my health issues, and he couldn't seem to get a girl to like him in the way that he liked her. *But we had each other. Sammy baby, if you can hear me right now, can you lead the right man to me? I think he might need some extra guidance. I just miss you terribly.*

Sammy was unlike any other person I've ever met in my life. He lit up any room he walked into. He went out of his way to make other people feel good about themselves. He would often have deep, spiritual conversations with my adult friends, and they were always astounded. How could I fill this horrible void I felt in my heart while waiting for whoever my Emperor was to get his shit together? *It was like torture.* I wasn't sure how much more I could take. *God, I know you never give us any more than we can handle, but I'm about to snap!*

I knew missing Sammy would never go away, but I needed to make a solid plan on how I going to get through January every year. The first year after his death, I was still in shock. The second yahrzeit we held a memorial with all of our friends there to support us. But year three there was *nothing,* no event or memorial. And between his English yahrzeit and birthday, there was also the Hebrew date, which is a totally different day. That January dragged on and was *brutal.* I even took a molly just to try and escape *feeling,* only to realize I *hated* rolling, and that's probably why I hadn't done it in years. *It is not a Xanax you idiot, you actually feel everything more!*

So year four I devised a very sound plan, I would only memorialize the English dates, not the Hebrew dates. I felt that this would make the process not drag out for the whole month, which had made it too emotionally burdening. So on January 8th, Sammy's yahrzeit, my girlfriend came over and I lit the candle and then we got silly drunk. She made me laugh so hard I almost peed my pants. Then she nicknamed the day as my "Sammiversy". *I lover her, I have the greatest friends.*

The next day January 9th would've been his 20th birthday, so I decided to throw him a little party. I knew Sammy would want us to celebrate his life instead of mourn his death on that day. I bought a cake and some snacks and invited a few neighbors over. I didn't make a big deal of it, *but it felt really good to laugh and drink wine to celebrate instead of drinking wine to avoid feeling pain.*

One neighbor I invited over had lost her husband 6 years earlier, and she was amazed at how well I was doing. She admitted that on her husband's birthday, she would just try and not think about it. I joked to her that I probably wouldn't throw my dead son a birthday party *every* year, but it just felt like the right to do. As I talked to this neighbor, I realized that I wasn't giving myself enough credit for how far I had come in my healing. I know others that have lost a child and it is so painful for them that no one ever *dares mention it.* Yet here I was, able to talk about it and able to feel and process the emotions. *I was joking and laughing again!* I knew that grief would never go away, but I also knew it wasn't healthy to stuff down my emotions into my body. All that would do was land me in the hospital. I almost wanted to pat myself on the back, *again*. Maybe I could stop beating myself up for not having everything figured out, *I was doing pretty damn good.*

Although I had come a long way in my healing, I still wanted some kind of confirmation that Sammy was happy and okay. I knew he was always with me and giving me messages, but I needed to hear it from someone else. Judaism is against using a psychic medium to communicate with deceased loved ones, yet doesn't explain why. I think it's because some of these mediums have no integrity and use a person's grief to exploit them for money. I had seen it happen to a friend of mine Debee, who lost her only son. I also believe that Judaism might be against using a medium because it's something we can all learn to do ourselves. *There's even a science behind it.*

Debee's son had died around the same time Sammy did. Every week, she would talk to him through a medium, *until the medium tried to extort her for money.* Debee was heartbroken for a while, she really missed talking to her son. One day Debee jumped in her Mercedes Benz and drove hours and hours north of here, to this community that was famous for having a lot of mediums living there. When she sat down the woman said: "Your son is laughing at you right now. You already talk talk to him...*Don't you?*" Debee was dumfounded, but she couldn't deny it. *It was the truth.*

When is everyone going to realize that we *all have psychic abilities, we all can talk to dead people, and that we do it through our intuition.* Yet people are doing things *because everyone else is doing them,* like injecting themselves with something and they have no idea what it is, or taking a pill that is going to mess with their brain chemicals. *They're certainly not following their intuition.* There are other people that insist on announcing to the world on TikTok that they now no longer wish to identify with *either gender, yet somehow I am the weirdo?* The whole world has gone mad and everyone is just sitting around as if nothing is wrong? *Where is my Oscar for pretending like everything is normal? I've kept up this act for so long, I think I deserve it.*

I decided I needed to talk to a medium anyway. I just wanted confirmation, to make sure I wasn't really going crazy. So I called up my sister, who's into that sort of thing. She had gone to a weekend convention with John Holland, a world renowned psychic medium, because she wanted to communicate with our mother. She sat there the whole weekend without getting any messages from her and was a bit disappointed. At the end of the weekend, a guy came up to my sister and gave her some messages from our mother. My sister suggested I call him, *because our mother had chosen him.*

When the Medium first started talking, I noticed he had a thick Texas accent, he was a jolly old fellow. I could envision him rocking in a rocking chair on his porch wearing a big cowboy hat, chewing on a toothpick. Sammy came through right away. He said that he was greeted by an ancestor that was wearing a military uniform. I said that was probably my grandfather, who we called Pop-pop. He said Pop-pop was taking him all around the world and he was visiting every place he had never been. He was learning all about Sacred geometry. But the most exciting thing for Sammy was that he got to see all of the movies *before* they came out in the theater, and the *uncut* version! *He was really excited about that!*

Now it was starting to make sense! We are a *huge* movie family, it's how we've always bonded. Every weekend I'd buy a new movie that we would all watch together. The boys always went to the *opening night* of every movie which started at midnight, even when they were very young and had school the next day.

The messages I had been receiving from beyond the veil that were movie scenes were from Sammy! *I knew that now. My guides were way too serious to show me a scene from a movie.* When I was in the midst of black magic hell and evil sorcerers were trying to get me to kill myself, Sammy showed me a scene from the movie The Devil's Advocate starring Al Pacino and Keanu Reeves. Keanu's wife was played by Charlize Theron, and she ends up killing herself when she sees a demon in the mirror. Sammy explained that that's what these witches were doing, sending demons to try and get me to kill myself. *Only it didn't work, and surely it will come back on them in a horrific way.*

I had had a particularly horrible date with the most shallow man I have ever met in my life. That one hour lunch we had a Soho House was absolute *torture*. This man kept asking me if I had gained weight during the pandemic, and was like "No". Then he asked me if I ever made a living at modeling because he said: "Anyone could get some pictures and call themselves a model." I'm not a size 2 anymore, *I get that*. But I thought I looked pretty good that day and wondered if he needed to get his eyes checked. While I don't require validation from any external source for my self esteem and confidence, somehow what he said shook me. Sammy showed me that movie Shallow Hal, with Jack Black and Gwyneth Paltrow, where what he sees is her internal beauty, and not what she actually looked like. Sammy explained that spirit had *made* me look fat/ugly or whatever because it protected me from ever seeing the guy again. *Thank God for that, because I never wanted to see that shallow jackass ever again.*

After I hung up the phone with the Medium, my eyes widened with delight and a sly smile crept on to my face.

Now I was understanding so much more about my life purpose. *It is a really big deal!* No wonder I had so many haters trying to stop me. *Why would anyone think I'd kill myself when life was about to get exciting and exhilarating?*

After the therapy with the Theta healing therapist, I knew I needed to reach out and ask for assistance in my healing, *even though I'm so stubborn that I had tried to do it all on my own.* I didn't have to wait very long because the next day I met the *Healer. The Healer* is the only way I can describe her. I had run into my friend Elisa in the lobby of my building, and I told her how *amazing* she looked, I couldn't get over it. She swore she wasn't on some special diet or anything, but her *glow up* was *noticeable.* From the time I had met her two years ago until now, *she was a totally different person.* She asked me how I was doing, I said, "Oh, the usual, warding off evil eyes and returning black magic to senders…no big deal.". I told her I wasn't focused on that because I wasn't going to give it more power, I was busy taking action to get myself out go this *horrible situation I had unintentionally let myself get trapped in.* She said, "*What?*" Her eyes widened with surprise. I said, "Oh my God, when was the last time I spoke to you?" I had seen her briefly at her mother's funeral and had made a Shiva call, but she was grieving and surrounded by people and couldn't really talk. *I knew what that was like.*

She grabbed my hand and said: "I have someone, you need to call her right away. She's a massage therapist, but *not really,* she's more like a *healer.* She clears your chakras and all that, do you know what I mean?" I told her I *did know* exactly what she meant, and indeed, *I fucking needed that, and pronto.* She instructed me to text, not call her, because she rarely answered her phone. I nodded and I told her I understood. *I was mentally taking notes.* Elisa told me to text her and *drop her name,* otherwise I might not get a response. *Duly noted.*

I texted this woman *right away.* I already knew she'd be in my building tomorrow for Elisa's uncle, so I asked her if she had time the next day, could she squeeze me in? The Healer informed me she'd be available after 1pm the next day and that she would text me. The next day she texted me at exactly 11:11am, to see if I was available. I had just finished journaling and my son was still asleep, so I told her *yes. Wow, the good Lord could not an extra two hours... this must be important!* Later, I found out that the Healer was so popular that she had billionaires flying her around the world to heal their family and friends, and she had just gotten back from a trip around the world. All it took was her healing someone of Bell's Palsy after one session, and these people *took notice.* I was grateful and felt *very blessed* that not only was she was in town and available, but that my spirit guides had *led her right to my doorstep. Thank you to my spirit guides. You are a badass team, and I couldn't do any of this without you.*

She came in with her massage table and asked me what was going on and how could she help me. I almost started crying, but then composed myself. Elisa had instructed me not to *say too much,* she would figure out what was wrong and how to fix me. I told her I wasn't actually sick, but that I was constantly nauseous and burning up all the time. *Ascension flu? What was happening to me? Yet, this is what I had signed up for?* She was nodding. I told her that something was about to explode over here, I felt like a storm was coming! She said: "The storm is already here honey", and I knew she was right. My life and writing this book had become a constant battle, and it *wasn't over yet. God, would these spiritual attacks ever be over? I hope so, because I'm super exhausted right now.*

The problem I had was: I was already in *my new life.* I had visualized that new life so much so that I was *already there. I had forgotten, momentarily, about the present moment and this hell of a situation.* I was already at an undisclosed location with the love of my life, doing nothing but writing, self care, meditating, yoga, eating good food and drinking good wine and *making love under the stars. I was already* traveling the world with him. We were busy fulfilling our Divine mission. *But back to reality and the present moment. I felt this panic of what could happen next. I was living in survival mode, my cortisol levels were probably off the charts!*

The Healer and I ended up talking for almost an hour before we even got started with her healing treatment. She was doing the *exact same thing I was,* taking every religion and spiritual tradition and trying to *piece it all together.* Except she was *ten steps ahead of me! I was amazed!* She had a *degree in theology,* and studied *all of the spiritual traditions* as well, Wiccan included. She was planning on going back to school and getting her PhD in theology, and she was *also writing a book.* I wondered if she even needed the extra schooling, she seemed to know *exactly what she was doing.*

The Healer had been speaking with spirits from beyond the veil since she was a child, she came from a long line of natural born mediums. Her upbringing encouraged and supported it. I began spilling it *all out* to her, all the bullshit, the curses, the whole shebang. Well, *not everything.* I haven't told one person the *full story* yet, and I didn't feel the need to. But I felt like I had finally met someone who was *speaking my language,* besides my sister.

So she began to massage me, and tap into my energy. She hovered around my sacral chakra, and told me there was *huge problem.* She asked if I was close to my mother. I *gulped,* and I told her she had died. I had never really known her, and spilled all about the guilt I felt for so long that she had sacrificed herself for me. *Then, the tears started to roll. I couldn't help it.* I know I had already forgiven myself, my mother had told me that I couldn't feel any guilt for a choice that *she made,* and I knew she was right. But it didn't make it any easier. In my ascension process I was *so sensitive,* and everything was *heightened* from my sense of touch, to my emotions, even my *sense of smell.* And not everything smells *pleasant.* I could smell alcohol of someone's breath, even if they hadn't had a drink in hours. Plus, I had almost thrown up after guzzling down a glass of rose and munching on a steak. It didn't matter that both were kosher, my body suddenly couldn't handle normal things like this. *Oh no…* I wondered if I really wanted Ascension after all…*God, please, I still need to be able to have a glass of wine and a kosher steak occasionally. Could you make that happen? I would really appreciate it.*

The Healer informed me that a curse had been placed on a woman, *one of my ancestors, to lose children and have familial sorrow.* I thought of all the barren women in my family, and those that had lost children. My maternal grandmother had lost *two of her four children* in her lifetime. It was heartbreaking. I had remembered some past lives where I lost a child as well. *Was it really a curse?* She said this curse went *way back,* to a time when… a curse was *actually curse.* She asked if I knew what that meant. I said, of course I did…I asked if it was the time before Abraham and Sarah in the Bible? She said "Yes, the whole reason

Sarah couldn't give birth for so long was *because of this same curse." Oh no...this was really bad...* My eyes flipped open and I looked directly at her and said: "But Sarah gave birth to Issac in her old age. *That is Sammy's Hebrew name, Yitchak!"* I knew what she was saying was true. I knew that I was the one *meant to break that curse, and she was the one that was going to tell me how to do it.*

At one point in our discussion of this topic, she said "the curse is what brings in the blessing". I said back: "Yes, the curse is what, in fact, brought Abraham *back to God* and his *coming back to God* is what brought in the blessing. The curse is what *in the end, brought in the blessing...*because everything happens for a reason, even curses." I wondered who I was exactly, because now I wasn't even acting like myself. *Where was this profound insights and information coming from?*

When I had been instructed to write this book, I balked, I tried to negotiate, and *I procrastinated. All to no avail, my guides persisted and prodded me that I fulfill my mission.* So I told my guides that I would need some help, and I asked for an extra spirit guide, one with extraordinary literary skills. Later, I asked God for a "walk-in", like Dolores Cannon had talked about. I figured that would be better, I could have this information with me *at all times, and no one could try and cut me off from the communication because it was already inside of me.* I asked that I keep my original memories and all that jazz because I would need it, duh, to write a memoir. It seems like God had *answered my prayers,* because I didn't even *recognize myself, but in a good way! But who knows, maybe I was just giving myself the permission to be even weirder than I already was.*

I knew I would want a few more sessions with the Healer. I was already aware that I could heal myself and I was *my own damn guru.* Which is the only way to go, one cannot follow another's path. It is up to every individual to listen to their own intuition and *do what was right for them.* But I knew she had more information for me…and she knew it too. She told me to call her next week. I said: *For Sure.* She instructed me to run out and buy the book: "Eastern body, Western Mind" by Anodea Judith, and that I needed to do chapters 1 and 2 *immediately.* My first two chakras were clogged and *blocked, and it was not a good thing.*

She instructed me exactly *how to break this curse.* I ran to get a pen and paper to write it down. She said…to break generational curses involving children and fertility… you're going to need to bring an offering to Yemanya, the goddess of the ocean and mother of fertility, or something of that nature. *Say what? Ok…I'm listening.* I needed to go and buy a full watermelon, seeds and all, and put a letter in there requesting Yemanya to *break the curse and restore tranquility and love to may familial line.* Also, I would need to drizzle molasses all over the watermelon and rub it up against my womb. *I didn't have a uterus, but hey- whatever works.* She suggested I go to Key Biscayne, where no one would be so I could have some privacy. I would need to rub molasses all over this watermelon with my note in it, and I guess people *might think I'm weird. Hello? I'm already beyond normal and no longer cared.*

I told the Healer I would do the ritual. It sounded kind of silly, *but if there is was a generational curse and I was the one meant to break it, then I had to at least try.* At the end she said: "Oh, and don't turn your back on the ocean, walk away backwards *out of respect.*" *I could do that.* Writing a note and not turning my back while walking away was something I did every time I visited the Western Wall in

Jerusalem. The only thing I didn't tell the Healer was that while I'd mention the name Yemanya, *I would not be praying or offering anything to her...I pray only to God. I'm no fool.*

When the Healer left, she told me she had already met three people on my spirit team. I knew the first two were my mother and Sammy, but the third? I had been feeling another soul close to me lately...and I knew it was *a child yet to be born. He even told me his name.*

When I got the book, I learned that the first chakra can get blocked in the developmental stage. Chakra one disruptions happen within the first 12 months of life. I was what the book called a Schizoid Creative, and I had a problem trusting and obeying. *Oh no way, this book already knew me.* These types are battling with the most basic *right to exist.* Our biggest fears are "falling apart" or "going crazy". *Well, it was a good thing to find out that I wasn't actually going crazy.* I got to work unblocking my first two chakras. Because if the foundation is messed up, *everything else goes haywire from there. I hoped that this was the last missing piece keeping me from union with my Divine Masculine.*

At that moment, being single not only *made sense,* it was a *good thing.* My energy had shifted from "heartbroken and lonely", to this *sense of urgency to take action!* The meeting of two souls was the *wake up call. Hey! You need to heal yourself!* The separation period was necessary, it was required for me to finish healing to get ready for union with my Divine Masculine. *I would have a union, it was only a matter of time.* I no longer had time to sit here and feel lonely or sorry for myself, I was taking action and was *guided on how to set myself free and finally heal!*

THE LAST THING I WAS REALLY GRAPPLING WITH WAS forgiving all those who had persecuted me, cursed me, and wish me dead. I knew I would *need* to forgive them all, not because they asked for it or even deserved it. I had to forgive because I needed peace in my heart. Louise Hay says: "All dis-ease comes from the state of un-forgiveness." If I could not forgive, then I was only hurting myself. *Although it wasn't easy. I told God if I never had to see them again, I'd be able to fully forgive. And so it was.*

Then it occurred to me that my *entire life* was designed to be this way, and *my soul had agreed to it*. My life was set up, as some sort of pressure cooker, *meant to explode*. All the persecution showed me how to be strong and stand up for myself. The massive heartbreaks of being dumped, ghosted, disappointed or not chosen and all of my failed romances taught me how to truly *love myself*. All of the lies, deception and betrayal showed me how important honesty is. The profound loss of my mother and Sammy forced me to stop ignoring my spirit guides and just accept that I could connect beyond the veil. All those years of loneliness and isolation *forced* me to do my inner healing and shadow work. I realized *there was no other way I could've discovered who I truly am*. It was like one bad thing after next, *in rapid secession until I exploded, like a God damn supernova!*

A light bulb turned on in my head. *That was it!* I knew enough about science to know that a supernova actually creates a new star. I didn't need to get a rocket ship or find a wormhole to get to that shining Star that was calling my name. *All I had to do was reach my maximum breaking point and self implode!!! Seriously!*

On second thought, *maybe I do* identify as a Phoenix rising from the ashes! The fire in me completely incinerated the old me, and the new me was a *badass.* I had the strength and courage to say whatever I wanted and to *stand alone.* I believed in the vision I had seen, and *no one could deter me.* I felt like I was on top of the world… nothing was stopping me now! *I am invincible.*

I was *grateful* for every shit thing that has happened in my life, because it helped me to discover my own powers. I learned how to transmute pain. I found out what my God given gifts were and how I could use them for good, the whole purpose of my trials and tribulations was so that I could finally realize *who I am.*

I AM LITERALLY THE *PHYSICAL EMBODIMENT* OF THE Tower card in the tarot deck. I bring people their "tower moments"; I serve it right up on a silver platter. Whether they got bad karma or had a sudden realization depended on who I was dealing with. It wasn't always negative or destructive, a tower moment can be a sudden awakening. Sometimes I had to energetically *bitch slap* someone who wasn't seeing their own worth. Other times I'd need to *harshly chide* someone for not realizing that not only their negative mindset, *but the very words they spoke,* is exactly what *created their reality.* I was specifically designed *to ignite a spark or send a shock* to anyone who came across my path. Part of my purpose is to be a *catalyst* for *others'* spiritual awakenings. It is not a coincidence that I actually live in a condo building *named Tower House. Here you go honey, no need to thank me.* I *finally* understood who I was, what I was supposed to be doing in this incarnation, and *where I was supposed to sit. I am the Empress!* Although…I'm not into labels. I'm just a walking, talking, sarcastic, hair flipping *contradiction. You can call me Rebecca.*

After months of hibernating while healing and writing, I decided it was time to come back down to earth and rejoin society. I was invited to some soiree, and it seemed like the perfect time to re-emerge. It felt exciting to get dressed up again, and the anticipation of meeting new people had my spirit soaring. *Rebecca is back, and better than ever!* Although I was forever changed, some things about my personality will always be the same. The social butterfly in me was reentering society as an actual butterfly, *not* a slimy caterpillar, *but with the wings of the immortal Phoenix!*

It was fancy black tie party, and upon entering I grabbed a glass of champagne and surveyed the atmosphere. People conversing and laughing, introducing friends to others. I had missed people and the spirit of community, and *it felt so good to be back. I smiled to myself and was so happy.*

Then, out of the corner of my eye, I see a very handsome and confident man looking and heading directly towards me. It was *The Emperor!* He smiled at me, and I guess I couldn't hide the way my eyes lit up when I saw him. *Maybe I'm not that good of an actress, I can't hide certain emotions.* We went to the bar to have a drink and catch up. I had met him at least a dozen years ago, but we never really knew each other.

He asked me out on a date. He was a complete gentleman. But this was no ordinary date, our *souls* knew each other, and we silently understood each other. It was like being reunited with a loved one from many, many lifetimes. We finished each others sentences, our connection was almost telepathic. We couldn't be fake or hide from each other, *not that I'd ever want to.*

Over the coming months as our bond deepened, I felt an overwhelming sense of peace and tranquillity in my heart. I had finally found *my person.* He was my best friend, I could tell him anything. We supported each other's goals and ambitions. We both let the other one just be our authentic selves and our values aligned up perfectly. While we didn't agree on everything, we both would truly listen and try and understand the other's point of view. *We were both committed to making it work, no matter what.*

I'm so grateful his identity was finally revealed to me after so many years. I'm happy that I spent so many years alone because I needed to discover who I was, and what I wanted in a partner. When people go through a heartbreak, they often run out and just try and *replace* the person. They're afraid to be alone, *or just don't like it.* In today's culture, this has gotten out of control. The swipe and replace of online dating makes it seem like there are so many options. They find a substitute, and never break the cycle of co-dependency. But it is so worth it to take the time to heal, and find the lesson from the sadness. I had learned what I wanted and what I didn't want in a partner. *No relationship is ever a waste of time if I learned something from it.* Then, I could really find my *true match. Because believe me, there are some people that can never be replaced.*

I finally understood that real and *unconditional love* was the greatest power in the Universe. Love has the power to *heal and transform.* It was the last missing piece that I needed to be fully healed. Of course, I loved myself enough, that was the first step. I couldn't love someone else until I had fallen in love with me. But there's something about *physical touch* with a man that I completely trusted, and it made our love *out of this world.*

I knew our relationship wouldn't be this blissful forever, especially after the "honeymoon" period ended. We were both focused on the *mission* and excited to build an empire together. For the first time in my entire life, I felt loved, protected and nourished. *A woman cannot surrender to her feminine nature unless she feels safe. She has to trust her man,* and I fully trusted him with my heart and *my life.* I was able to fully *surrender* and reclaim my femininity because I finally felt *safe. It is Divine.*

Last night I got a good night's sleep for the first time in *years.* I awoke and rolled over to see the Emperor already awake and staring at me. He looked so handsome, and his wavy brown hair was an adorable bed head mess. He smiled at me, kissed me gently and said "Good morning beautiful". I couldn't help but smile back, *he is so handsome.* I decided right then and there that I wasn't going to call him the Emperor anymore, I was going to call him Mr. Dreamy, because he was a dream come true. Life is good. *And so it is.*

Now you may be disappointed when I admit to you that I just made up that last part. I wasn't sure how to conclude this memoir because I'm living it. *I'm still calling in the Emperor,* but because of free will it could be *anyone and I could meet him at any moment. My life was exciting again!* But things are different now, I have a fresh perspective. *I had died, was buried, and was reborn. I am completely transformed.* I was now tapped into the Divine Matrix and swimming in the sea of *infinite possibilities.* I had stepped *into the unknown,* only to find out that's where the *magic* was happening. I was no longer confined to my subconscious programming, and I didn't care about fitting into society or what people thought of me. *I am truly living life on my own terms. I know without a shadow of a doubt I that I can make all my dreams come true.* Manifesting my life vision didn't even require faith anymore, *because I had seen it.*

I am the *Star* of my own movie entitled *My Life.* Not only am I the Star, I'm also the executive producer, director *and* casting director. I *get to decide which actors are in my movie, and which ones suck ass and don't make the cut.* In addition, I get to decide what My Life is all about. It may have started off as a depressing tearjerker, then it turned into some dark murder mystery with abusive narcissists and disgusting sorcerers. So I had grabbed the Wheel of Destiny *myself,* and turned My Life into a kinky, *kind of freaky,* romantic comedy. Unexpected things happen in My Life, *I can't control everything.* Although, if My Life suddenly becomes a zombie apocalypse or slasher horror film, *you better believe that I will be the only survivor.*

My guides told me I could manifest the life of my dreams, so long as I followed my intuition. I needed to go where it led me, and not get hung up on any certain outcome. As I evolve more spiritually, so will my vision of how I want my life to be. I needed to stay open to any and all possibilities and *go where my heart led me. Logic is overrated anyway. I knew* could have anything I desired, so long as I stayed humble and grounded and it was for the *highest good of all. I was giddy, like a school girl!*

The other day I was laughing so hard I almost peed my pants. *Except I wasn't wearing pants, I didn't even have on my Hankys.* The whole point of wearing a maxi dress is that you don't need to wear panties. *What was even happening to me? Maybe my Ascension is complete?* Whatever it is, I simply can't wipe this shit grin off of my face, *not that I'd want to.* My spiritual awakening had set My Life on a completely different path, *the one I was meant to be on.*

My overly active imagination proved to be quite useful, because I learned that t*hat is how one manifests.* Author Neville Goddard calls imagination *God. I am dreaming My Life into existence.* I refuse to attach to any of these tragic stories, *I will not be defined by my past.* I know that I can create the life I have always desired, *I am already doing it.* I am having a full on love affair with *myself, and it is absolutely incredible.* This not the end...*My Life is only just beginning. Mic drop.*

Mind Blowing Book Recommendations

Allen, James. *As A Man Thinketh.* Tarcher edition, Penguin Group, 2008.

Bhavnagri, Khoeshed. *The Laws of the Spirit World.* Jaico Publishing House, 2009.

Boland, Yasmin. *The Moonology Diary.* 2023

Chopra, Deepak. *Reinventing the Body, Resurrecting the Soul.* Three Rivers Press, a division of Random House, 2009.

Dispenza, Joe. *Becoming Supernatural.* Hay House, 2017.

Goddard, Neville. *The Power of Imagination. The Neville Goddard Treasury.* A Tarcher Perigee Book, 2013.

Grout, Pam. *E-Squared.* Hay House, 2013.

Hay, Louise. *You Can Heal Your Life.* Hay House, 1984.

Hill, Napoleon. *Law of Success.* The Napoleon Hill Foundation, 53rd ed printed in 1997.

Holland, John. *Bridging Two Realms: Learn To Communicate With Your Loved Ones On The Other Side.* Hay House, 2018.

Judith, Anodea. *Eastern Body, Western Mind. Psychology and the Chakra System as a Path to the Self.* Celestial Arts, 1996 and 2004.

Lipton, Bruce. *The Biology of Belief. Unleashing the Power of Consciousness, Matter & Miracles.* Hay House, 2005.

Moorjani, Anita. *Dying To Be Me,* foreword by Dr. Wayne W. Dyer. Hay House, 2012.

Murphy, Jospeh. *The Power of Your Subconscious Mind.* Published in India by Embassy Book Distributers, 2010.

Nicholas, Chani. *You Were Born For This. Astrology For Radical Self-Acceptance.* Harper One, 2020.

Pescatore, Dr. Fred. *The Truth. 310 hidden cures "they" hoped you'd never discover.* OmniVista Health Media LLC, 2018.

Walsch, Neale Donald. *Conversations With God, Book 1: An Uncommon Dialogue.* 1995.

Webster, Richard. *Communicating with the Archangel Michael for Guidance and Protection.* Llewellyn Publications, First Edition, Sixth Printing, 2010.

Weiss, Dr. Brian. *Many Lives, Many Masters. The True Story of a Prominent Psychiatrist, His Young Patient, and the Past-Life Therapy That Changed Both Their Lives.* A Fireside book, Published by Simon and Schuster, 1998.

Made in the USA
Middletown, DE
15 September 2023

38556923R00156